We Won't Get Fooled Again

We Won't Get Fooled Again

Where the Christian Right Went Wrong and How to Make America Right Again

Gregg Jackson & Steve Deace

JAJ PUBLISHING

WE WON'T GET FOOLED AGAIN
Copyright © 2011 Gregory Jackson, Steve Deace
Published by JAJ Publishing

For further information, please contact:
Annie Fischer at annie@conservativecomebacks.com

We Won't Get Fooled Again
Gregory Jackson and Steve Deace
First printing: October 2011

Printed in the United States

1. Title 2. Author 3. Political Science

Library of Congress Control Number: 2011940359
ISBN-13: 978-0-9837238-1-3

"A nation can survive its fools, and even the ambitious. But it cannot survive treason from within. An enemy at the gates is less formidable, for he is known and carries his banner openly. But the traitor moves amongst those within the gate freely, his sly whispers rustling through all the alleys, heard in the very halls of government itself. For the traitor appears not a traitor; he speaks in accents familiar to his victims, and he wears their face and their arguments, he appeals to the baseness that lies deep in the hearts of all men. He rots the soul of a nation, he works secretly and unknown in the night to undermine the pillars of the city, he infects the body politic so that it can no longer resist. A murderer is less to fear. The traitor is the plague."

–Cicero

"So many sheep without! So many wolves within!"

–St. Augustine

"Let him begin by treating the Patriotism (conservatism) or the Pacifism (liberalism) as a part of his religion. Then let him, under the influence of partisan spirit, come to regard it as the most important part. Then quietly and gradually nurse him on to the stage at which the religion becomes merely part of the "cause," in which Christianity is valued chiefly because of the excellent arguments it can produce in favor of (his political causes). The attitude which you want to guard against is that in which temporal affairs are treated primarily as material for obedience. Once you have made the World an end, and faith a means, you have almost won your man, and it makes very little difference what kind of worldly end he is pursuing. Provided that meetings, pamphlets, policies, movements, causes, and crusades, matter more to him than prayers and sacraments and charity, he is ours—and the more "religious" on those terms the more securely ours. I could show you a pretty cageful (of men just like this) down here (in Hell)."

–C.S. Lewis,
The Screwtape Letters
(parentheses added)

See to it that no one takes you captive through hollow and deceptive philosophy, which depends on human tradition and the basic principles of this world rather than on Christ. —St. Paul

This book is dedicated to our two sons, Jacob and Noah-Andrew, as well as our beautiful brides who gave birth to them. For it is boys like our sons who will one day soon become the men called upon to carry on this great commission to disciple the nations in accordance with the Law and Love of Christ. May its words inspire and inform them, as well as those of you reading this book now.

Christos Kurios!

Table of Contents

Foreword—Lions Led by Lambs

By E. Ray Moore, Th.M.

———•◦◉◦•———

As World War I deepened into the futility of static trench warfare, hidebound French and British generals attempted to break the stalemate by flinging their willing troops in massed waves across open ground against German machine guns, barbed wire, and impregnable fortifications. Unspeakable carnage was the result. On a single day at the Somme River in June 1916, 60,000 British soldiers fell. Watching the slaughter of his heroic enemies, a German general remarked sadly, "Nowhere have I seen such lions led by such lambs."

We Won't Get Fooled Again by Gregg Jackson and Steve Deace tells the story of lions led by lambs in another protracted conflict. This is the "culture war" that has convulsed our country in recent decades, transforming it from a free constitutional republic founded on biblical precepts into a godless, collectivist empire in which Christians themselves, as well as biblical truths, are being increasingly disenfranchised.

The lions? The dedicated and hard-working Christian activist of the modern Christian Right and pro-family movements. The lambs? Their so-called leaders.

In their book, Jackson and Deace analyze the failure of the Christian Right and pro-family leadership, also sometimes identified with the political wing of the evangelical movement, to halt the cultural and moral slide of the family, church, and culture in the USA. I have been part of this movement since my college days and have participated in many of the organizations and political campaigns described in this book. Regrettably, I must affirm that their analysis, tone, and overall conclusions are valid. You only have to look around at the state of America today to see the failure of Christian cultural and political regeneration writ large.

"Lions led by lambs" captures the current status of the evangelical political movement and its Christian Right political allies, marching under the banner of the major pro-family and Christian Right organizations. It is a failed movement, and we are long overdue for this fundamental reassessment and evaluation. That *We Won't Get Fooled Again* is so late in coming shows the patience of many activists who have doubted the value of these major pro-family organizations for years, yet continued to hope and pray for wise and effective leaders to emerge.

It's a sad task for me to write this foreword and no doubt was the same for Jackson and Deace to write the book. But today we have to face the reality that the Christian Right is manifestly a failed movement. It has not reversed, nor even appreciably slowed, the process of moral, cultural, political and legal degeneration in America. The culture is inexorably "slip-sliding away" to the Left.

Christians' lack of political and cultural success is of enormous significance, yet most evangelical and pro-family voters who support Christian Right organizations with their votes, lobbying, and funds seem oblivious to the gravity of the losses and depth of cultural demise. This book will awaken many of the rank and file to the real record of their leaders, although it is not just about these failed leaders and their organizations, but also about the future of our families, our churches and yes, our country, too. Nevertheless, though we are all in some ways at fault, such poor leadership needs to be evaluated and held to account and no longer blindly followed.

My own journey into cultural and conservative politics began in 1962 when I attended the Draft Goldwater Convention in New York, and continued through the '60s, '70s and '80s. In 1980, while serving as a campus minister at Purdue University and having recently completed my seminary education at Grace Theological Seminary in Indiana, I was invited to serve on Dan Quayle's U.S. Senate campaign staff. I was also present at a founding meeting of the Moral Majority in Indianapolis in late 1979 with Jerry Falwell. I participated in several Congressional and local campaigns until 1986 when I was invited to join the presidential campaign of Pat Robertson. So I may claim, modestly but accurately, that my experience as a loyal foot soldier in both the conservative movement and Christian Right organizations is considerable and spans four decades.

In 1997 I launched the Exodus Mandate Project with the goal of encouraging K-12 Christian schools and home schooling in the evangelical Christian community, and in hopes the effort would eventually find wide support in both the conservative movement and major Christian Right and pro-family organizations with whom I had worked all my adult life. I believed that families and churches recovering their God-ordained role in the education of their children would lead to family, church and culture renewal.

As a result of my mission to promote Christian education, I began to be aware of the failure of the older conservative movement and Christian

Right to concern themselves with the moral and Christian educational development of the children in our churches. Five years ago at a major conservative leadership meeting, I had an extensive conversation with legendary conservative political leader Paul Weyrich, now deceased. Paul said to me, "You're doing the right thing by getting families and churches to place their children in Christian school or home schooling. When conservatives and their Christian allies win elections they still lose because the left controls primary and higher education, the media, the arts and our legal system. Thus, they control the culture-forming institutions. We lose even when we win *because culture always trumps politics.*"

In February 2009 I attended the National Religious Broadcasters convention in Nashville and published a report card on the major Christian Right organizations involved in the culture war and on their failure to fully support K-12 Christian education or home schooling over the public schools. Most organizations received grades of C and D. This was a difficult step, but I came to a realization that these organizations would never commit to save their own children from the damage to their Christian worldview and to their moral and academic development at the hands of the state-sponsored public school system.

The full report card can be viewed at www.exodusmandate.org. This event and my subsequent interview with national columnist Kathleen Parker on the failure of the Christian Right in *The Washington Post* published April 5, 2009, entitled "Political Pullback for the Christian Right?" represented my official break with the Christian Right leadership.

How is it that such a potentially potent movement as the Christian Right has failed so miserably and at such an important time in U.S. history? There are estimates that evangelical Christians number 40 to 50 million Americans and comprise 20% of the population or more. These are good, moral, honest people who contribute immeasurably to the well-being of their local communities. It is indeed a tragedy that this great potential for good has not been effectively mobilized to reverse the moral, cultural and political collapse of our nation, an outcome well within Christians' grasp had they done things differently and been better led.

Jackson and Deace have done considerable research into the causes of the failure of the Christian Right and pro-family movement and offer invaluable insights. I can only hope the Christian Right will begin to heed them.

One of the main reasons for this failure is theological, including a refusal to follow long-established biblical principles characteristic of the evangelical movement in other arenas. *Sola Scriptura* should be followed in the realm of public policy and politics as well as in doctrine, missiology, and church affairs. But no, many Christian Right leaders are supremely pragmatic and operate under the lesser-of-two evils approach when deciding between candidates and issues. The choice between the lesser of two evils is still evil. Jackson and Deace give a good critique of this approach and how it has been used to defeat good public policy and superior Christian candidates from a Christian point of view.

As Paul says in Romans 10:3, it's a case of "Going about to establish their own righteousness, but have not submitted themselves to the righteousness of God."

It grieves me to say it, but it appears that many of our Christian Right and pro-family leaders have been naïve and vulnerable to the con-artistry of the political establishment in Washington, and especially of the Republican Party. The GOP now has a virtual lock on the Christian and pro-family voter, while doing little to further their agenda except dropping rhetorical crumbs from the table from time to time. The Republican Party has become a master at fooling Christian leaders into thinking they make a difference and are important players in Washington politics. In turn, our so-called leaders have tried to con the average evangelical Christian voter and contributor with reports of energetic political and lobbying activities, even though these efforts do nothing to arrest the moral, cultural, and political rot. As Paul Weyrich pointed out to me, even our occasional political victories don't last. They don't reverse the inexorable drift to the left because conservatives and Christians have failed to address the cultural component which always trumps politics.

Even though the conclusions of Gregg Jackson and Steve Deace are at times withering, it is important to note that their critique is based fully in their commitment to the goals (if not the methods) of the Christian Right and the evangelical movement. My hope is that all who want to save what is left of our country and begin the vital work of regeneration and restoration will heed its invaluable insights.

We must start with repentance followed by intercessory prayer. Then we must recover a sound Christian worldview and apply it in all areas, in public policy and political activity as well as in ecclesiastical activity. We need a renewed vision of effective Christian action and service at all levels, in the hearts of those who aspire to lead, among pastors, and especially in the Christian people who support them.

E. RAY MOORE, CHAPLAIN, Lt. Colonel, USAR Ret., is founder and President of Frontline Ministries, Inc., and the Exodus Mandate Project (www.exodusmandate.org) a ministry to grow K-12 Christian education and home schooling. He was awarded the Bronze Star for his participation in Gulf War I.

The views expressed by those interviewed in this book do not necessarily reflect the views of the authors. In addition, the claims made by those interviewed regarding specific incidents, people, or issues represent the recollections and opinions of those individuals and do not necessarily reflect the views of the authors.

The authors of this book intentionally interviewed a list of people from different philosophical, eschatological, and theological persuasions on the subject matter here presented to get as wide a sample of opinion as possible. At times the information from one source in an interview may conflict with another, and the authors have determined therefore to let you, the reader, draw your own conclusions.

Finally, the authors also want you to know that no animals were harmed during the making of this book.

Introduction

"By their fruit you will know them."

JESUS CHRIST, MATTHEW 7:16

———

During the pivotal presidential election of 1980, Republican nominee Ronald Reagan poignantly gazed into the camera during a nationally televised debate with then President Jimmy Carter. He asked an American people at a crossroads, struggling under the crushing weight of inflation, an energy crisis, a national malaise, coupled with the potential threat of Soviet domination, a question that cut right to the heart of the matter.

"Are you better off than you were four years ago?" he asked.

Game, set, and match. It was clear the American people weren't better off, but instead were much, much worse. The country could endure a heinous scandal like Watergate, but it couldn't endure four more years of cowardly and incompetent leadership.

At this point in America's history, it seems fitting to use Reagan's $64,000 question as the premise for this book, since it was that same 1980 election that launched Christians into the political mainstream as an organized force to be reckoned with in America for perhaps the first time since abolition. Through the early work of pioneers like Paul Weyrich and Jerry Falwell's *Moral Majority*, Christians were given credit for being a key cog in a new conservative coalition that elevated Reagan to the presidency. Ironically, the man Reagan defeated in 1980 was one of the most outspoken, self-proclaimed born-again Christians in public office at the time.

It has been 30 years since the movement known as Christian Conservatives, the Religious Right, the Christian Right, Social Conservatives, or Values Voters hit the big time and became simultaneously the most feared and despised political advocacy group of the modern American political era. Therefore, it's well past time to subject it to the same scrutiny it has sought to impose upon candidates who don't share its convictions in every election since its ascendancy. Or, to be even more blunt, it's about time to hold ourselves to the same standard we demand of others.

Let's begin that process with a multiple choice test. Which President of the United States did the following?

- Actively campaigned against a state standing up for the sanctity of life while never bothering to physically appear at the "March for Life" held each year in Washington D.C.[1]
- Selected a vice president who was in favor of same sex marriage.[2]
- Gave vocal support to civil unions, which is marriage for homosexuals by just another name.[3]
- Nominated to the U.S. Supreme Court someone who once did pro bono work for homosexual activists attempting to overturn a state constitutional amendment protecting religious freedom in Federal court.[4]
- Nominated a homosexual activist as his AIDS czar, and had his Secretary of State preside over his swearing-in ceremony where he placed his hand on the Bible while his male partner stood next to him. Afterwards, that same Secretary of State referred to the boyfriend's mother as the new AIDS Czar's "mother-in-law."[5]
- Said on national television that Muslims who reject the saving grace of Jesus Christ go to Heaven,[6] and that the Bible is not literally true.[7]

Your choices are:
- Jimmy Carter
- Bill Clinton
- Barack Obama
- None of the above

The answer is, none of the above.

More specifically, and sadly, the answer is George W. Bush. That reality may surprise some, because he was the "Christian" politician most aggressively marketed as such of his era.

Unfortunately, the list of urgent email alerts from the most prominent Christian pro-family political advocacy organizations warning of all the sin and wickedness coming from the Bush Administration was embarrassingly short.

The conservative talk show superstars also failed to spend the hours of precious broadcast time exposing how Bush and some people close to him were a threat to America's traditional values the way they certainly would have if the occupant of the Oval Office were named Clinton or Obama.

In the same way, those ministers who are nationally-known for being outspoken on social and moral issues, failed to appear on Christian television to use the platform to hold Bush accountable for "threatening America's moral foundation" with the frequency and fervor they seem to reserve for Democrat presidents.

Sin and wickedness know no political affiliation, but for reasons known only to them, many Christian organizations, talk hosts, and television preachers held Bush to a far different standard than they did his predecessor or his successor.

And herein lies the problem.

For a generation those who believe "righteousness exalts a nation but sin is a disgrace to any people," have been hoping to save the collective soul of America through engagement with the political process. Hundreds of millions of dollars have been raised and spent on behalf of this crusade, not to mention the countless hours millions of believers have volunteered for the cause.

Christian involvement in the political arena has largely been driven by the Biblical principle, "when the righteous rule the people rejoice but when the wicked are in authority the people mourn." A major goal of this movement has been to help scores of men and women of Christian conscience, like George W. Bush claimed to be, to attain public office. The hope was that once there, they would advance a Biblical worldview for the betterment of society as a whole.

Unfortunately, it appears Christians were fighting for something most Americans no longer understand. In this day and age everyone does what is right in his own eyes, ethics are situational, truth is a matter of perspective, and everything is relative. Therefore, in order to honestly evaluate results, you have to clearly define your terms.

By fighting for "righteousness," which the Bible says only comes from faith in Christ[8] that produces good works,[9] and using politically correct code language like "traditional values," the vast majority of Americans who have never seriously been taught the Bible are left even more confused about who God really is and what it is He really demands of us.

Depending on the office, those same Biblically confused voters are given the opportunity to have a referendum on how their elected officials are performing. Each time a candidate stands for re-election, their constituents determine whether or not to retain their services. This book intends to challenge the reader to do something similar, but instead it's a referendum on a movement more than on any individual.

We, the authors of this book, believe this level of accountability is absolutely Biblical, and frankly way overdue. The movement has been so influential in both the city of man and the city of God that it's likely far more Americans could identify Pat Robertson or Ralph Reed, thanks to their myriad of appearances discussing political affairs in the news media over the years, than could tell you who prominent contemporary Bible teachers like John Piper or John MacArthur are.

To mainstream America, it's often those who carry the name of Christ into the highly-publicized political arena that symbolize the Body of Christ in America, not those who lift up the name of Christ from its pulpits. As a result, it is imperative that the body of believers in the United States honestly evaluate those who have so profoundly influenced the mission field we call home. In addition to their impact on politics and public policy, this movement has had a direct impact on our ability to fulfill the Great Commission.

As you read the pages that follow, ask yourself, "As I share Christ with my neighbor, will their perception of Christians in the public arena help or hinder their decision to repent?" The impact of those who carry the banner of "Christian conservative," "values voters," or the "moral majority" has permeated far beyond the political arena.

Therefore, as Uncle Ben once told Peter Parker before he became Spider-Man, "with great power comes great responsibility." The Bible agrees with Uncle Ben, by the way. Jesus says that "to whom much is given much is required,[10]" and he commands us to "judge not" unless we are willing to be consistent in applying our own standard "for in the same way you judge others you will be judged, and with the measure you use it will be measured to you.[11]" In addition, the Apostle Peter taught us that "judgment must begin in the house of God.[12]"

So it is with the approval of the King of Kings and Lord of Lords, as well as one of the church's patron saints, that this book will paraphrase former President Reagan and ask a simple yet difficult question—is America better off than it was 30 years ago before Christians invaded the political arena?

Let's put an even finer point on it by asking some uncomfortable follow up questions:

Is the culture more or less secular or humanist then it was 30 years ago? Are Christians more or less Biblically ignorant then they were 30 years ago?

According to leading worldview trend analyst George Barna, despite decades of standing for Biblical truth in the most visible arena in the culture, the answers to both of those questions are disappointing. Only 34% of adults believe that moral truth is absolute and ethics are not situational and only 46% of Christians do. Just 27% of adults believe Satan is a real force, and only 40% of Christians do. Only 40% of adults believe Christ lived a sinless life on earth, and more than one-third of born-again believers do not. Only 28% of adults believe that people can't earn their way into Heaven by being good as opposed to grace alone, but only 53% of Christians disagree. Add this all up, and Barna concludes that since he started surveying American belief systems in 1995 the percentage of adults with a Biblical worldview—defined by Barna as belief that absolute moral truth exists, the Bible is totally accurate in all of the principles it teaches, Satan is considered to be a real being or force and not merely symbolic, a person cannot earn their way into Heaven by trying to be good or do good works, Jesus Christ lived a sinless life on earth, and God is the all-knowing and all-powerful creator of the world who still rules the universe today—has increased from just 7% to only 9%[13] while at the same time 83% of Americans consider themselves to be Christians.[14]

Is Planned Parenthood more or less powerful than it was 30 years ago?

For example, did you know the income for America's top infanticide merchant increased by 24% and its government subsidies have grown by 33% since 2005 alone?[15] More revenue has allowed Planned Parenthood to get even more gruesomely innovative in its brutality. After aiding and abetting the deaths of over 50 million babies in America[16], life is so disregarded abortions are now available via teleconference[17].

Is the homosexual lobby more or less powerful than it was 30 years ago?

In 1980, homosexual activism was pretty much relegated to San Francisco and a few other liberal locales. Today, it's a national social and political force benefiting from multi-million dollar sugar daddies[18] like Tim Gill,[19] and has major corporations vying for its affection.[20] All this despite the fact it represents less than 5% of the U.S. population[21].

Furthermore, even though the homosexual lobby has lost every voter referendum on the definition of marriage so far, thanks to the relentless dissemination of dogmatic disinformation recent polls show increasing public support for the state allowing homosexuals to marry.[22] That which has failed in every public referendum, and which was unthinkable as recently as 2000, let alone 1980, is still managing to make inroads through slick marketing and shrewd political maneuvering.

Is government education in America more or less dominated by leftists from places like the NEA than it was 30 years ago?
Through decades of well-orchestrated political activism, the NEA has basically gained control of the Democrat Party[23] and remains firmly entrenched as a leading expositor of progressive indoctrination[24] despite a terrible decline in American government education.

Are judges more or less in line with their Constitutional parameters when issuing rulings than they were 30 years ago?
Time and again, judges have attempted to redefine marriage by thwarting long-standing legislation and now even voter ratified state marriage amendments.[25] They have trampled on private property rights[26], and have attempted to give tax-payer subsidized welfare and education to illegal aliens.[27] They have issued rulings stating that parents have "no constitutional right" to determine how to educate their children nor to protect them from "contemporary secular values."[28] Perhaps worst of all, they are increasingly and stunningly using foreign court precedent[29] to render decisions as they did in the landmark *Lawrence v. Texas* Supreme Court ruling on sodomy laws.[30]

Is the government smaller or bigger than it was 30 years ago?
In 1980, the federal government collected $244 billion from individual taxpayers.[31] Just 30 years later, in 2010, that number was projected to climb to just over $2.3 trillion.[32] Keep in mind this is only *individual* income taxes, and doesn't count Social Security, capital gains, or other taxes like excise taxes, which are applied to things such as gasoline, firearms and other weapons, tobacco, alcohol, tires, trucks, and fishing equipment. King George III would be envious of the ways by which our government now extracts taxes from Americans.

One example comes from co-author Steve Deace's home state of Iowa, where the state budget more than doubled from $2 billion to $4.5 billion after 16 years of having a Republican governor![33] By contrast, the $700 billion increase in the federal budget under President George W. Bush was far and away the biggest in American history at the time. Fortunately for former President Bush, President Barack Obama made all previous budgets appear austere when he proposed growing it by $1.3 trillion.[34]

al budget was $590.9 billion before Ronald Reagan
en George W. Bush left office in 2009 it was $3.51
1-2009 Republicans were in the White House for 20

publicans set the stage for the even bigger spend-
k Obama. According to projections from the Inter-
Fund, U.S. deficits could reach 100% of our gross
which is the total worth of a nation's economy) by
ves office, if he's elected to a second term.[36]

abies born out of wedlock than they were 30 years

study, the out-of-wedlock birth rate in the United
States has skyrocketed from 28% in 1990 to an incredible 41%.[37] Just
compare either of those numbers to the out-of-wedlock birthrate in
1980, which was 19.6%,[38] and it becomes obvious that the 30-year
trend is anything but encouraging. Despite much more awareness,
acceptance, and access to birth control, as well as millions of taxpayer
dollars invested in abstinence programs, more and more children in
this country are conceived by parents who are not married.

So while overall abortion rates have slightly dipped since 1980, it
doesn't appear to be a result of a return to family values, but rather
unwed mothers having their babies as opposed to murdering them.
Obviously the unwed mother having her baby is always preferable. In
fact, one of the authors of this book was born to a 15-year old unwed
mother. However, while it may be preferable it's still not God's ideal,
which is a married man and a married woman procreating and raising
the next generation within the bounds of holy matrimony for the betterment of society.

Is the marriage covenant in our culture more or less honored than it was 30 years ago?

The current divorce rate in America for first time marriages is 41%. For
second marriages it's 60%, and for third marriages it's 73%.[39] While
divorce rates did decline from 1981-90, for the first time in American
history a couple is just as likely to be parted by divorce on average as by
death.[40] For the first time in American history, the majority of Americans adults are living together or are remaining single rather than mar-
rying as the rate of married adults has fallen below 50%.[41]

Is our children's innocence more or less protected than it was 30 years ago?

According to *The Center for Media and Public Affairs*, sexual content is found every four minutes on network television. About 98% of that sexual content has no subsequent physical consequences, 85% of it has no lasting emotional impact, and 75% of its participants are unmarried.[42] A March 2000 study by the *Kaiser Family Foundation* found the percentage of primetime television shows that included sexual conduct tripled from 1990-2000.[43] According to *Family Safe Media*, the pornography industry grosses more revenue than all the professional football, basketball, and baseball franchises combined. They also assert that the average age of first exposure to pornography is 11, with 12 to 17 year olds comprising the largest consumer demographic of online porn.[44] Iowa State University Professor of Psychology, Craig Anderson, recently concluded an exhaustive study on the explosion of violent video games and their impact on children. His research "proves exposure to violent video games makes more aggressive, less caring kids—regardless of their age, sex or culture."[45]

Despite the overwhelming political support given by Christians to Republicans, who promised to stem the counter-cultural tide, we can't imagine that the answers to all of those questions are anything close to what was promised, or what was hoped for.

Republicans appointed a majority of the current federal judiciary (including two-thirds of the current Supreme Court justices), won five of the eight presidential elections since 1980, and for several years had control of both houses of Congress. Additionally, many of the state legislatures and governorships were held by Republicans during that time span as well.

Even more disappointing, a Republican Party that was a minority party in America until grassroots Christians made the ranks of its base swell with new voters in the 1980s, is now openly and routinely shunning its most loyal voting bloc. They not only duck the issues that drive people of faith to the polls, but continue to mock anyone who continues to look for political leaders that would share their values. Even though issues such as the right to life and the sanctity of marriage are the foundation of any civil and prosperous society, the GOP establishment is adamant that those issues be abandoned.

Here are just a few examples:

- The 2008 Republican presidential nominee, John McCain, worked to defeat an amendment to the U.S. Constitution defining marriage as one man and one woman while in the U.S. Senate,[46] supported taxpayer funding of the destruction of human embryos,[47] and voted to confirm even the most leftist judges like Ruth Bader Ginsburg to lifetime appointments on the U.S. Supreme Court.[48]
- McCain's campaign manager in 2008, Stephen Schmidt, encouraged a pro-homosexual GOP group known as the Log Cabin Republicans to "keep fighting for what you believe because your day is going to come."[49]
- Former Republican National Committee Chairman Ken Mehlman revealed he was a homosexual in 2010, and that over the years he used his lofty perch within the GOP to fight back against efforts to defend marriage, essentially admitting to sabotaging the moral principles of his party's most loyal voters and activists that empowered him in the first place.[50]
- Rep. Pete Sessions and Sen. Jon Cornyn, the two men most responsible for getting Republicans elected to Capitol Hill during the last election cycle, were the keynote speakers at a pro-homosexual group's banquet leading up to the 2010 midterm elections.[51]
- On July 29, 2010, talk radio titan Rush Limbaugh came out in favor of civil unions, which is just same sex marriage by another name.[52]
- Less than two weeks later, fellow talk radio titan Glenn Beck—a self-proclaimed devout Mormon—said that destroying marriage was "no threat to the country" and that he had "bigger fish to fry."[53] In Mormonism the family is the central institution of the religion,[54] which is why Mormons have fought so hard and spent so much money to defend marriage in places like California, so Beck abandoning the family as a Mormon would be similar to a Catholic abandoning the sacraments.[55]
- Former vice president Dick Cheney has frequently exhibited public support for homosexuality,[56] as has prominent conservative activist Grover Norquist who joined the Advisory Council of GOProud in 2010.[57]
- Former First Lady Laura Bush said that she was pro-abortion and pro-homosexuality in several interviews while promoting her book in 2010.[58]
- CPAC, the most influential perennial gathering of conservatives, included pro-homosexual GOProud as a "sponsor" in 2010[59] and a "participating organization" in 2011.[60]

ᴀSH THIS
BEFORE
E SPECIAL
ESS USED
BEAUTY
NT MAY
LOR
ST BE
ᴀTELY.

d about these acts of moral malfeasance is that they come at
more Americans than ever before are describing themselves
opinion surveys,[61] and are taking place in the growing wake
jection of gay marriage in every referendum held so far. The
attempt to pander to a segment of the population that rep-
than 5% of the U.S. population at best, and is already solidly
in the Democrat Party to begin with, flies in the face of not
ral sensibilities of the conservative base, but also that of logic
mathematics.

le Republican establishment is telling the truth when it says it's
winning elections no matter what, why would they sell out to a
iority comprised of homosexuals? What is it about the political
position that has lost 31 consecutive elections (at the time of this printing)
in states that have considered whether or not to defend marriage? Who
takes the losing side of an issue that has an electoral record of 0-31, including votes in notoriously liberal states like Maine and Oregon, and calls
that political pragmatism?

What's even more tragically ironic is that Christians engaging the
political arena have allowed their entire worldview to be defined by the
mainstream media as simply pertaining to life and marriage. While we
agree those issues are the two most important and that they determine
the direction of an entire civilization, the Bible also has a lot to say about
monetary policy, banking, economics, education, just war, and a host of
others. The Bible has just as much to say about the issues that most Americans actually vote on as it does about the so-called "social issues" that get
so much attention.

We've allowed the political elites and the media to misrepresent our
worldview, and misdirect our energies. As a result, the kitchen-table issues
are only debated from a secular philosophical viewpoint, wrongly giving
Americans the impression that the Word of God does not have something
to say about every aspect of our lives.

As you can already see, the most troubling conclusion of this self-
assessment is that we're ultimately left with one rather troublesome
truth.

That inconvenient truth is that despite all of the time, talent, and treasure presumably spent to stand for righteousness in America, this country
is careening toward a leftist and pagan collision course with historical
oblivion. It is beginning to look like the result of 30 years of Christian
Conservatives in politics may be the very antithesis of its Biblical founda-

tion. This is why Dr. James Dobson in his farewell address to the staff of *Focus on the Family* in 2009 admitted that after decades of political activism, "we are absolutely awash in evil."

God Almighty Himself says, "My Word that goes out from My mouth; It shall not return to me void, but it shall accomplish what I please, and it shall prosper in the thing for which I sent it."[62]

If that's true, how could it be that despite all the hard work, good intentions, and ballot box successes of faithful Christians, the United States is following in the footsteps of the secularization and socialism that has already occurred in Western Europe? Furthermore, what can be done to reverse our collision course and put this country back on the narrow road?

Before any real change can take place, there must first be an honest assessment of how we got here in the first place. That's exactly what this book attempts to do. The two authors are fathers and husbands concerned about the future. We are aware of God's rich blessing on our country and of our unique providential history. We desire to preserve the God-given liberties we have enjoyed and pass them on to our children and grandchildren.

Gregg Jackson wrote the conservative best-seller *Conservative Comebacks to Liberal Lies*, which was endorsed by conservative heavyweights like Thomas Sowell and David Limbaugh. He's been the emcee at CPAC, a talk show host for WRKO in Boston and KDAR in Los Angeles. He has rubbed elbows with a literal who's who of conservative and Republican elites.

Nationally syndicated radio talk show host Steve Deace is also the former afternoon drive host for the legendary 1040-WHO in Des Moines, one of the top news-talk radio stations in the nation. WHO was where Ronald Reagan served as the station's first sports director, and from that 50,000-watt vantage point in the first-in-the-nation caucus state, Steve got an intimate look at many of the nation's leading political figures and organizations.

Yet despite our combined expertise (or lack thereof depending on your perspective), neither one of us presumes to have all the answers regarding how the fight for righteousness in America went wrong, which is why for the past few years we set out to discuss this with some of the leading Christian political activists in the country.

We began doing this independent of one another through our respective radio programs and various contacts. After a while, we realized that the answers we were getting, or more noticeably *not* getting in some cases, deserved as wide an audience as possible. We hope the information that follows can help stop America from being lost on the scrapheap of history. We decided the best way to accomplish that was by joining forces and compiling these interviews into a book.

Since there is "wisdom in a multitude of counsel" we will give you, the reader, a chance to pick the brains of those that have been fighting the good fight on the front lines for years. Our hope is that we can learn from both their successes and failures. As much as possible, we have removed our own opinions from each discussion until the conclusion. We have chosen to rely heavily on direct quotes from the interviews we conducted. That way the words of these political operatives, power brokers, and insiders can speak for themselves. In the end, you will be left to make up your own mind about what they mean.

In his farewell address to the Ephesian elders, the Apostle Paul warns them that "savage wolves will come in among you, not sparing the flock. Also from among yourselves men will rise up, speaking perverse things, to draw away the disciples after themselves. Therefore watch, and remember that for three years I did not cease to warn everyone night and day with tears."[63]

We pray that we can humbly follow in Paul's footsteps and warn you, the reader, with tears. We take no glee in revealing some of the things you will learn by reading this book, or have already learned in this introduction. In fact, we are heartbroken ourselves, but the truth must come out before whatever hope that America might rediscover her original intent and purpose vanishes entirely.

If there is not earnest revival in this country by the end of our generation, we believe our children will inherit a nation that looks more like a post-Christian Western Europe drowning in debt than it does the nation our Founders designed. We hope the next generation will know an America that would once again inspire the words that became famous with Dwight Eisenhower's 1952 presidential campaign:

> I sought for the greatness and genius of America in her commodious harbors and her ample rivers—and it was not there...in her fertile fields and boundless forests and it was not there...in her rich mines and her vast world commerce—and it was not there...in her democratic Congress and her matchless Constitution—and it was not there. Not until I went into the churches of America and heard her pulpits flame with righteousness did I understand the secret of her genius and power.

*America is great because she is good, and if America ever ceases to be
good, she will cease to be great.*

Even though both of us are a part of "Generation X" we each share a
fondness for The Who. It's their Magnus Opus, "Won't Get Fooled Again,"
that serves as one of the inspirations for this book. Guitarist Pete Townsend
wrote the song, and he has said that the core of its message is a warning
to not fall for political spin and empty rhetoric but instead critically think
for yourself lest you become exactly like that which you loathe.

Or, as the Apostle John put it, "test the spirits."[64]

However, while we believe critical thinking and accountability are
healthy for the discerning Christian, we are also concerned that the following pages may cause some Christians to want to abandon the public
square altogether. A general retreat from the culture to some modern day
manifestation of monasteries is the last thing America needs. Quite the
contrary, this self-governing nation needs Christians to see its halls of
power as a mission field before it's too late.

The harvest is plenty, but the workers are few. Our intent is to take you
on a journey that empowers you to keep the faith, not lose it.

In the book of Hosea, God said, "My people are destroyed from a lack
of knowledge."[65]

That will no longer be the case for you if you turn the page, but while
knowledge is power ignorance is also bliss. If you read this book there will
be no turning back. You may no longer blindly and emotionally follow
leaders, or swoon at the politicians they support, as you once did—as we,
the authors of this book who once would have voted for *any* Republican
over *any* Democrat, once did. You may also end up unintentionally alien-
ating those close to you who refuse to reevaluate what they have thought
to be true through the prism of the words of the very people they have
been following.

On the other hand, those of you gutsy enough to read this book are
about to find out just how far down the rabbit hole goes. Consider yourself
warned.

Soon it will be another generation's turn to lead. We hope when they're
finished reading this book they will be inspired to "get on our knees and
pray, we don't get fooled again."

Well, Who Are You?

For I know that the hypnotized never lie.

PETE TOWNSEND

───•◦•───

The first step on this journey is for you, the reader, to know more about each of us and what specifically happened that led to the writing of this book. It's important for you to know a little about the authors, so you can make informed decisions as you draw conclusions from the contents of this book.

Let's begin with Gregg's story:

No doubt. I had really arrived! I was now a recognized conservative mover and shaker.

Well not quite a celebrity conservative like Ann Coulter, Sean Hannity or Rush Limbaugh. But as I, Gregg Jackson, sat on stage at the 2008 Conservative Political Action Conference as the emcee of the "Presidential Sessions," for the second year in a row I looked out at thousands of grassroots conservatives and knew that hundreds of thousands more were watching on TV. I was on top of the world.

At the time, I was on the radio on one of the oldest and most prestigious talk radio stations in the country, WRKO in Boston. I was the author of the nationally best selling *Conservative Comebacks to Liberal Lies*; spoke regularly on college campuses and to conservative organizations around the country; and had written articles that were published by *Townhall.com*, *Human Events*, and the *Washington Times*. Several of my "letters to the editor" were also published in the *Wall Street Journal*.

So being chosen for the second year in a row to emcee the presidential sessions at CPAC, the largest and most important gathering of conservative heavyweights and grassroots activists in the country, was the icing on the cake.

Still, amidst all the exhilaration of rubbing elbows with, and introducing GOP presidential candidates like John McCain, Rudy Giuliani, Mitt Romney, Sam Brownback, Duncan Hunter and Ron Paul to a nationally televised TV audience, I had a nagging sense that something was not quite right.

The year prior, at the 2007 CPAC, I sat about five feet to the left of the former governor of Massachusetts, the state where I had worked and lived, as he addressed the CPAC gathering. He read directly from a teleprompter, and drew tendentious comparisons between himself and Ronald Reagan.[66] Although I was clapping along with the rest of the crowd on all the red meat applause lines, I remember thinking that this wasn't the guy who I covered on the radio in Boston who during his time as Governor (2003-2007):

- Illegally instituted gay "marriage."[67]
- Signed into law $50 co-pay, taxpayer-funded abortions, as a component of his quasi-socialist healthcare plan[68] (three years after his supposed "pro-life conversion.")[69]
- Boosted funding for homosexual "education" starting in kindergarten.[70]

His Reaganesque rhetoric at CPAC certainly didn't line up with his actual far left record in Massachusetts.

I remember sitting only a few feet away from "conservative" columnist and pundit George Will, who I had just introduced. I listened as he then introduced Rudy Giuliani. During his glowing introduction of the liberal former mayor of New York City, Will equated the firmly held convictions of some, to the pragmatic pliability of others when he said like ice cream "conservatism as we all know, comes in many different flavors."[71]

I could not believe my ears. Was Will actually claiming that a man who is in favor of tax-payer funded abortion on demand[72] and gay marriage,[73] and the man who dressed in drag at a gay pride parade,[74] was a "conservative" in Will's estimation?

According to Will, since Giuliani agreed with conservatives on 80% of the issues (tax cuts, crime, war on terror) conservatives could overlook the fact that Giuliani is ok with killing babies in the womb and allowing homosexuals to marry or adopt children.

At that moment I had to fight every urge that I had to grab the mic away from Will and denounce the entire fraud that CPAC had become. Looking back, perhaps I should have done just that, but like many of you reading this I went along with the partisan hypocrisy because the Democrats were supposedly so much worse.

Politicians who were pro-abortion, pro-socialized healthcare, and pro-homosexual like Romney and Rudy (who Ann Coulter claimed in a personal e-mail to me would be her "dream ticket") were now "conservative" because they had "R's" near their name and claimed that they shared Reagan's conservative political philosophy?

It was a surreal moment for me. Had the powers that be in the "conservative movement" lost their mind? How could they allow these liberals in a Reagan Costume (Rudy, Mitt, and McCain), who had spent the vast majority of their careers thwarting conservative legislation and values, to speak at the same CPAC that Ronald Reagan helped launch decades earlier?

Furthermore, why was I, a virtual unknown, selected two years in a row to emcee the presidential sessions at CPAC? I had not lobbied David Keene, the president of the American Conservative Union and head of CPAC, for the gig.

Well, I have no doubt now in retrospect that this was indeed a "God thing."

No doubt God orchestrated it all, I believe, to enable me to "peek behind the curtain," to witness first-hand the compromised and corrupted conservative movement. He literally gave me a front row seat.

After all, I had not lobbied David Limbaugh to suggest to pro-family Christian activist Janet Folger of *Faith 2 Action*, who coordinated the Values Voters Summit, that I emcee that event either.

Nor had I lobbied to be selected by Folger to attend a private, three-day meeting of "conservative leaders" at her home in Florida—including *Movie Guide* president Ted Baehr, Rev. Rick Scarborough, former head of the Southern Baptist Convention Jimmy Draper, Matt Staver of *Liberty Council*, and Peter LaBarbera of *Americans for Truth*. All this was no doubt orchestrated by God to provide me with a behind the scenes perspective of the conservative movement and its compromising leaders.

Time and time again, what I witnessed at gatherings like CPAC, private meetings like the one at Folger's home, in radio interviews I conducted, and through personal e-mail exchanges, was that a movement founded upon Judeo-Christian values and principles had sacrificed those core values at the altar of "getting a seat at the table."

It soon became clear that the core social/moral convictions such as life and marriage, which brought tens of millions of grassroots evangelical "values voters" to the polls for Reagan, and then for the two Bushes, were now merely two political positions among many. The two issues that serve as barometers for the health of a society were lumped in with others that could be altered or spurned altogether if it meant winning the White

House or seats in Congress. The founders of the conservative movement, such as Russell Kirk and T.S. Eliot, sought to preserve the "permanent things" in society like life and marriage, but it was increasingly obvious to me that the conservative movement had devolved into a movement whose central purpose was access to and acquisition of political power.

I then had to admit to myself that I had adopted the same pragmatic, anti-biblical worldview of much of the "conservative movement" around me. I had become just another political pawn who believed that everything would be good in America as long as Republicans were in control of government.

After all, I had voted for George W. Bush—twice. I cast those votes in spite of the fact that he and the GOP grew the federal government more than LBJ, and increased funding to the nation's largest abortion provider, Planned Parenthood, at a greater rate than under Bill Clinton. I took tremendous pleasure in verbally filleting liberals on the radio in Boston, while simultaneously ignoring liberals in the GOP who were guilty of the exact same things I criticized liberal Democrats for.

"Republican good, Democrat bad" was essentially my motto and mindset.

By the grace of God, I came to see that what ailed America was not too many liberals. I came to understand instead that America's major problem is not political but spiritual, and that therefore the only real solution is not political but rather it's spiritual. God helped me to understand that those I had railed against were merely a symptom of the problem…a symptom of a nation under judgment whose Christians have largely rejected God's Natural Laws. I came to understand that the reason the conservative movement had been infiltrated by liberals and materialists, and the reason the Left was winning the Culture War, was largely due to the fact that God's people were less serious about defending their core values and beliefs than the liberals were.

That realization is at the root of why I decided to co-write this book. That God brought my co-author Steve Deace to a similar epiphany at roughly the same time has been both a confirmation and an encouragement. My hope is that as you read the following pages, you will take courage in knowing that we are not taking you where we haven't already been.

The bottom line is that the conservative movement, founded on the protection, preservation and advancement of Biblically-defined morality, has essentially devolved into a huge money-making industry whose leading organizations and pundits have too often compromised the core values and beliefs of the Christian grassroots for power, prestige and prosperity.

You, the reader, deserve to know the truth about who some of the wolves in sheep's clothing are. It's as simple as that. If Christians are truly going to preserve America from totalitarian socialist-Democrats, we must acknowledge that the enemy within the gate is more dangerous than the enemy outside.

The Founders recognized that political factions within our nation posed a more significant threat than foreign enemies. Steve and I have come to the sad realization that many of the "conservative" and Christian organizations, media publications and pundits have actually done more to advance the Left's agenda than the recognizable leaders of the Left could have ever accomplished on their own. So, before Christians endeavor to help preserve the American Republic in the 21st Century, we must first come to grips with the enemy within.

Steve's story, and his first encounter with the enemy within:

He just looked me right in the eye and lied to me. I can't believe it, he lied right to me. And if he isn't lying, then he doesn't even know the record of the candidate he's trying to convince us to support!

I kept playing the conversation over in my head as I sat at the back table of a Perkins restaurant in West Des Moines, Iowa, one snowy Saturday in December of 2007.

The "he" in this case was James Bopp, Jr., a well-known attorney in political circles for his work with the National Right to Life Committee. He had joined our table for an appointment with an intimate group of local Christian conservative activists as part of his effort to shill for his favored presidential candidate—former Massachusetts Governor Willard Mitchell Romney.

I had been tipped off to the meeting by another local activist concerned over Romney's apparent ability to "persuade" folks to overlook the gaping holes in his claimed conservative record regarding our key issues. I'll leave it up to your imagination to determine what "persuade" means, but here's a hint—team Romney had already begun to "persuade" Iowa activists the way a "john" "persuades" a prostitute to have sex with him. My tipster was especially concerned because one of the activists slated to be there was Steve Scheffler, the head of the Iowa Christian Alliance.

Scheffler was a man that, at the time, held sway with thousands of Christian conservatives across the first in the nation caucus state. During the 2008 cycle, he parlayed that influence into a position as Iowa's Republican National Committeeman.

My tipster invited me to crash the meeting, saying that a deal could be struck between Bopp and Scheffler to shutout other candidates like Tom Tancredo, Fred Thompson, Ron Paul and—my favorite at the time—Mike Huckabee, and keep them from gaining access to this key voting bloc. He was concerned no one would be there to rebut Bopp's anticipated pro-Romney propaganda.

I'm not normally shy when it comes to confrontation, and I couldn't resist the invitation. However, my wise wife didn't trust my tendency towards a short fuse and made me promise to take our pastor with me. She figured the former military policeman who had become my pastor could keep me on a short leash.

So Pastor Bob and I drove through the early winter Iowa snow and just showed up uninvited to a small meeting of Christian conservative activists. We were Christians, conservatives, and activists, but we quickly realized we might be the only ones not ready and willing to be "persuaded" towards Romney by Mr. Bopp.

Romney had run scorched earth ads against his competition in Iowa, just as he had in other races, with what seemed like an endless supply of money. He actually outspent all of his competitors in Iowa combined. Often, the ads attacked his opponents' weak spots, and some of the accusations were even valid attacks. The problem for Romney was that he was often weaker on the very issues he was attacking his opposition on than they were! What a tangled web he had to weave in order to deceive Iowa's strong Christian conservative voting bloc he was one of them, despite being labeled by *Human Events* the nation's # 8 RINO (Republican in Name Only) as recently as 2005.

Thanks to the ceaseless negative advertising and Romney's long line of flip-flops and outright untruths, the worst-kept secret during the 2008 Iowa Caucus campaign was that perhaps the only thing the other Republican presidential campaigns could agree on was their shared loathing for the Romney campaign.

So Pastor Bob and I sat down at the table designated for the meeting in the back of the restaurant. We were the first ones there. I wish I had brought a camera to record the looks on the faces of the other activists as they arrived. They tried to put on their best poker faces, hoping we didn't see their combined grimaces and nervous twitches, but it was too late. My pastor isn't known for being bashful, and I'm certainly no shrinking violet and it was obvious our reputations had preceded us. I had already spent months exposing Mitt Romney's deceptions on my 50,000-watt radio show heard by thousands of Iowans per week, and as each guest arrived they likely knew that the meeting was not going to be a walk in the park for Bopp.

When they sat down we initially engaged in some small talk about sports. I silently prayed inwardly not to get diarrhea of the mouth and totally alienate everybody before the real fun was sure to begin. *Please God*," I prayed, "*help me to be a good boy and just listen to start with for a change*."

Then Bopp showed up, brushing the snow off his coat he greeted the gathered group warmly. He acted as if he didn't know me, and then sat down right next to me. As coffee and food was being consumed, Bopp suddenly and awkwardly made an off-handed comment about how he's pro-life, but he doesn't want to have to support "big government" and a governor who was known for giving clemency to felons to do it.

He was making a clear reference to Romney's attack ads against Huckabee. The comment appeared to be directed at me and seemingly only me. How did he know I was a Huckabee supporter? I thought he didn't know me? I thought he didn't know of my radio show?

So we went back-and-forth for a few minutes until he had finally had enough of me and said, "I didn't come all the way here to debate you."

I asked him, "Why did you pick a fight then?"

At this point a couple of the activists stepped in and let me know they were here to hear him and not me, and that they get enough chances to hear me already. It was a fair point, so I kept quiet and gave Bopp the chance to make his case.

Right away he began to lecture the group about coalescing behind one conservative candidate, the one who was conservative across the board, and the one who could win.

The "one" in this case was Romney.

Bopp made it clear that Huckabee was an Iowa phenomenon only because of the large evangelical population in the GOP caucus, that evangelicals were only voting for him because he was a former Southern Baptist minister, and that Huckabee had no chance in more mainstream Republican states.

You know, like all those "mainstream" states that Romney won during the 2008 Republican presidential primaries. But I digress...

It was amazing to hear Bopp cynically refer to his own constituency as if they were a herd of cattle just waiting to be told where to go. His hard-sell devolved into a lecture with the patronizing tone of a teacher scolding his pupils. I had heard Christian Conservatives talked to, and about, like this before—by liberals. Now the condescending disrespect was coming from one of their alleged "leaders."

The activists expressed skepticism that they could pull the people behind Romney. It is important to note that Romney's connection to the Mormon religion was never even discussed as the reason why, contrary to the urban legend promoted by so many sellout Republican elites. Romney's Mormonism didn't even register as a reason for not supporting him when compared to his record. The activists just simply thought that with less than a month before the Caucus, it was too late for such a move to take place for such a troubled candidate. With only weeks to go, and Christmas just around the corner, the die was cast.

Still, Bopp would not relent. He kept pushing and pushing the men gathered around the table. His antics reached a point where his tone communicated more than his words, delivering a clear "how dare you not obey me" message. Just when he had appeared to brow-beat them into silence, Scheffler finally spoke up.

He asked Bopp about something Phyllis Schafly at the *Eagle Forum* had written about Romney. He asked if Romney, and not the Massachusetts Supreme Court, was actually responsible for homosexual marriage in that state. He pointed out that Romney had enforced the State Supreme Court's immoral ruling despite the fact the Massachusetts Constitution explicitly forbids the Court from legislating from the bench.

How did Bopp respond?

He dismissively shrugged his shoulders and said to Scheffler it would've been "political suicide" for Romney to oppose the court and "you can't expect any politician to do that."

There you have it. The oldest Constitution in America handwritten by (among others) John Adams himself, and the moral law of Almighty God, cast aside in Romney's home state because there was a presidential race to gear up for.

Finally the conversation came back around to whether or not Romney was truly pro-life. In both his 1994 U.S. Senate campaign[75] and his 2002 gubernatorial campaign[76] Romney was an outspoken supporter of killing babies. Then, coincidentally enough, shortly before running for president he claimed to have a pro-life epiphany after talking it over with an embryologist.

There were lots of doubts about the sincerity of Romney's pro-life conversion given the timing. Everyone knows you simply can't win the Republican presidential nomination unless you can convince enough primary voters you're pro-life. It was interesting to note that even after his alleged pro-life conversion, Romney signed his infamous "Romneycare" state-mandated healthcare plan into law, which included a provision for taxpayer-funded, $50 co-pay elective abortions.[77]

After remaining silent for quite a while and just listening to the exchange, I finally spoke up and said I didn't believe Romney was truly pro-life. Bopp of course said he was. As evidence for my position, I told Bopp that Romney had given three different positions on the Human Life Amendment in the Republican Party Platform championed by Bopp's National Right to Life Committee, and pointed out that all three positions were asserted in just the last six months alone. Bopp steadfastly said that was absolutely not true and Romney had stood for it the entire campaign.

He just looked me right in the eye and lied to me. I can't believe it, he lied right to me. Or, at the very least, he's more interested in promoting his candidate than knowing the truth.

At this point my adrenaline went over a cliff. My voice was quivering. I looked at this man who had been allegedly fighting the pro-life fight longer than I've been shaving, and realized he was just another political operative for-hire, not a pro-life warrior. If this was really about saving babies, how could he support a guy that was willing to make it easier for unwed mothers like my own back in the day to abort their babies for only $50 in the first place? Instead, in exchange for a seat at the table, he was willing to cover for Republican politicians willing to sacrifice babies, like those in my own family, on the altar of political pragmatism to a modern-day Molech.

He just wanted a seat at the table.

I told Bopp he wasn't telling the truth. He denied it.

I invited him to take a trip downtown to my studio and hear for himself the audio clips of his candidate I had collected going back years. He refused. He really had no other alternative. Those recordings would've exposed him as just another so-called Christian conservative leader whose character had been swallowed whole by the system. Mitt Romney was just the system's latest Manchurian Candidate to take those "seat at the table" leaders like Bopp for a ride on a magical, monetary tour.

It is moments like that, and those Gregg wrote about, that are the reason the Christian conservative movement is at a crossroads today. After more than a quarter century of high-profile political action that has often led to victory at the ballot box, the larger war for the soul of America has clearly been lost.

Let me urge you—don't just take our word for it. Turn the page and hear it directly from those who have been there.

Steve Baldwin

Interviewed by Steve and Gregg—March, 2010

———•◦•◦•———

If you want to understand the major players within the pro-family and pro-life, conservative, and Christian organizations in America, there may be no one better to speak with than the man who from 2001-08 was the Executive Director for the Council for National Policy (CNP).

CNP is a largely confidential group of around 500 leaders from conservative think tanks, organizations and policy groups. Steve Baldwin wasn't just hired to run this elite organization of insiders, he was also tasked with keeping its members informed of key issues and candidates.

Baldwin has been involved in the movement for almost 30 years. In the Reagan era he worked as a fundraiser for the resistance in Nicaragua, and was a member of the California legislature from 1994-2000. He also served as National Executive Director of Young Americans for Freedom and has authored two books, *From Crayons to Condoms: a Critique of Public Schools,* and *The Revolution Lobby.* Baldwin is currently a freelance writer and political consultant based in San Diego, and has never been shy about ruffling his fellow conservatives' feathers over his attention to facts. It didn't take Baldwin long in our conversation with him for his blunt assessment of the movement to emerge.

"As (my) time went by (in the movement) it started to dawn on me that there's a lot of money here being raised by a lot of groups, mostly via direct mail, that doesn't seem to be used for what people think it's being used for," Baldwin said. "As time went by it started to dawn on me that there's a lot of money here being raised by a lot of groups, mostly via direct mail, that doesn't seem to be used for what people think it's being used for.

For example, I found that Jay Sekulow (President of the American Center for Law and Justice) was raising tens of millions of dollars, and had three homes and a private jet. He would do one highly visible lawsuit on religious freedom each year and the rest of the year he'd just golf and cruise around the country to his different homes in his private jet.

The Christian Coalition was pretty much a shell at that point but it was still fundraising and yet doing nothing to educate Christians about political action. They were nothing but a fundraising front. When I went on a tour of the Family Research Council I was shocked. They had all these conference rooms, media rooms and empty offices all throughout their building and you could hear a pin drop. They have this huge building and everything was quiet. There wasn't any activity, and yet I think they have a $30 million budget. To this day, I can't really tell you what they do on Capitol Hill (laughter)."

Where did most of these groups and people come from?

"I came to the conclusion that most were folks left over from the Reagan era, who were no longer warriors but are now either too old or unhealthy, and had compromised and become comfortable with the Republican establishment. They turned these organizations into pretty much direct-mail fund-raising fronts and were making tons of money and living the good life in very beautiful mansions. Overall I found a couple hundred million dollars a year flooding into these groups.

Most of these groups are based in Washington, D.C., but the groups that really did the work of the movement were the grassroots groups struggling on shoestring budgets and having a difficult time making ends meet. The whole thing kind of struck me as bizarre that the people who do the work have absolutely no resources, and the people who don't do the work have all the money from all the little old ladies in America who get the direct-mail letter in the mail and write their monthly $20 check.

The conservative movement had transformed itself from a very dynamic, principled organization in the Reagan years to a bunch of compromising, useless, and ineffective moneymaking machines."

Baldwin then gave his assessment of several of the top leaders in the movement. beginning with the aforementioned Sekulow, who uses his nationally-syndicated radio show, humbly named "Jay Sekulow Live!," to promote his ACLJ as the righteous antidote to the leftist ACLU.

"The idea that he's fighting religious freedom cases on a daily basis is just not true," Baldwin said. "Most of the religious freedom cases in America are being fought by smaller groups and smaller organizations and by guys like Gary Kreep out here in California (Executive Director of the United States Justice Foundation) and Alan Sears (President of the Alliance Defense Fund). They tend to do the bulk of the religious freedom cases. The cases where someone is fired for wearing the cross around their neck at their workplace things like that. The bulk of the real battle in religious freedom is being fought by groups out in the grassroots. But if you didn't know any better, and you're a little old lady, and you're worried about religious freedom slipping away, all you see is Jay Sekulow because he is promoted all over the place. You hear him on Christian radio and television stations and he is very effective at promoting himself. But the reality is they have very few cases they're involved in."

How would Baldwin rate Sekulow's integrity on a scale of 1-10, with one being totally dishonest and 10 being a pillar of integrity?

"(Laughing) I'd give him a two," Baldwin said. "I had a confrontation with him about Romney and he told me flat out that Romney appoints conservative judges who are faithful to the Constitution. I told him that's a flat out lie, and he got all mad at me and said 'you don't know anything about it.'

I said I actually know about all of Romney's judicial appointments. I know who they are. I know what their party registration is, and they're mostly Democrats, liberal activists, and even homosexuals. They were feminists and environmental wackos. He appointed all kinds of nuts to the bench. There's not a record of Romney appointing conservatives to the bench and that's a flat-out lie. I took his head off and he tried to backtrack."

Dr. James Dobson, founder of the largest Christian pro-family organization in the country, has been one of the titular heads of the movement for decades. Baldwin has known Dobson for over 20 years and shared his impressions.

"James Dobson is a very confused man. He's done a lot of great things but he seems confused and misled by people around him. He allowed Tom Minnery to pull him away from a lot of important battles and misinform him on other important battles. For example, he did everything he could to confuse Christian voters about Romney, and while not endorsing Romney, he gave the impression repeatedly that Romney was the guy that Christians should line up behind. By openly criticizing everyone but Romney it pretty much left the impression that Romney was the last guy standing and should be the guy. Instead of coming out and criticizing Romney the most, he criticized Romney the least, and then his colleague Minnery would show up at various events and promote Romney. We always had intense conversations about Romney, and Minnery would defend Romney.

Then they put out that video, along with Tony Perkins, as part of the political action wing of *Focus on the Family*, called *Citizen Link*. They openly lied about Romney, and made outrageous remarks about Mike Huckabee. I mean Huckabee wasn't perfect, either, but they made Huckabee look like a horribly liberal guy, and Romney look like a superstar of the conservative movement. It was such an outrageous video clip that Mat Staver (Founder and Chairman of Liberty Council) fired off a letter threatening to sue *Citizen Link* for violating their 501(c) status. Over and over again I caught Minnery working behind the scenes to promote Romney.

I sent a detailed e-mail about Romney's positions early on in the 2008 presidential campaign to Dobson. I knew him and his wife well, and I would usually e-mail his assistant and his assistant would then forward the e-mail to his private e-mail which no one really had. He would generally respond to me and suddenly my e-mails started getting hijacked. They were rerouted to Minnery, and Minnery would add his comments, and try to debunk my e-mails and then forward them on to Dobson. The reason why I know that is Minnery forwarded one of my e-mails to people on his staff and he somehow left me on by accident in the CC space, and in this e-mail message he's saying 'I need you guys to debunk Baldwin's allegation's before I show this to Dr. Dobson.'

So he's instructing his staff to debunk the $50 abortion thing and Romney's promotion of gay marriage, and his staff came up with bogus propaganda they picked up from the Romney camp. It looked like they just hand wrote it word for word right from Romney's campaign literature, and then they would forward it to Dobson. They were just parroting Romney stuff. It was just disheartening to see how they were doing absolutely no independent checking of my allegations whatsoever—none."

Baldwin spent a lot of time discussing the connection between Romney and Minnery, which prompted us to ask Baldwin what he thought connected the two men.

"I think it was two different individuals that I will call enablers. One was Tom Shields (Chairman of the Coalition of Marriage and Family) and the other was Ray Ruddy. Both men were very close to Romney and very close to the *Focus on the Family* Empire. They were the go-betweens who ran interference and kept evil people like me away from Dobson. Shields grew up with the Romneys, and was head of a *Focus on the Family* affiliate in Boston. He's a very wealthy man. I think he's still on the board today, and he's on the board of Family Research Council.

Ruddy is a very wealthy man who's made his fortune off the federal government. His company made millions off of welfare-to-work contracts with various social services during the Bush years. He dumped his money into pro-family and pro-life groups and causes. He became friendly with Romney when Romney was governor because he was trying to convince Romney to promote this abstinence program specifically designed for public schools getting contracts from the government. Romney was looking for ways to promote himself as a conservative because he was approaching the time period in which he was going to declare his intention to run for president, and he jumped on the abstinence bandwagon and claimed to be a champion of abstinence. Do a little research on Romney's and Ruddy's connection to abstinence and you'll find abstinence is carried out in maybe a half dozen schools in the whole state of Massachusetts, and they refused to abolish the Planned Parenthood program in the same schools. It was not abstinence in place of Planned Parenthood, but alongside Planned Parenthood.

On that basis Romney is able to brag in his campaign literature that he promoted abstinence throughout Massachusetts, which was a complete lie. Ruddy is also one of the largest donors to *Focus on the Family* and the Family Research Council, and has been at meetings convened by Minnery in Colorado Springs with leaders of the pro-life movement in which he would stand up and promote Romney."

But didn't Dobson officially endorse Huckabee for president in 2008?

"He endorsed Huckabee after the race was over. It was completely and totally useless, and a wasteful endorsement from a very powerful man who could have had far more impact during the primaries, but I believe was yanked away from having any impact whatsoever by Minnery. Still, you have to hold Dobson responsible. He is a very busy man. He's more of a writer and spends probably more time each day writing his books and doing family counseling on his radio show, and he ends up relying on Minnery for all things political which was a dangerous decision to give Minnery that kind of power. Dobson was basically made ineffective and useless during this (2008) campaign cycle."

While it wasn't our intention to have so much of our discussion with Steve Baldwin focus on Mitt Romney's failed 2008 presidential run, he insisted that Romney's candidacy was pivotal in exposing the compromised nature of many leading organizations in the movement. Baldwin's observations expose a conundrum. Was Romney a mere manifestation of a problem that had existed for years and that manifested itself in someone with the right resources, capabilities, and a willingness to exploit it, or did Romney carefully manipulate and craft a scenario that led to the grassroots eventually breaking away from many of their leaders?

Baldwin speculated that it might just be a little bit of both.

"I think there's probably a little bit of truth in both, there's always been a problem in the movement with those who will go with the candidate who they think has a chance of winning even if the candidate is horrible in policy. We've always had an element of sellout in the movement from the very beginning. Old veterans of the movement going back to 1950s and '60s can tell you a lot more stories about that than I can, but I know that's always been a trend that's been there in the movement. Pragmatism over principles is how I would term that.

Romney, though, exploited that more than anyone. I mean his people really were brilliant when I watch what they did and they were spreading money around from his foundation and his PAC (political action committee). They knew he was going to run for President so a couple years out they were spreading money around way in advance. He had over 100 consultants on his payroll that did nothing but control his image. They reached out to the movement. There was a couple of them tasked with reaching out to Christians like James Bopp and other pro-lifers. I mean each one had a role and they would go in there and tell people complete lies about Romney's record on these issues. We all know Romney's record on virtually everything—not just abortion and gay rights—but affirmative action, taxes, immigration, and global warming. I've got documentation. He was horrible on *everything*.

This has always been a problem in the movement, but Romney exploited the pragmatic side of the conservative movement more than anyone I've ever seen in the movement's history. His team was brilliant at how to find the weakest links. How to get into the Heritage Foundation's inner sanctum, how to get invited to speak to the Federalist Society, and how to how to get on Dobson's radar screen. At the very least, if they couldn't get some of these guys to endorse them they got them to not endorse their opponents. The Romney people made sure that if they couldn't get their personal endorsements for Romney, at least they would not be endorsing anyone else in that race. It was amazing how years in advance all the strategy was completely laid out by the Romney machine."

Baldwin had already mentioned how pragmatism won out over principle, but how could that happen to a movement supposedly built on a Christ-centered foundation? How seriously do leaders of the movement take their Christian faith? Does it seem like an integral part of their political engagement?

Baldwin didn't shy away from the question.

"I think if people will compromise politically on foundational issues like life, they must also be compromising in their faith life as well. I cannot imagine how any Evangelical or conservative Catholic person could endorse and support Romney knowing what we all know about him. And most of these people had encountered the correct information about Romney at one time or another. It tells me they've been compromised on their faith and they're choosing power and money over commitment to their own faith. I think this is a serious moral failing here going on."

Early on during the 2008 presidential primary, the indomitable Phyllis Schlafly was asked if she would try to encourage other conservative leaders at CNP to endorse Congressman Duncan Hunter since he was arguably the most conservative candidate across the board. She responded in an email to co-author Gregg Jackson that while she liked Hunter, she wanted to wait to see how things "shook out" before endorsing a specific candidate. We asked Baldwin why neither Schlafly, nor most other Christian leaders, endorsed a more proven conservative like Hunter early on in the primary. Why did he think they were never even willing to expose Romney's far left wing record? Were there any Christians leaders who placed their faith over political pragmatism? Are there any other leaders like the late Paul Weyrich, considered the founding father of the Religious Right, who in New Orleans at a CNP meeting wheeled himself out to the front of the room to repent of his Romney endorsement by saying, "before all of you and before almighty God, I want to say I was wrong."[78]

"I think Hunter was probably the most principled candidate in the whole pack and no one backed him. They all said Duncan is great, but they didn't think he could win. Well, if everyone had gotten together and said 'Duncan's great let's all get behind him,' it would have changed the whole complexion of the race. Instead they all unilaterally kind of like distanced themselves from Hunter because they didn't think he had a chance to win.

A few did expose Romney's record, but Schlafly didn't, and she knew about it. Weyrich had the guts to admit he was wrong. He got the information that completely contradicted the information he was being given by the Romney forces, and he went out there and nationally proclaimed himself to be in error. I have to tell you that I do have some praise for that. Nonetheless, had Weyrich gotten behind Hunter, or if 100 of the 500 CNP leaders had endorsed Hunter early on he would have been described as the front runner and money would have flowed to him.

I think the serious flaw in the leadership of the movement was that a lot of them will not get behind the most solid candidates. They stayed neutral in the presidential race, and a lot of them did it because they're afraid of losing supporters and donors for their organization. So they stay neutral, they wait to see who wins the primary and then they get behind that guy."

Did Baldwin get a sense the movement's leaders really searched the Scriptures for the candidates they supported, for the positions they took, and for how to run their ministries? Did they utilize a Biblical worldview or was it a more humanistic one?

"You know it's hard to say, so much of this stuff is in a person's soul and outwardly they all look like they're committed," Baldwin said. "They all pray at our meetings, and they all prayed with me at the dinner table. If you didn't know any better you would just assume they were all very committed Christians, but obviously some of these people were deluding themselves. Obviously some were being used by people who were not Christians, or by candidates who held non-Christian positions like Romney. How do they reconcile that? I don't know. It was a shock to me to see the degree that millions of people would go to endorse a candidate whom they knew had a very liberal record on social issues and pray for him—pray that he would be the President of the United States."

If it's humanistic pragmatism over a Biblical worldview for these leaders, who holds them accountable for the decisions they make? Are these leaders open to scrutiny? Do they explain to their supporters, on Biblical grounds, why they took the positions they took and supported the candidates they supported?

"There is very little accountability. I would send out information about Romney's real record to all kinds of leaders for years. If I saw Tony Perkins (of the Family Research Council) saying something favorable in the newspaper he'd get an e-mail from me that night saying, 'did you know about Romney?'

"I am playing that role because I felt that if the movement completely sold out to Romney it would be the end of the movement as we know it. I viewed my role as a defender of the movement and viewed Romney as a major threat."

After spending a decade interacting with a who's who of the movement's leaders, whose integrity does Baldwin still respect?

"Dick Bott (President of Bott Christian Radio Network) remains in contact with me to this day, and loves the idea that I was willing to go out there and try to inform others of the dangers of Romney. Bott never compromised.

Paul Pressler, a retired judge out of Texas, is another. He doesn't head up any groups right now, but he was one of the guys that led the conservative resurgence in the Southern Baptist Convention when it was going liberal a decade ago. He was one of the guys that had the conservatives take over the Southern Baptist Convention Board and purge all the liberals. I never understood why Schlafly wasn't more anti-Romney, but I trust her as well."

We asked Baldwin who he would recommend a Christian concerned about the future of America donate his money to, given the fact that so many of the leading pro-family organizations seem to be compromised in his estimation.

"I would recommend that they find a grassroots based group that has a board that's accountable, that has people on it they can trust, and that has an agenda that you can easily follow. As a donor you can see what they're doing with their money and its finances are open to you at any time you want to look at them. I recommend all of us nowadays not give money to these national based groups anymore. They're direct mail front groups and they're not using the money wisely. The movement needs to be at the grassroots, and the faster we can switch over the donors to support local based groups with boards that are accountable to God and accountable to one another, the faster we can clean up this mess in the movement."

We asked Baldwin for his take on the superstar syndicated talk show hosts, whom millions of Christians rely on each day for information, encouragement, and marching orders. Does he think they've also been compromised?

"I had e-mail exchanges, sometimes long-winded ones, with Laura Ingraham, Mark Levin, and Ann Coulter, all of whom I've known for many years," Baldwin said. "All three were given extensive documentation on Romney. I also gave Sean Hannity and Rush Limbaugh stuff, though they never really responded to my e-mails. None of them can claim they were uninformed, and yet all of them did things to promote Romney, if not issue an outright endorsement. They did everything possible to make it appear like they were endorsing them. These five are all personal friends, and they all get on the same song sheet when it comes to presidential campaigns. I think they all convinced each other that Romney was the most electable, and they lied to their listeners because they refused to broadcast information I sent them that clearly showed Romney being off the charts liberal on just about every issue. They would never talk about it on air. So unfortunately we have a talk show monopoly that, all as a group, got on board the Romney bandwagon and misled millions of American listeners who look up to them as sources of accurate information."

How effective has the last generation of the movement's leadership been?

"These (leaders) have done very little to stop liberals within the GOP, and they've done very little to stop Democrats. They've done very little to win the battles, and many of them weren't even in the battles. I can cite you battle after battle after battle where national groups in DC were non-players, or they got active just enough so they can` brag about it in their next direct mail fundraising letter. They really didn't do much at all, and I just saw so much money going to those groups—hundreds and hundreds of millions of dollars.

I know all the direct mail consultants. I know all their clients. I have their client lists. I mean you won't believe how much money these groups raise. I mean there is probably 400 conservative groups in D.C. that raised anywhere from $1 to 60 million a year. Collectively the movement fundraising may be worth as much as a half a billion dollars. And what do we have to show for it? Not much.

We're losing on every front."

David Barton

Interviewed by Steve—February, 2011

———————

Few Christian Conservatives are more in demand today than David Barton, who heads the influential organization *Wallbuilders,* which specializes in reclaiming America's providential history.

A much sought-after speaker, respected author and historian, and also a political activist, his work has been tremendously influential on many Christian Conservatives in both the previous generation as well as the emerging one—including the two co-authors of this book—have grown to respect Barton and his work.

Steve spoke to Mr. Barton just as the Republicans were beginning to take power following massive victories at the polls in the 2010 midterm election. Barton began our conversation by saying the signs are there for a civic revival in America.

"I've never seen a time like we have right now, it used to be when I went to speak somewhere they'd say give us 30 minutes on history and now they're saying give us two and a half hours," Barton said. "I've never seen churches do what they're doing right now, which is teaching full Constitution courses. It's just a whole other climate. I think that's a good thing. When I look at the demographics of what happened in the last election in the exit polling, there was a lot of stuff that never got talked about, but I think that's indicative of what's happening. I think with what's coming up now as we look forward there are several things that have to be considered and balanced, especially for a new generation of folks coming forward."

Such as?

"I think we're now starting to figure out that what we're engaged in is not an event, an election is not an event, a president is not an event—it's part of a process. We're looking now at economic problems that are 40 years old. They're not going to be solved with a motto, or a platitude, or a 30-second TV commercial. We've got to start looking beyond what we've done in previous years. That's what I liked about this last election. We really elected a lot of people that should have been non-electable. We broke the mold on guys that looked like politicians, acted like politicians, tell us the right things, and we instead elected a ton of folks that don't fit any political mold, except they're common sense people. They're average everyday people, they're not particularly great communicators, but they've got a positive vision that's long term. I think that's one of the healthiest things I've seen in a long time. We got beyond just electing political people and we started electing citizens."

Barton believes the media-driven conventional wisdom of a divide between moral and economic issues is largely a myth.

"One of the things that really, I think, was very key was all the stuff that we've been told since the election that 'well there's going to have to be a truce between social issues and economic issues because the economics of the nation is so bad.'

Fine, but what didn't get brought out is that you had the same percentage of people in the exit polling that wanted a change in the direction of the morals and values of the country, *and* wanted a change in the economics of the country. Those two were equal. You had a majority of voters that opposed same-sex marriage.

Let's back up to another issue. Two years ago when voting occurred, only 6% of voters said that abortion was an issue one way or another either pro-life or pro-death. In this election 30% of voters said it was the issue on which they voted. Then you had 22% that said they voted strict pro-life, while only 8% straight pro-abortion. That's a 14 point advantage for pro-life candidates. When we look at Congress two years ago and the House of Representatives out of 57 freshmen we had 23 who were pro-life, pro-faith, and pro-family. In this class, we had 97 freshmen and 81 of the 97 are pro-life, pro-faith, pro-family which is an 84% freshman class. That's a pretty significant change and people are saying, well, you can't get the social stuff involved. You have to agree that we're going to win on economic stuff. That's nonsense. You actually had 52% of voters who said that political people were ignoring the heritage of the nation. That's a pretty strong

number. That's a majority in anybody's count. That's one of the
things I think does stand out."

Barton has further evidence that instead of a dividing line between
moral and economic issues, the data actually proves that where someone
stands on moral issues will determine where they also stand on the economic ones.

"If I know where a person stands on the life issue, I can tell you
where they are on the START Treaty, where they are on bailouts,
and everything else within 90% accuracy. Occasionally there's an
anomaly, but if you take the economic voting record of all members
of Congress according to *Americans for Tax Reform*, or any of the
economic groups, and you bump that voting record up against the
right to life voting record, it's almost a complete correlation. You
will find that you don't get solidly economic conservatives unless
they're also social conservatives. If they say I'm an economic conservative and I don't care about social stuff, that's usually a schizophrenic, and you'll get a 50% economic conservative which is a
moderate. I've been able to show even an economic group that ok,
you don't care about abortion or marriage, that's fine, but if you
really care about economics the best indicator of what you're going
to get economically is to find someone that has the right value system on God-given rights, and that's the best economic vote you'll
get. That's something that was really validated in this last election,
the paradigm that economic conservatives *are* social conservatives.
You can't separate the two."

Barton says our contemporary debates about social issues wouldn't be
lost on our Founding Fathers.

"They talked about if you will not protect the first of all inalienable
rights, which is life, you won't protect the rest of them. Sam Adams
and all these guys said the right to life was first, and yes they were
talking about abortion. We have their specific writings. That was an
issue of the day. Thomas Jefferson passed pro-life legislation in the
1770s in Virginia, for example."

Barton should know about the writings and actions of our Founding

Fathers, as he is in possession of what may be the largest private collection of their works in the country.

"We own about 100,000 (documents) from before 1812, so I have thousands of hand-written documents from Jefferson, Washington, Adams and all those guys, and we've got a lot of things the Library of Congress and the National Archives don't have. Scripture says there is nothing new under the sun and that is what we find, because just about everything that we deal with today they already dealt with. They had health care debates back in 1805 whether it was a state issue or federal issue. They went through the issue of gays in the military in 1778. George Washington led the debate on that, and created the policy that the Pentagon had used up until the last lame duck session.

There's just so much back there that still relates to today, particularly they're good with what they meant in the Constitution and what those 18 enumerated powers are. What the general welfare clause is. We have a lot of fun taking current issues that we're dealing with right now and going back and saying, 'here's the Constitutional documents, and here's the guys that wrote them, and here's how they relate.' So, within that framework, we try to combine really the aspect of some Biblical principles, along with Constitutional principles, along with statistics, along with public policy, and try to craft things that reflect all four of those traditional issues."

What drove Barton to get involved in politics?

"I got into this about 20 years ago when I was a school teacher. I actually became principal of the school, and had been a coach, and I taught math and science and other things. I came across some really old documents, and in reading those documents I realized what I'd been taught they meant in school was completely different from what I read. That got me really curious. So, we started looking for more documents, and we started collecting them, and now we've got this great repository.

Within that, I kept hearing the political debates. I'd been somewhat involved in politics as a citizen. I would at least vote and if I was going to vote, I'd at least know who I was voting for. Doing that minimal amount of work, I heard a lot of arguments and a lot of positions, and when I started thinking about them and started going back and looking at the history, it started changing my entire paradigm. That's where I really got involved in this thing, almost in a full time way, trying to get this information that really shifted my life out to others. To let them at least be exposed to original documents and original information. That kind of led to where we are today."

Back to the topic of a civic revival, does Barton believe we can return to the ideals of our Founding Fathers without experiencing a spiritual revival as well?

"One of the things that has stood out to me in the study of history is societal change and from a spiritual sense, people call them revivals. They tend to span decades. They're generational, or even trans-generational. Very few things politically happen in a short period of time.

The first Great Awakening, without which there is no America today, was a 40-year revival that ran from 1730 to 1770. Out of that revival came a lot of the political leaders that we had, like Sam Adams and Benjamin Rush. It was a multi-faceted strategy they used to take on the British system and replace it. It was a long term process. They made plans that were often 15-20 years in the future."

Does Barton believe that is a model we should try to replicate today?

"I recently went through and did a categorization of the 250 folks that we call the Founding Fathers that did the *Declaration of Independence*, Constitution, and Bill of Rights. I looked at their professional groupings and backgrounds and what kind of strategies they used," he said. "They had a group that was doing letters to the editor and op-ed pieces. They had another group doing marketing, what we would call online stuff, the committees of correspondence. You had another group that was publishing books and newspapers. Another group was working on policy in the legislature. Another group was working on training the next generation of legal minds. There were 15-18 different things they did simultaneously to touch the nation. I think that is still the model.

That's what I've learned from history. This stuff doesn't happen as rapidly as we would like, and therefore you have to make plans at all levels and all spheres in areas that I might not be an expert in, but I still need to get involved in and help others in those arenas. With the Founders it took 15-18 categories to achieve the American Revolution and the Constitution."

While we're discussing what we can learn from history, why does Barton believe the last generation of Christian engagement in politics didn't bear the fruit that was hoped for?

"There was political change in the name of party affiliation, but there was not much change in the way of philosophy. Part of that goes back to what most Americans believe.

A great example of this that I would point to is what's done by the guys that come out with the survey every year about what do Americans actually know about themselves. They took 13 questions off of our immigration test and gave it to people who've gone through 17 years of schooling in America. They gave it to college graduates and 71% of college graduates didn't know enough to become citizens of the United States. What they did last year that was different than all previous years, is they also gave the test to public officials. Whereas 71% of college graduates failed the test, 80% of public officials failed the test. Get this: 62% of public officials did not know the three branches of government.

Now, I don't care what party affiliation you are, when you are so depleted in fundamental knowledge, how can you argue separation of powers? How can you argue keeping judges under control? How can you argue any of the things that the Founders gave us when you don't have a clue what the branches are? We've had a lot of people that have wanted to get into office because they like the power, they like the name, they want the perks, but they don't have the philosophy to be there."

Barton said not only have we failed to maintain our heritage as a people, but that Christians have failed to follow the Bible's guidance in determining their leaders.

"If I go back to a Scriptural thing, we as people of faith have also goofed up. In Exodus 18:21, which was used often by the Founding Fathers, it says, 'choose out from among you able men that fear God, tell the truth, and hate dishonest gain.'

We got the fear God part right, but we didn't get the able men. We've got a lot of people in office that have decent values, but they're not competent to be running government. They don't know the basic stuff about economics or separation of powers, or anything they need to know. That's what we have to change."

Barton believes those who share his view of where we're at as a nation, need to start investing for the long haul.

"If you don't start a farm team right now, getting the right people with the right value system and the right kind of worldview, the right kind of skill set, I don't care if its Rs or Ds, the Ds are taking us into the bad stuff faster than the Rs are, but they're both headed in the same direction.

I think you need to work in the short term, the medium term and the long term. I'm going to work my tail off in this next election, but at the same time I'm working with candidates that might not run for office for another 10 years."

Barton believes a return to citizen legislators who can be groomed to become statesmen is a key to returning America to its founding vision. He believes some important first steps in that process were taken in the 2010 elections.

"A lot of these guys should never have gotten elected, because they don't fit the profile, they're just a bunch of average citizens. Let me give you one example I love.

Several weeks after the election, I was all over the country and being asked to train these freshmen on worldview of government. One was in Arkansas in the little town of Hot Springs that's been a mafia or gambling town since the 1920s. There was a pastor's wife at a church there. She had to do some business down in the city and the mayor was drunk behind the desk. She looked at that and said, you've got to be kidding me I can do better than that.

She stuck her name on the ballot and got elected as the mayor of Hot Springs. She's never done a political thing in her life. She and 20 others took over the whole thing and they don't have a political credential among any of them, but they have common sense and logic and they're running it like a business.

That's the kind of stuff that will make a difference when you start getting some common sense involved, and not just actually candidates and consultants. The consultants are worse than the candidates often. That's what we have to get, people with the right worldview. They have to be competent. They might not have the pedigree, but they have to have common sense and the right worldview. That's exactly the type of citizen legislators that we need that think right and will not compromise their principles."

Barton believes that in a republic such as ours we get the very government we deserve, therefore the policies—even the ones Christians may disagree with—of our government are simply a reflection of the people it represents.

"I think we are displaying the same characteristics that we don't like in our government, but it's ok because it's us doing it," Barton said. "Two examples come to mind. How can we yell at the federal government for being in deficit spending when the average credit card debt for the average American is $13,000? We ourselves live in debt, we stay in debt, we buy stuff we shouldn't and we just elect people that think like we do. We have to get our own ship in order. You're looking at a starter house nowadays being 2,300 square feet! You've got to be kidding me. We're way the heck over our head and we wonder why everyone won't stop spending. It's because our whole mentality is that way.

I have a friend in Congress, one of the great guys that won't buckle his backbone to anyone, named Len Westmoreland out of Georgia. He's a Tea Party favorite and he was talking to these guys before the election and said 'you guys want us to cut all this federal spending, right?' Everyone was cheering and hollering. He said 'if we get in office and pass a budget that stops federal spending, and the president wants it to go on and he vetoes our budget and shuts the government down, do you want us to shut the government down if that's what it takes?' They all hooped and hollered and cheered. Then he said, 'You need to understand, if we shut the government down, that means that grandpa's not getting his check from the veteran's administration' and he went through all these things and then asked do you still want us to shut it down.

He said it was completely silent, no response at all, because what we have is 75% of Americans get at least some assistance from government, 50% get 50% from their assistance from government, 25% get 75% assistance from government. We start talking about trimming stuff back and it starts getting personal. And that's where these guys in office, if they don't have a backbone, I guarantee you the well organized groups will yell at them and holler at them and they'll get thousands of calls and they'll say 'Well, I've got to back off on my position, and I've got to compromise here.'

That's what kills us, is we ourselves as citizens are doing the very things that we don't want our elected officials to do. Until we change that mentality and demand that change in ourselves, it's going to be very hard to get the right kind of people with character and backbone in office."

Barton believes Christians must also become shrewder in how they participate in the political process, beginning at the primary level. By not aggressively participating in primaries Barton believes Christians have allowed the two major political parties to nominate candidates with similar worldviews, so that the best the allegedly conservative Republican can do is "slow down the bad progress."

"The only way you reverse that is you get something different in the pipeline coming down the stream, and that's what we have not worked on. We wait to see who's going to pop up every election. We wait to see who puts their name on the ballot. There's nothing aggressive in getting good people in the pipeline. So what happens is, every two years we get a choice between the bad and the worse. That's what it was in (the 2008 presidential election).

The way to solve that is you have to go back and say, 'kid, you may be president 20 years from now and here's the path you have to be on right now to prepare yourself for that. Here's the convictions you have to know. Here's the Constitutional issues you're going to have to deal with and you've got to resolve.'

We're not doing that."

Barton is also concerned that the sort of big money it takes to compete in modern politics may discourage potentially good Christian candidates from running for office in the first place. He believes this inevitably leads to liberal Republicans, who have openly opposed righteousness in the political realm like John McCain, winning primaries by default.

"One of the things that disgusts me right now, with the next presidential race, is the fact that a lot of folks now are bowing out because Obama already has $1 billion in his war chest and there's no way they can compete with that. In the last three presidential elections, 52% of votes have been cast on the basis of TV commercials. So it doesn't matter what the guy believes, it's about the platitudes he puts out on TV. We have to get ourselves weaned from what the candidates say about themselves. Until we get past that, we're going to have the same situation of having one of the worst choices (for Christians) winning the primary. That's just the way it is.

We have to ask 'what am I going to do to make sure that McCain is not the nominee or a McCain-like person is not the nominee next time?' I think part of that is we can't get our guys to run because we can't pony up with a billion dollars, which is an abominable system when that happens."

What's the first step to overcoming those money and media advantages?

"We have to get involved in the process a lot earlier. We can't just show up every election and cast a vote. We've got to get involved in the process back in January after the election is over. We have to get them into training. It's just an ongoing process. As long as we're going to take our politics casually, and only show up every two years or every four years to cast a vote, we will get nothing better than what we've had for the last forty years."

Barton believes savvy Christian voters need to start treating primaries as just as important as the general election, if not even more so.

"I try to help people think right in primaries, and a primary is not about who can win. A primary is about moving your values and getting them as far down the road as you can. If you're only going to look at who the handicapped winner is, my gosh, you would not have done well in the last couple Super Bowls, and you would not have done well in the last couple NBA titles, because the favorite doesn't win it most of the time. It's just not the way it goes. You have to look at the primary process as a chance to advance your values and make a statement.

That did happen in 2010 for the first time in at least 25 years, and the primaries made statements all over the place including throwing out some sitting senators in Utah and Alaska. Primary voters made a lot of noise in the right direction. The kind of folks they chose out of Florida, what they did with Charlie Crist, etc. That's what a primary is supposed to be about, but that only works if you have high voter involvement in the primaries.

If you have low voter involvement, and the involvement is radically different than your general election, then what it does is embolden the other side. So, if we can't get high voter turnout in the primaries, and keep that same voter turnout when we go to the general to reinforce what we said in the primaries, we become schizophrenic and the other side goes, 'Ah, that person's primary is out of the mainstream so don't help them move down the road.'"

According to Barton high voter turnout in primaries is a good way to get candidates to listen to their constituents and not their consultants.

"I'll just point to what really disgusted me in the last two cycles from the Republican side in recruiting candidates was the Republican National Committee. In my opinion, the RNC isn't worth the powder to blow it up, and their position was if you're a self-funding candidate you're exactly who they were looking for to run for Congress. Really? That's all it takes is to be able to fund yourself?

Well, fortunately people like Lynn Westmoreland out of Georgia got involved in recruiting these candidates rather than just looking to see who would put themselves forward, and we got a lot of really good guys this time because we aggressively went out and twisted their arms and said it's your duty to public service, it's your duty to God to get in there and carry these convictions and this worldview."

Barton believes those efforts are already bearing kernels of fruit.

"I worked with (new Republicans) on the rules package, and I love the fact that the current Republican rules package will allow no new entitlements of any kind whatsoever. They have a rule that now says, anything that will increase federal spending $5 billion within a 10-year period over a 40-year span, is not allowed to be introduced. You can't even introduce that kind of legislation! That's huge stuff and that's a product of actively and aggressively recruiting better candidates and getting them in there."

Barton agrees that flawed past Christian political engagement damaged the integrity of the Gospel in America, but he also believes the next generation is learning from those mistakes.

"I think we've hurt our integrity, but I think that is now a thing of the past. A lot of that was a reflection of the fact that we came through a paradigm where we were very top centered in our organizations. In other words, you had the Moral Majorities, and you had these other groups, and you had a spokesman for them and everybody marched to that tune. That is really fragmented now. You no longer have a national spokesman to do these things. You now have a thousand local groups that are doing these things. I think that has returned some credibility in the sense that they're just not shills. You have to deal with local leaders now and you have to deal with local groups. You have to deal with things at different levels.

I remember doing an interview with the *New York Times* and they said who's leading this national marriage movement and I said 'nobody.' Every state is picking it up on its own. The guys in Hawaii don't even talk to the guys in California, and they don't even know the guys in Maine who are doing it. And that's one of the good things that's developed in the last four years or so is there's no longer top centered organizations.

Who's the leader of the Tea Party groups? They don't have a leader. Nobody has a clue, and I think that's a healthy thing because that's virally driven, grassroots working up.

We just had an incident here in Texas where for the first time in my lifetime we had 142 groups come together on a political issue telling the Speaker of the House, you've got the wrong committee chairman. I've never seen 142 groups come together on anything, but that's because they're all now philosophically united and they come from all spectrums—some are economic groups, some are social groups, but they all have a united vision."

Barton thinks one of the main issues that must be tackled by the next generation is the rise of a judicial oligarchy. He believes we must reverse the trends that have given courts and judges a final authority on the Constitution and the rule of law that our Founders never intended for them to have.

"Part of that is a result of our education and all the stupid arguments that are being put forward. If those arguments were put forward 100 years ago, they would've been laughed out of court.

The idea that the judiciary is independent of the will of the people, or that you can't politicize the judiciary by holding judges accountable, you've got to be kidding me. The Founding Fathers were so clear about those issues, but of course we never study history and we don't read the Constitution.

One of the things that I find so fascinating is that right now with our current public education knowledge that we have and, by the way, Christian school knowledge as well, only 6% of Americans can name the rights listed in the First Amendment. Now if that's all that can list the rights in the First Amendment, how do you defend those rights, how do you talk about when they're being violated, and how do you know where the line is?

Barton says the Left's ability to dominate the government education system for a generation is having far-reaching and disastrous consequences for the country.

"If 63% of folks don't know what the three branches of government are, how can you talk about the separation of powers or the role of the judiciary? That's the easiest part of the Constitution. Article 3 is really short. There's only a few clauses there, yet no one reads it. We're really looking at a situation where we give in to the Left's arguments because that's what we hear all the time.

If we'd read the documents ourselves, and a Biblical passage I really like on thinking is 1 Peter 3:15, 'be able to give a reason for the hope that's within you,' we ought to be able to line out the reasons that we believe what we believe. This is not in our textbooks or our schools. We're going to have to read things by ourselves which means a little more work on our parts."

What about the oft-debated question in Christian political circles of "the lesser of two evils?" How does Barton apply that? What can Barton tell us about what the Bible says about how much evil a Christian can do and/or endorse and still consider himself good?

"Look at 2008, instead of looking at (two liberals) like McCain and Obama and saying, 'how can I do this?' I'll take it back a step earlier and ask my more important question which is how do I never have a choice like this again? How do I make sure that I never get to the point that it's between a McCain and Obama?

By the way, I was really hopeful that we were going to have that solution fixed with the primary in Arizona with McCain, but the citizens of Arizona decided that they really liked McCain and they overwhelmingly put him back in and gosh, there's not a whole lot I can do to stop that particular situation when the citizens themselves demand it. This goes back to the Scriptural example of God giving the people manna and they said no, we want quail. They demanded quail. He said okay then, I'll give you quail until you're sick of it."

While he did criticize McCain's moderate to liberal record, during the 2008 presidential election Barton's *Wallbuilders* also published a voter guide that painted a more conservative picture of McCain than his actual record would support. Does Barton believe that was a "lesser of two evils" compromise on his part?

"I look at McCain and say yup, he voted for all the wrong guys to get on the Supreme Court, for example, but one thing I could say about McCain is he did put Jay Sekulow (of the American Center for Law & Justice) in charge of choosing his judges, and Sekulow I do trust. I would, in a heartbeat, go with Sekulow in choosing judges. That makes it really easy for me to vote for McCain because Sekulow's going to do the choosing.

Still, out of the nine Republicans running McCain was my eighth choice in 2008. So I think again, we react too much to what's in the current rather than looking down the road and saying how do I prevent this? What steps can I take right now? Who can I start working with right now so that when we get to 2020 I don't have a McCain choice? How do we make sure we don't get in this spot again which means I'm having to work 10,12, or 14 years down the road."

But what happens if a Christian's conscience simply won't allow him to vote for a McCain type of candidate no matter who the Democrat is? Considering how hard some people like McCain have worked over the years to defeat Christians on issues they care deeply about, aren't there times when there simply isn't a God honoring choice?

"I have a really easy response to that one. Thirty times in the New Testament we're told to protect the rights of conscience. So, for example, I can argue with a Quaker all day long from a Scriptural standpoint why war is a necessary thing and a justified thing. But, I will not go against his conscience that says they won't vote for anything that deals with war—period.

I'm not going to argue with somebody's conscience. That's between them and God and that's why we've protected that constitutionally. That's why the Scripture says 30 times to protect the rights of conscience.

I'll sometimes rate arguments and say, 'have you thought about this? Have you looked at this?' If they still say, 'yes, but my conscience won't permit me.' then I've got nothing left to say. I'm not about to tell someone to violate their conscience because they answer to God about their conscience and not me."

Ann Coulter

Interviewed by Steve—February, 2009
Interviewed by Gregg—10 interviews
between 2004 and 2007

———

Like many conservatives, we had been fans of the bombastic Ann Coulter for years. Gregg had the pleasure of interviewing her on his radio shows in Boston and Los Angeles on numerous occasions. When he emceed the presidential sessions at the CPAC in 2007, he met her in person backstage, and spoke with her briefly right before she went on and uttered her now infamous "faggot" comment, which was directed at Senator John Edwards.

Gregg ended up developing a relationship with Coulter that included regular email communication. One such e-mail was sent from the "green room" on the set of the Donny Deutsche Show on CNBC. Coulter made the gross error of attempting to witness her supposed Christian faith to Deutsche (who happens to be Jewish) by telling him that her ideal picture of America would be "like the 2004 Republican National Convention" where everybody is "happy" and "Christian."

Coulter frantically texted Gregg after her exchange with Deutsche likely because she knew he is a Jewish believer in Jesus the Messiah:

"Didn't you tell me you're writing a book titled 'The perfected Jew?' Donny Deutsch just got very angry at me for saying we Christians wanted him to become a perfected Jew. It was strange and alarming—I wasn't sure if he was serious at first but he was. I even explained that Christians believed the Old Testament and that Jews go to heaven, but that requires man to follow a lot of laws and Christians have the fast track program which is a continuation of the Old Testament, but he just kept saying I had offended him—SERIOUSLY. It was as if I had said I support Adolph Hitler and all his goals. I still don't understand what happened, though the cameramen and make-up people told me they understood me completely. I hope they don't run that segment, I don't want to be personally offensive to anyone—not over that anyway."

Gregg responded to Coulter that, based on what she said, she had used inaccurate terminology and that it probably wasn't the best way to share her faith with Deutsche and his audience. He then offered to put her in touch with a Jewish Pastor friend who could help educate and guide her. Unfortunately, she only stubbornly persisted in claiming that what she said was factually correct and didn't have to apologize for anything.

This incident was a real eye-opener for Gregg, who had always thought that Coulter was intellectually honest and therefore open to correction. He expected her to be humble enough, as a Christian, to seek forgiveness from Deutsch. Instead, he was just beginning to see a very disturbing side of Coulter that very few in the general public ever witness.

Leading up to the 2008 presidential election, Gregg was a radio show host in Boston and trying to use that platform to warn as many Americans as possible who former governor Mitt Romney really was. He was being portrayed by many in the conservative media as the second coming of Ronald Reagan who was forced to do some liberal stuff. He was, after all, the governor of a very liberal state. However, after having covered Romney closely for three years Gregg knew that Romney had more in common with Hillary Clinton, Teddy Kennedy and Planned Parenthood (all of whom endorsed his quasi-socialist healthcare plan) than he had with Ronald Reagan.

In 2007, Gregg received a call from one of Fred Thompson's California campaign directors asking if he would consider endorsing Thompson, and speaking on his behalf at a campaign event. He replied that he needed to do more research on Thompson's record and get back to him. He proceeded to e-mail Coulter, and asked her what she thought of Thompson. Her reply was very revealing:

"I AGREE WITH YOU 100%! I'm as torn as you are, except that I'm worried it will be Rudy by default if social conservatives split their votes among the Huckabees, Thompsons, Tancredos and so on (even Duncan Hunter, whom I adore!). After watching the debate last night, I just realized that in terms of stature, gravitas, speaking ability etc, Rudy is always the winner (by far, unfortunately) and Romney a closely-controlled 2nd.

Obviously, between those two, I'd prefer Romney. I think Romney is probably pretty conservative on all the social issues we care about, but threw liberals some rhetorical bones because he was running in Massachusetts. Consider that if he had knocked out Teddy Kennedy, that would have been one of the greatest victories for social conservatives since Reagan was elected. Also Mormons are generally very conservative (I know it's a nutty religion, but I think that's just what he is by birth and doesn't spend a lot of time thinking about Joseph Smith's golden tablets).

Rudy is SUCH a good debater—he's the only Republican that doesn't give me a pit in my stomach when he's asked a question because I'm so worried he'll blow the answer. I wish he would just switch on abortion. I guess I'm secretly hoping for a Romney/Rudy ticket—or a ticket with Rudy as the designated AG or something. I just love when he gets that crazy-ass look in his eyes.

The thing about Rudy and Romney is: you know they were as liberal as they will ever be governing INSANELY liberal jurisdictions like Mass and NYC and are probably a lot more conservative, whereas Huckabee and Thompson and McCain are probably a lot more liberal than their records suggest coming from states with sane voters. I doubt this helped, but that's my basic view."

Romney/Rudy was Coulter's "dream ticket" in 2008? Was this the same Romney who signed $50 tax payer funded abortions into law three years after his supposed "pro-life conversion?"[79] The same Romney who was America's Founding Father of marriage between homosexuals?[80] The same Romney who opposes bans on homosexual scoutmasters?[81] The same Romney who forced Catholic Charities to place children with same-sex couples even though he wasn't required to by law? The same Romney who boosted funding for homosexual, bi-sexual and transgender "education" starting in kindergarten?[82]

And was this the same Giuliani who supports abortion on demand, including late-term abortions funded by taxpayers?[83] Was this the same Giuliani who told George Will that *Roe v. Wade* was "good constitutional law?"[84] Was this the same Giuliani who supports homosexual "marriage" and as mayor marched in the Gay Pride Parade[85] and once dressed up in drag?[86]

Coulter was "secretly hoping for a Romney/Rudy ticket?" It was hard to imagine someone who is perceived to be so conservative deciding to overlook the flaws she admitted in Giuliani, but had she really not done her homework on Romney's across-the-board, far left-wing fiscal and social record? Gregg replied:

"I have to tell you as an ex-Mass resident I really detest Mitt. He is a 'Republican John Kerry' through and through. Google the 'Mitt Romney Deception' for full documentation on this deviously slick politician. He also threatened to fire justices of the peace who would not issue licenses to same sex couples. He also changed the certificates from 'husband' and 'wife' to 'partner A' and 'partner B.'

He also bragged about having the most stringent gun control laws in the country and that he never took money from the NRA. Finally, he left Mass with a socialist healthcare plan Hillary would have been proud of. I wrote an article outlining it a few days ago published in Human Events.

Sorry, but he is a liberal through and through and a dishonest one at that. At least Rudy is semi-honest about his pro-abortion including tax payer funding, pro-same sex marriage, and pro-gun control positions. But what is up with the fact he won't sign a 'no new taxes pledge?' What the heck is the guy conservative on?

Unfortunately, I believe that Hillary will wipe the mat with Rudy or Mitt or John because RINOs don't win national elections. Even if they did, I am not very confident that either would appoint Alito-Scalia-Roberts-Thomas justices. I think we would have a bunch more Kennedys and Souters.

So that is why I was hoping Fred would be the one, true conservative with a real shot at getting the nomination. I am with you regarding Hunter. I have had him on the show a bunch and introduced him at CPAC and talked to him privately and love the guy (minus his isolationist/Lou Dobbs trade streak), but don't think he is a viable candidate. Actually Alan Keyes would be my choice if he were running.

So, I take it that you are advising me that Thompson is not the true conservative Christian candidate I am looking for, correct? If he is not, then I probably will not "endorse" or speak on behalf of any candidate. Why don't you run? :-)"

As his concluding comment clearly illustrated, at the time Gregg believed that Coulter was merely a misguided, but well meaning, authentic conservative who had just been fed a bunch of inaccurate information about Romney.

The very next day (October 11, 2007), Gregg sent Coulter the link to the "Mitt Romney Deception,"[87] which fully documented Romney's far left-wing record including the fact that Romney:

- Signed $50 tax-payer funded abortions into law (three years after his supposed "pro-life conversion.")
- Illegally and unconstitutionally instituted of same-sex "marriage."
- Boosted funding for homosexual, bi-sexual, and transgender "education" beginning in kindergarten.
- Opposes a ban on homosexual scoutmasters and supports special rights for homosexuals.
- Forced Catholic Charities to give children to homosexual couples even though he was under no legal obligation to do so.
- Opposed the Bush tax cuts.
- Raised taxes and fees by a billion dollars which decimated the Massachusetts economy.
- Instituted a quasi-socialist healthcare plan which has been an abysmal failure.
- Passed over GOP lawyers for three-quarters of the 36 judicial vacancies he faced, instead tapping registered Democrats or independents–including two openly homosexual lawyers who have supported expanded same-sex rights, according to *The Boston Globe.*

Gregg's e-mail to Coulter read:

"Ann, Here is the 'Mitt Romney Deception.' I would print and read it when you get a few minutes. It is a real eye opener."

To which Coulter promptly acknowledged receipt and replied:

"Excellent—thank you!"

Just over two months later, on December 19, Gregg followed up with Coulter and sent the following e-mail:

"Ann, Why have you yet to write one article on Mitt Romney's blatant violation of the oldest functioning constitution in the world—the Massachusetts Constitution—that he violated by illegally imposing 'same sex marriage' in Massachusetts? As head of legal affairs for Human Events, I am surprised that you have not covered this enormous story yet? What gives?"

Coulter replied the next day:

"I told you! HE (Romney) WAS FOLLOWING A COURT ORDER! I would love for some Republican, someday, to do the very ballsy thing of defying a court order. I wish Bush would do it on trials for terrorists in Guantanamo. He's the commander in chief! But not doing something shocking, that no Republican has ever done before, and in defiance of a court order is not disqualifying in my opinion. Reagan never did it!"

Unfortunately for Coulter, there was no "court order" forcing Romney to authorize the issuance of marriage licenses to same-sex couples, nor was there any court order instructing him to make alterations to the wording on those state documents.

Had Coulter done her homework, she would have found that the justices themselves, in the majority opinion, admitted that for same sex "marriage" to become legal, the legislature and the legislature alone would have to actually change the current marriage statute (chapter 207 in the Massachusetts General Laws) to accommodate same-sex "marriage."

Something the Massachusetts legislature, to this day, still has not done.

In an effort to set the record straight, the following e-mail was sent the very next day, December 21st, in response to Coulter's:

"No. You're wrong, Ann. There was no order. And it's much worse than that.

As one law professor (who testified before Congress re: Goodridge, etc.) responded to the arguments I will just barely touch on below, 'Not only are you right, but you're obviously right' (responding to a prominent attorney who presented it to him).

A retired senior jurist hired by Romney to advise him heard what I'm about to clue you into and responded: 'How did we miss this?' (Who missed it, Ann? The entire 'conservative' legal community—almost.)

It was a declaratory judgment. Remember those? Black's Law Dictionary: 'without consequential relief.'

No order.

Nothing like an order.

Merely legal advice to the Legislature, as per the Massachusetts Constitution.

No role mentioned or even imagined for anyone in the executive branch unless the legislature changed the statutes.

Sit down right now and beg God to clear your head.

This is probably the most important decision OF YOUR LIFE—other than accepting Christ. You, and I and many others will now know what you are willing to give up to obey Christ at whatever cost.

You will now know whether you fear God or man. The rest of your life may depend on what you do in the next few days. The recovery or death of Judeo-Christian values in America and the rule of law may depend on whether a small number of people, including Ann Coulter, obey God on THIS issue, now—possibly even before the Iowa caucuses.

What have Romney's orders to public officials and statements to the media and the public after Goodridge wrought?

Remember the Maggie Gallagher article 'Banned in Boston?'

Remember that she interviewed over a dozen law professors? Remember that the consensus of those pro and con homosexual 'marriage' was this: it will strip away religious freedom, first by stripping tax exempt status from every church, school, ministry, adoption agency or other non-profit in the country that does not hire and promote active sodomites in the pulpit and all the way to the TOP of their personnel structure and offer all benefits to homosexual couples?

Remember David Parker, Lexington, Massachusetts father (and personal friend of mine) arrested for strenuously objecting to his 5-year-old son being brainwashed to accept homosexuality in kindergarten? Remember that the town and the federal judge nullified what the U.S. Supreme Court has called 'possibly the oldest principle in Western law,' going back at least to the Romans, the right of parents to control the education and upbringing of their own children?

Remember that the school and the judge cited the supposed 'legalization' of homosexual marriage as trumping parents' rights (and unmentionably, freedom of religion) and asserting that the schools now have not merely a right, but an obligation to teach children about the normalcy of homosexual relationships?

Remember two months ago the Quebec government threatened to take Mennonite Christian children from their parents to force them to learn homosexuality and evolution?

Remember World Net Daily's coverage of the German state seizing Christian children from their homeschooling parents ruling that the state has an interest in preventing the rise of parallel societies? This 'parallel society' is called 'Christianity.' The statute used was imposed under a fellow by the name of Adolf Hitler. Still in force.

Did you notice WND's coverage a few days ago of a Utah judge threatening to take Christian children away from a homeschooling mother because, he said 'Homeschooling always fails. I won't allow it.' (And Columbine worked better?) She and her husband left their home and belongings behind and fled the state rather than risk losing their children. Where do you go if you leave Utah to get a more conservative state where you can home school in peace?

Remember that Scalia wrote 'This could be the one that swallowed the rule of law?' He was talking about Lawrence. If you liked Lawrence, you'll love his son. Well, meet Goodridge, 'Larry's' son. He swallows children.

Hate crimes. Human Rights Commissions. Add it up, Ann. Romney stood on the boundary of civilization and fascist barbarism. Having sworn a solemn oath in the name of a Holy God, under a Constitution that implies that putting your career ambitions above fulfilling that oath is a felony punishable by thirty years behind bars (blame John Adams, not me, if you think violating a solemn oath, taking God's name in vain and then failing to defend a constitution is a misdemeanor.)

Oh, but Ann, it gets much, much worse than this. Romney knew he was not forced to 'obey' the court, and that there was no order. He also knew that the court has admitted it has no power to order the governor or the legislature. And that the court has no subject matter jurisdiction over marriage policy.

Oh, but Ann, it gets worse.

And everything I'm telling you has already been vetted with dozens of lawyers, law professors, professors of jurisprudence. People you know, Ann. People who publish in fancy venues like the National Review and the Wall Street Journal.

If you want to know why and how Willard Mitt Romney violated just about every principle of American law and, oh, maybe eight articles of the world's oldest functioning constitution, just tell me this: Ann, what are you going to do, if I and others take the time to prove, point by point, beyond any doubt—not reasonable doubt—ANY doubt that Romney's entire story is a fairy tale?

If I prove all this and much more, Ann, what are you going to do?"

That same day, Coulter back-tracked by admitting that she didn't actually mean that Romney was "ordered" to commence homosexual nuptials," and resorted to accusing me of being a "Romney-hater."

"Gregg—you are going crazy with hatred for Romney. There's a lot not to like about him—though less than there is not to like about Rudy or McCain or Thompson or Huckabee—BUT THIS ISN'T IT.

A declaratory judgment still requires the parties to conform their conduct to the judgment. They may not be 'ordered' to, but failure to abide by a judgment to which you are a party would be basis for contempt or other sanctions. The Massachusetts court would have loved to start throwing contempt citations around and Romney would have been considered a nut by even 90% of the Federalist Society.

I don't know what nuts you are talking to, but this is crazy. AND I'M SOMEONE WHO SUPPORTS GOVT OFFICIAL IGNORING SOME COURT ORDERS. Yes, it would have been fun, but then it would also have been fun for Bush to send armed troops into Florida to save Terry Schiavo (as I argued he should have done in a column at the time). Still, I would not impeach the guy for not doing it.

Roy Moore tried that kind of thing, and that bleeding heart Arkansas AG BILL PRYOR ran him out of office. If you don't know, Pryor is among the most right-wing Christian lawyers in America, often praised in my columns. Should we impeach Bill Pryor from the federal bench because he wouldn't help Moore defy court decisions on the Ten Commandments in the courtroom?

You and I might prefer Roy Moore for president—I wrote up his 'Man of the Year' tribute for Human Events a few years ago—but he's not running. No other candidate—not even Duncan Hunter and DEFINITELY NOT that Mike Huckabee—would have done what you are describing."

Was Gregg a Romney "hater?" If so, it would be completely appropriate for Coulter to use the blunt tone of her e-mail to grab his attention. That's what friends are for.

If that were true, however, we ought to send him for treatment as his "hatred" seems to have taken root in a number of areas. It also appears that he is "going crazy with hatred" for abortion, and sodomy-based adoption. Instead of co-writing this book, perhaps he ought to be in counseling. This "hate" stuff can drive a guy crazy.

Before calling the men in the white robes, a quick look to the Scriptures reveals that Christ was "really going crazy" with "hatred" for the lawyers, writers, (scribes) and sanctimonious profiteers. I mean look at the extreme and nutty things he said to them. They weren't the barbarian, sodomizing Romans. These were the good guys Jesus was talking about in Luke chapter 11:

And the Lord said unto him, now do ye Pharisees make clean the outside of the cup and the platter; but your inward part is full of ravening and wickedness.[88]

Woe unto you, Pharisees! for ye love the uppermost seats in the synagogues, and greetings in the markets. Woe unto you, scribes and Pharisees, hypocrites! For ye are as graves which appear not, and the men that walk over them are not aware of them (and defile themselves ceremonially).[89]

Then answered one of the lawyers, and said unto him, Master, thus saying thou reproachest us also.[90]

And he said, Woe unto you also, ye lawyers! For ye lade men with burdens grievous to be borne, and ye yourselves touch not the burdens with one of your fingers.[91]

Woe unto you, lawyers! For ye have taken away the key of knowledge: ye entered not in yourselves, and them that were entering in ye hindered.[92]

That Jesus was crazy with "hatred."

As to Coulter's contention that "a declaratory judgment still requires the parties to conform their conduct to the judgment," Mitt Romney was not a party to the Goodridge case. She's too smart not to have known better.

Gregg shared with Coulter a letter co-authored by many prominent pro-family Christian leaders such as Paul Weyrich and Bob Knight called "Joint Letter to Romney from Pro-Family Leaders."

(The letter is available for review on-line at: http://www.massresistance. org/docs/marriage/romney/dec_letter/letter.pdf)

The letter explains in detail that according to the oldest functioning constitution in the world, the Massachusetts Constitution co-authored by John Adams and others, only the people and their legislative representatives can make, revoke or amend any law in any way. It asserts that the judiciary possesses no constitutional subject matter jurisdiction in the area of marriage, and clearly explains that there was never any court order forcing Romney to alter and issue marriage licenses to same-sex couples. The letter goes on to point out that the legislature never changed the marriage statute to accommodate same-sex "marriages," and that Romney unilaterally, illegally, and unconstitutionally instituted same-sex "marriage" in Massachusetts.

There was no response from Coulter, who eventually endorsed Romney for president in 2008, but she can never say that she had not been made acutely aware that Romney was blatantly lying about the court forcing him to unilaterally issue marriage licenses to same-sex couples.

Coulter persisted in claiming that Romney "had no choice" but to "follow the court order" to institute same-sex "marriage." Gregg went so far as to publicly offer Ann Coulter one million dollars on co-author Steve Deace's radio show if she could produce the "court order."

Coulter has never been able to produce the "court order" at the center of her argument. Gregg went further, and invited her on his show in Los Angeles numerous times to debate the issue. She instead stopped responding to his e-mails, and never again came on the show.

She did however agree to an interview with Steve Deace.

When Coulter did appear on Deace's radio show, they spent the first 30 minutes discussing her latest book and all the evils of liberal Democrats and socialism. As the discussion turned from the book to a more broad discussion of the political landscape, he played a clip of Mary Matalin (who was with Fred Thompson's 2008 presidential campaign at the time) regarding the man Coulter claimed was "manifestly the best candidate in the race," Mitt Romney. Here is the exchange:

Matalin (clip)> Mitt Romney's health care plan that he's applauding, as you know you can get an abortion for $50 in his health care plan. I mean come on, I don't know what he's saying. I mean I know what he's saying, but what he's actually done, what he's bragging about having done, is a healthcare program that pays for abortion.

Deace> Now I know that you are a seeker of truth, and you were on the late D. James Kennedy's special going after Darwinism. Which was phenomenal, and he's a heck of a character witness in my book, and he was somebody I looked up to. Mary Matalin came on this show and said that Mitt Romney signed into law legislation in Massachusetts that would provide $50 co-pay abortions. That blew our audience away at the time. Is that true?

Coulter> I don't know the details on that. He was in Massachusetts, what his defenders say—this is something obviously a lot of people have looked at—is that state law already covered abortions. This was changing how healthcare would be paid for. It wasn't going in and fixing everything that was...that was wrong with health care. It never would've gone through..."

Is Coulter telling the truth here when she tells Steve "I don't know the details on that?" Considering how meticulous Coulter has footnoted and documented her work in the past, is it possible the woman who wrote the best-seller *Godless* about the Left's lack of morals and promotion of a culture of death endorsed someone for president without knowing whether or not they signed into law taxpayer-funded, $50 abortions?

Coulter then went on a rant for about 10 minutes about all the evils of Obama, socialism, and Democrats. All the while, she went out of her way to ignore the RINO in the room—the question of Romney's record. The exchange continued:

Deace> You wrote a book, Godless, *which I thought was a phenomenal exposé on the party of death, and how they essentially on the left have profited politically and financially off of perpetuating death, and I could not agree more. Both myself and many of the people that are closest to me in my family were conceived in less than ideal or tragic circumstances where virtually every Democrat and too many Republicans think allowing abortion is okay...*

Coulter> Wow, what a fabulous story!

Deace> So, I mean this is an issue I care very deeply about, and I know that you do as well. So let me ask you this question: if they came to you and said you have to sign this into law, and also guarantee that we're going to provide $50 abortion co-pays, and put Planned Parenthood on the state board, knowing how much of a conviction the life issue is for you would you have done that?

Coulter> I don't know. I don't know the details. Look, I already told you I'd sign the Constitution, and the Constitution didn't get rid of slavery and that doesn't mean I'm a fan of slavery."

So, self-proclaimed pro-life Ann Coulter, the author of *Godless*, doesn't know if she would sign a healthcare plan into law that subsidizes abortions, including late-term/partial birth abortions, at $50 each?

Keep in mind, Coulter endorsed Romney for President of the United States and makes a living as an author and political pundit. She has a virtually encyclopedic memory when it comes to politicians' stands on issues.

Furthermore, Coulter had, on numerous occasions, been explicitly presented with the "details" of Romney's entire record by Gregg. On top of that, the details of Romneycare's abortion coverage was at the time making national news and going viral on the Internet.

Coulter was invited to conduct a follow up interview prior to the publishing of this book but declined to respond.

Bob Enyart

Interviewed by Steve and Gregg—May, 2010

———•••••———

Bob Enyart is the Senior Pastor of Denver Bible Church and for 20 years has also been a mainstay on local television and radio in the Denver area. Enyart is also the spokesman for American Right to Life and Colorado Right to Life. From his association with these two groups, Enyart has accumulated a wealth of experience within the pro-life and pro-family movements over the years.

Enyart says the foundation of the message he takes, both to the pulpit and into political activism, is that "there is a God. He's revealed through the Bible right and wrong, and that Christians need to honor Him above all else."

However, Enyart goes on to say that his message has been met with "opposition from many national Christian and pro-family organizations, and so that's made the battle even more difficult." Enyart has been a committed Christian since 1973, but it was many years after that before he became politically active.

"I didn't become active in the pro-life movement until the time of *Operation Rescue* at the 1988 Democratic National Convention, when I saw Randall Terry on CNN and hundreds of Christians being willing to risk their freedom and their livelihoods by sitting peacefully and praying in the front of the doors of abortion clinics," Enyart said. "I realized that this is what Christians should be willing to do, if in fact we're going to honor God and love our neighbor, because these babies are being ripped apart by the hands of Planned Parenthood abortionists. So that got me involved in the pro-life movement and I've been involved ever since.

I was the director of Operation Rescue Colorado and started a daily talk show in 1991, and it's been a joy to be on the air all those years—but for the interaction with many in the pro-family movement. In fact, you could almost call it an industry. For example, the partial-birth abortion ban took 15 years to pass, brought in a quarter of a billion dollars, and it never saved a single human life, and that's according to Dr. James Dobson who promoted it. So it's an industry that has brought in many hundreds of millions of dollars, and along the way they have openly shown that they are no longer following God's commands and His Word. They've compromised politically, and have increasingly become secular humanists in their policies."

Enyart isn't one to pull any punches. Especially when discussing *Focus on the Family*, which has become perhaps the largest and most influential Christian parachurch association in the country. Enyart has had many dealings with *Focus on the Family* over the years. He lives in Colorado, where *Focus on the Family* has its headquarters.

"I'd like to provide evidence that we've documented that (*Focus on the Family*) has become moral relativists in their public policy such as the Partial Birth Abortion ban fiasco, their support for Mitt Romney, and our interactions with various *Focus on the Family* state affiliates. We document this in our *Focus on the Strategy* DVD series.

The elder board of Denver Bible Church went down to Colorado Springs and met with *Focus on the Family's* public policy group, Tom Minnery, and their judicial analysts. We recorded that meeting. Then we made an identical presentation to 300 national Christian activists in Denver at a local church. We presented *Focus on the Family's* tragic reaction.

I'll give you some examples. Their abortion and pornography policies are very similar. They have long opposed efforts to ban abortion and only support efforts to regulate abortion. Similarly with pornography, they believe that the pornographer has the right to produce pornography and to sell it, they only seek to regulate it. (e.g., how many feet from a school can pornography be sold, what kind of graphic sex should be allowed in pornographic videos and so on). Of course, this is as counterproductive as it is to try to regulate the murder of innocent children. If Christian leaders cannot agree that it is fundamentally criminal to traffic in human sex, then how can we ever expect secular politicians and judges to agree with us?"

Enyart said he bases his convictions concerning the banning of such things on the teachings of the Bible.

"There are sins and then there are sins which are also crimes, but broadly God has written in our heart and our conscience the crimes that are so outrageous that they are not only sins but are also against the law. For thousands of years, in the Jewish law from the Old Testament and through to the New Testament and in Christian legal tradition, behaviors like homosexuality and adultery were criminal because human sexual activity was only permissible within marriage.

God designed sex that way to protect women especially, and to protect children, because human sexual activity is how we produce children. So if sex outside of marriage is decriminalized then you end up harming millions of children because it becomes commonplace to have sex even anonymously and recreationally with people we have no commitment to. In First Timothy chapter 1 Paul says we know that the law is good if you use it lawfully knowing this that God did not give the law for the righteous but for the unrighteous.

For example, from the time when Thomas Jefferson was the Governor of Virginia up until as late as the mid-1900s, homosexuality was a capital crime. If you wanted to check into a hotel and the clerk thought that you were not married, he would not permit you to check into a hotel. Adultery laws in our state of Colorado are still on the books. Adultery is a crime only they took away any punishment. So we still actually have in our criminal code a section on adultery only it no longer has a punishment. So we have decriminalized homosexuality, adultery, fornication, and through pornography we've decriminalized prostitution also because women get paid a lot of money to have sex with men, and as long as they videotape it and sell it it's supposedly all legal.

In the Bible when we see lists of crimes like murder, kidnapping, and adultery we realize that these are crimes that are not only sins. Murder is a sin. That doesn't mean that Christians should be tolerant of decriminalizing murder. Because it's a sin, we should realize that God authorized governments, and it's the role of governments to punish criminals. So of course you have to know what a crime is and you don't have the right to just invent or declare whatever you don't like as a crime."

Enyart believes a flawed understanding and application of the Scripture has led to a generation of failed Christian political activism.

"*Focus on the Family* makes it clear that they will not oppose pornography per se, but they want to regulate it. They don't oppose abortion legally per se but to regulate it even if in their heart of hearts they think abortion should be ended. They have spent years opposing efforts by Christians to end abortion, and they say that's not wise we should only regulate it. And of course then we are shown to be hypocrites, and we contradict our own position and we've lost the moral high ground and the blessing of God.

It would be as though we were in Germany and we said well, you can't kill Jewish children under the age of five you know because they're too cute. But over the age of five you can kill Jewish boys and over the age of eight you could kill Jewish girls. For Christians to spend 15 years advocating for such a law would not only be absurd, but it's dishonoring to God because it blurs the distinction between right and wrong. It invites wolves in sheep's clothing to come into the fold and become leaders. And that's what's happened.

Regarding the homosexual agenda, for example, during our meeting with Tom Minnery and his staff at *Focus on the Family*, we thanked them for leading Colorado's successful fight for Amendment Two back in the early 1990s, which made it clear that Christians and others could not be forced to rent to or hire homosexuals. Well, Tom Minnery told us as we're thanking them for fighting that fight that Focus would no longer support such a measure.

We said Tom, what does God want the law to be on this issue and on any particular issue and then why not work toward that goal? Minnery said directly 'We cannot do that. That is not how we come up with public policy objectives.'

And to us it's become clear that they are no longer overtly Christian in their public policy."

Enyart also believes Christians are too eager to praise recent Supreme Court appointments like John Roberts and Samuel Alito.

"After Colorado voted for Amendment Two, we had a homosexual group here called Equality Colorado and John Roberts was a partner in a leading law firm in Washington D.C. The homosexuals wanted to challenge our amendment at the Supreme Court, and they did. Roberts volunteered to craft the oral arguments for the homosexuals, and he did. His specialty was oral arguments before the Supreme

Court, and they succeeded. Roberts and the homosexuals succeeded in the Supreme Court and overturned Colorado's Amendment Two. Very few Christians spoke up to expose Roberts' role in this, and when George W. Bush nominated him to be the Chief Justice we were horrified. The pro-life community in Denver was horrified. On my radio show *Bob Enyart Live*, we began a full-court effort to at least educate Christians that Roberts supports a radical homosexual agenda. Roberts actually supports the radical homosexual agenda that homosexuality not only should be tolerated, but promoted by our public policy.

When we pointed this out, Dr. Dobson on his daily radio show came to Roberts' defense. He said that Roberts was acting like a secretary in a firm, and when a secretary is given papers to handle, she's not responsible for any moral consequence in those papers.

That just cannot be true. A lawyer, especially a partner of a prestigious law firm, is not forced to work for free especially for an organization that's determined to destroy Christian morality. So that's an example of *Focus on the Family* using their influence to promote those who have been undermining Christian morality.

A similar example was Samuel Alito. When Samuel Alito was nominated, *Focus on the Family* began lobbying for him to be confirmed to the Supreme Court, and we published—along with other Christians—a report card on Alito. It highlighted a half a dozen of his most egregious pro-abortion rulings. So we pointed this out to Dr. Dobson, and he sent us a written reply on *Focus on the Family* letterhead, which he signed, and included a hand-written note in shorthand. He said that Alito's ruling is exactly what we would want from a judge because he's following the rules."

Enyart is referring to the fact that Alito followed precedent, or *stare decisis*, in rulings he says actually affirmed abortion.

"We were grieved by that because when 'thou shall not murder' is discarded by a government, or by courts, you don't have the rule of law. You don't have precedent, because that is the greatest precedent. That is the oldest precedent. That is the foundation of all civil government. Just government is you cannot murder the innocent. You cannot murder children.

Alito used his authority to keep it legal in New Jersey, even to commit partial-birth abortion, and here you have *Focus on the Family* on both sides of that court case generally, where they're advocating for states to pass partial-birth abortion bans, and they're defending a federal judge who struck down a ban because they've lost their way. They no longer realize that if a law or a judge says that you could kill innocent children that that judge is guilty of murder before God, and he should not be defended or justified, but he should be admonished or rebuked or corrected."

Enyart believes fighting for measures such as partial birth abortion bans is a waste of time for the pro-life movement.

"Dr. Dobson admitted in writing, after the partial birth abortion ban was upheld by the U.S. Supreme Court, that it does not save a single human life. Now that's shocking, because for 15 years he fought for the ban and millions of Christians actually thought this would end all late-term abortions. Which, of course it didn't prevent a single scheduled abortion—not one—because abortionists are trained in multiple methods of killing children."

Enyart described the U.S. Supreme Court opinion that upheld the partial-birth abortion ban as "the most brutally wicked ruling" in the high court's history.

"If you read the *Gonzales v. Carhart* opinion of the Supreme Court, it's like a public relations move for the abortion industry. The ban does not use the term 'child' to describe the unborn baby, which we didn't like. In a previous case it used 'fetus,' and they said if we uphold this partial birth abortion ban the fetus might actually experience more pain not less compared to other methods of killing the fetus. Those other methods are more painful, and the partial birth abortion method is probably quicker and less painful. But this doesn't look good to the medical community to have a baby pulled out to the neck and stabbed in the back of the head and killed, so we're going to uphold the partial birth ban because it's not a threat to abortion rights, and it makes the abortion industry look a little better.

Now, I'm only slightly paraphrasing. We have analysis that we published within a week of the ruling, and we linked to the ruling so people could read it, and we quote from it to show how brutal it is. It's the most brutally wicked ruling in the history of the U.S. Supreme Court. When Alabama's former Chief Justice Roy Moore came out and praised the partial birth abortion ruling, he was echoing Jay Sekulow (from the American Center for Law and Justice) and others. American Right to Life took out a full-page ad in the *Birmingham News* and quoted from the opinion. Afterwards, I had the honor of doing a follow-up interview with Judge Moore. He publicly repented for having supported the *Gonzalez v. Carhart* opinion and he agreed that it's a violation of God's Law.

Enyart went on to describe *Gonzalez v. Carhart* as "a virtual late-term abortion manual."

"The Supreme Court Justices explain how to kill the same baby, saying if you're going to kill an older baby in the womb by partial-birth abortion, instead use a four-inch variation. Pull him out to the naval instead of the neck, and then you could kill the baby. You could dismember the baby. They literally include descriptions of ripping the baby's arms and legs off. They talk about injecting the baby with a lethal poison that would kill him. The Supreme Court, for the first time in their history, wrote a virtual abortion manual. It tells the abortionist you have to kill these babies with a more brutal method."

Enyart says he is not alone in that grisly characterization of *Gonzalez v. Carhart*.

"So many leaders came out and joined *American Right to Life* and condemned the partial-birth abortion ruling including Ambassador Alan Keyes, a co-founder of *National Right to Life* John Archibald, Notre Dame's Dr. Charles Rice, and the president of *Human Life International* Rev. Tom Euteneuer condemned it. Nelly Gray, one of the founders of the March for Life for all these decades, has completely condemned and exposed the fraudulent partial-birth abortion ban fiasco, as has Judy Brown at American Life League. We list dozens of pro-family and pro-life leaders who openly condemned the partial-birth abortion opinion and ban of the U.S. Supreme Court.

For those of us who lived through that 15-year period, we would get multiple fund-raising letters per week from different pro-life candidates, leaders, and organizations asking for money to fight for the partial-birth abortion ban. They did countless radio shows and commercials on helping us to fight for this and we are able to document that they raised over a quarter of a billion dollars!

Bob Dornan, a 20-year U.S. Congressman and pro-life hero, condemned not only the partial-birth abortion opinion of the U.S. Supreme Court, but also the ban itself because they're both immoral. He said those seven simple words which for the rest of my life I will use to evaluate pro-life legislation by asking does it end with 'and then you could kill the baby.' If it does, it's a bad law."

Enyart also believes pro-life bills that provide exceptions in certain cases to allow abortions aren't really pro-life at all.

"Exceptions are a window to the soul that means you are really pro-choice. Ultimately, this comes down to does God think that a particular politician is a murderer if he is guilty of shedding innocent blood? An exception still means a murdered child that is dismembered by an abortionist. God did not care about all the fruit Eve did not eat. He did not mention all the women David did not violate. He didn't list the children whom Herod did not kill. God looks at the exceptions, and they are a window to the soul.

What if we taught people to agree to lynch some blacks, to agree to gas some Jews in order to get a so-called victory? These exceptions have robbed Christians of the blessing of God on this fight for the last 30 years. Who would think that in John McCain's tenure as a U.S. Senator, by his current policies and approval, that 15 million children would be killed? If one child was killed intentionally by a politician's policy or authorized money, that politician is a murderer, and on Judgment Day that child will stand before that politician and that politician will be condemned and punished by God.

We add up the exceptions and the exceptions turn out to be of holocaust proportion."

It's no coincidence that the organizing of the modern pro-life movement seems to coincide with the ascendancy of the Republican Party. Remember that the coalition of Catholics and Evangelicals that came together after *Roe v. Wade* provided the final and largest faction within the three-legged Reagan Coalition of conservatives. Enyart believes that's why the GOP has responded since then with lukewarm attempts at stopping infanticide.

"This strategy turns the pro-life issue into a fundraiser and a partisan tool, because you know if abortion was outlawed the Republican Party would have a much harder time motivating its base. There are many Republicans who don't really care whether abortion is banned or not, but they market themselves as pro-life for the purpose of getting campaign funds and Christian votes. That should be obvious to us now, because it's been going on for decades, but many of the national Christian ministries have bought into that strategy because it provides them with a revenue flow that increases during primaries and during general elections.

Here is what their entire strategy boils down to: my mass murderer is better than your mass murderer. The Democrats have politicians who will kill millions, and the Republicans have politicians who will kill millions of innocent children. I believe this is an abomination in the eyes of God. He looks at Christian leaders and he sees that they've compromised. Their desire for victory is not much different than people watching the Super Bowl or the Final Four, and when you listen to these conservative talk shows whether on cable news or radio they become like the Dallas Cowboy cheerleaders."

Enyart also takes issue with the notion that President George W. Bush was our greatest pro-life president, as some pro-life leaders contend.

"South Dakota in 2006 introduced an absolute abortion ban, and Bush is nothing if he's not the consummate compromiser. He told ABC News, and this was reported around the world, that he did not support South Dakota's abortion ban because he has his exceptions of rape, incest and the life of the mother. So what he's basically saying is if I can't keep the right to kill a few of the kids I'm willing to kill, then I'd rather they just go ahead and kill them all. That's what he's saying.

So then in 2008, in a grotesque lack of wisdom by the pro-lifers in South Dakota, they tried to placate the president and they introduced an abortion regulation with exceptions. Now with the immoral exceptions advocated by President Bush where was he in his support? He was completely absent. He was not there trying to protect those children. So he'll speak at a fundraiser during a need for Republicans to do well in an upcoming election season. He'll speak at a fundraiser for a crisis pregnancy center, but he doesn't refuse to nominate judges because they're pro-choice."

While speaking of Republicans and their record on abortion, Enyart said that they've actually done more to advance infanticide in key areas than the Democrats who have embraced it as a party principle.

"In Colorado in 1967, it was Republican Governor John Love who signed our abortion law legalizing the killing of some innocent children. *Roe v. Wade* was decided by a Republican majority on a Republican Supreme Court, and it was written by a Republican Justice, Harry Blackman. The Supreme Court to this day is a Republican court, and it uses its influence to this day to deceive people into thinking that abortion has to be allowed. Sonia Sotomayor was nominated to the federal court by George H.W. Bush, so effectively she's another Republican Federal Judge who's pro-choice who's now on the Supreme Court. The Federal Judiciary for decades has been Republican, and for decades the Federal Judiciary has been overwhelmingly pro-choice and even now pro-homosexual and anti-Christian in its worldview."

Enyart also believes pragmatic pro-life strategy is "a lie."

"This is a lie that we're going to save the 99% and come back for the one with these bills that have exceptions. The Bush/South Dakota case proves it. Even if it were true, it's immoral. Jesus would leave the 99 to save the one. You don't say we're going to agree to kill the one child to try to save these others. It's an immoral illusion designed to keep money flowing into partisan coffers."

Seeing a need for accountability in the pro-life movement, Enyart was one of the people instrumental in creating the website www.ProLifeProfiles.com, which tracks the pro-life actions and statements of pro-lifers in all facets of public life. Enyart believes the standard for pro-life in the next generation ought to be what is frequently described as Personhood, or the idea that an unborn child is considered a person by the state at the moment of fertilization. Therefore, Enyart's website judges well-known pro-lifers accordingly, and it contains some provocative information about figures considered heroes to many pro-lifers.

"Pro-lifers cannot trust politicians who appoint Planned Parenthood board members to Supreme Courts like Sarah Palin did in Alaska. She praised this former Planned Parenthood board member (who is unrepentant) saying that she would be a fabulous judge for the state of Alaska.

They can't trust politicians like Mitt Romney, that authorized taxpayer-funded abortion-on-demand as he did with his Romney healthcare plan, which is awfully similar to Obama's health-care reform. They cannot trust politicians who oppose the personhood of the unborn child, and that includes Ron Paul who says that states have the right to legalize abortion and that the federal government would have to tolerate it if New York and California killed tens of millions of innocent children."

Personhood is what Enyart characterizes as "the dagger in the heart of liberalism." At the time this book was published there was personhood legislation pending in over 30 states.

"Personhood is the right to life from our Creator, that we are endowed with that does not come from the government, it doesn't come from the Constitution or from the hospital or the delivery doctor at birth. Our rights are endowed upon us by our Creator, so they come at the moment that we are created not when we're born. So the personhood movement affirms the God given right to life of every unborn child, boy and girl, and it is fighting for government to enforce that right to life."

Dr. Dobson was contacted for an interview, and offered an opportunity to respond to Enyart's claims in this chapter, but he refused.

Joseph Farah

Interviewed by Steve—July, 2010

Joseph Farah is the founder and publisher of *World Net Daily*, one of the top 500 websites online. It has become the No.1 independent news site according to *Alexa.com*, which is an affiliate of *Amazon.com*. Farah has spent 25 years working in journalism and media in various capacities, and one of his claims to fame was giving an early editorial opportunity at the *Sacramento Union* to then local talk radio host Rush Limbaugh. He's also authored and collaborated on several books, including 2008's *None of the Above* about the lack of principled conservatism represented in the presidential nominees of both political parties.

An outspoken evangelical Christian, Farah has connections throughout the conservative movement, as evidenced by the all-star lineup of columnists and contributors to his website. However, in 2010 Farah sent shockwaves throughout the conservative movement by rescinding an invitation to firebrand commentator Ann Coulter, who was scheduled to speak at his "Taking America Back Conference." Coulter was asked not to attend after she also agreed to speak at an event organized by homosexual activists called "Homo-Con."

The firestorm from his decision to publicly rebuke one of the conservative establishment's sacred cows was still burning in July of 2010 when the Farah interview took place. In August of that year, Coulter responded in typical Ann Coulter fashion by calling Farah and his staff at *World Net Daily* "fake Christians."[93]

"When we started planning our event, the Conservative Political Action Conference (CPAC) was going on and there was a controversy there stirred by a group called GOProud, which is supposedly a Republican homosexual organization. This group was allowed to co-sponsor CPAC, and I took exception to that and we withdrew our sponsorship as did a number of other groups. Sean Hannity and Sarah Palin both withdrew as speakers because of the controversy which isn't widely known.

We then started planning our event, and Ann was the first person we invited to be a speaker. This was going to be a no compromise kind of conference, and one of the issues that I believe the conservative movement is compromising on is the issue of same-sex marriage. Since Ann had decided to go and speak at this GOProud event, which had created the reason for us to have a conference, we were quite stunned.

We had a dialogue with Ann about it that didn't get anywhere, and I saw it as Ann affirming GOProud by appearing there. I've known Ann for 20 years, and remember when she was an intern at *Human Events*."

In 2010 several high profile conservatives issued public statements that were either indifferent about the marriage issue, or in support of same sex unions. Two high profile examples were Limbaugh voicing support for civil unions[94] on his nationally-syndicated radio program, and Glenn Beck saying the destruction of marriage was "no threat" to America on Fox News.[95] In response, Farah went on the offensive.

"This isn't just about Rush, Ann, and Beck. Grover Norquist is considered an icon in the conservative movement, and he sits on the board of GOProud. There are others compromising on morality that have even bigger names than Ann Coulter. We confronted some of them and they literally repented and stopped doing the egregious things they were doing to promote homosexuality, so we've had victories that we can't really talk about because we handled those issues privately."

Few in the modern history of the conservative movement have been more influential thinkers than the late Russell Kirk, whose book *The Conservative Mind* is considered one of the most prominent tomes defining conservatism.

Kirk defined conservatism according to "traditions," or time-honored beliefs/practices that have stood the test of time as proven correct, and therefore have been passed down from generation to generation. In Kirk's mind, several traditions were the foundation of contemporary American conservatism: belief in a spiritual order which in some fashion governs our mundane order; belief in political self government; belief in the importance to human persons of certain natural private rights; belief in the value of marriage and the family.

Farah echoes the same vision as Kirk, which is why he puts such an emphasis on the definition of marriage.

"The institution of marriage has been defined for 5,000 years so it's disappointing to see conservatives giving up on it. Really the movement is capitulating (to liberals) on every front imaginable, but when you give up on the Biblical institution of marriage you're giving up on the building block of Western Civilization. You cannot have self-government without the institution of marriage and you can't do all the things (liberals) want to do with it without unbelievably dire consequences. You can look at this issue spiritually, or you can look at this issue pragmatically. But regardless of how you look at it, when you redefine marriage you have redefined everything we hold dear in this country, and in Western Civilization, and the Judeo-Christian ethic.

I can't think of a more important issue for the future of this country than that."

From there the conversation with Farah turned to why so many conservatives seem willing to throw marriage overboard. He was asked to speculate as to why some conservatives compromise with a special interest group that had lost all 31 elections contesting the definition of marriage in America. Why, did he think, some conservatives were so willing to pander to a group that represents at best 5% of the nation's population?

"Well, I think it has to do with the fact that they don't have the proper worldview and grounding to fully understand, and to be able to articulate, their opposition to same-sex marriage. I would say most politicians don't know how to explain it, yet they feel in their gut like this is a bad thing. But they cannot explain it, because they don't have a proper Biblical or historical grounding to be able to articulate it in a way that will resonate with the vast majority of the people. So instead they have to articulate it to a reporter from the *Washington Post,* and that reporter will eat their lunch so they get the sense that there is no point in trying to have this dialogue anymore. They see the winds are shifting, and the times are changing, and they capitulate."

So what is the proper worldview?

"Self-government isn't possible if you do not have a strong family unit of a mother and a father rearing up the next generation that is exemplifying equally the characteristics of masculinity and feminin-ity. God set out a few rules for us to live by, and they're good rules. When you follow them you're blessed, and when you don't you're cursed. It's that simple. The only potential for retaining liberty and freedom in this lifetime is to live by God's standard.

The most loving thing we can do from a Christian or Biblical per-spective is to tell people that they're in sin, because we all are, and we all need to repent. That's the saving grace that we have as Christians, but if you don't give people an opportunity to take advantage of that, you're doing the worst disservice you can possibly do.

In Genesis we see He created this institution of marriage, and you can see Jesus affirm it in the Gospels, as well as Paul in the New Testament in places like Romans. So if you abandon an insti-tution like this, self-government implodes because the family is destroyed and then a society has to make a decision: are you going to worship at God's altar or are you going to worship at the altar of government?"

If this institution is so important, how come high-profile Christian political leaders haven't been more vocal in holding those conservatives accountable that seek to abandon it?

"It's very important for there to be consequences for people's bad deci-sions, and that's why we have a press, that's why we have things like talk radio, so that when people cross the line there can be account-ability. One of the things I've seen with the celebrity Christians, and celebrity conservatives, is there's not a lot of accountability in their lives and there needs to be accountability.

You know, I'm accountable to people. I'm accountable to my wife. I'm accountable to God. I'm accountable to a circle of friends, and people in the church and so forth. We need that because we are all tempted to cross lines we shouldn't cross, and when we do somebody needs to hold us accountable. I don't see many others doing it. Where are the pro-family organizations on this? Where is the church? When God gives you something He gives you a responsibility that goes along with it."

So if there's a lack of accountability in the movement, whom do we know we can trust to be people of integrity in accordance with God's Word?

"I don't look to men and women to tell me how to think, particularly contemporary ones, but I look to God's Word. That's the standard by which I measure the activity of men. There are still lots of good people in the movement, but it's shrinking. I can count on one hand how many famous people are willing to take a stand on this in public. That's the shocking truth.

We are living in very precarious times."

Michael Farris

Interviewed by Steve—October, 2010

———•◦•◦•———

The list of those in the Christian Conservative movement with a more complete resume than Michael Farris is a short one.

Farris is perhaps best known as one of the Founding Fathers of the American homeschooling movement. He is the founder and chairman of the *Home School Legal Defense Association* which got its start in the early 1980s. It's unlikely there is an organization that has done more to defend parental rights in education in this country than HSLDA has over the years. Farris also founded Patrick Henry College in 2000, which has the stated mission to "impact the world for Christ and liberty."

A Constitutional lawyer, and an ordained Baptist Minister, Farris has argued cases before the U.S. Supreme Court, is the author of several books, and is the father of 10 children. He's also helped start several grassroots organizations such as *ParentalRights.org* and *Generation Joshua*, which seeks to mobilize Christian youth in the political sphere.

Farris approaches his work from the perspective of both a movement insider and also a foot soldier.

"I got involved in standing up for Christian-oriented political issues when I was in law school," Farris said. "The first thing I did was to try to stop the city of Spokane (Washington) from opening up some taverns in the city park. The press never asked me how many members there were in our group, but there were just two of us. The other person was in her 80s at the time. We were successful in stopping one of the taverns and putting limits on the other one. Because of that, I got in the press and people started asking me questions. I was invited to join an umbrella organization that was basically a forerunner of the state family public policy counsel.

That group got me involved in a whole bunch of things. They sent me to New York City to be trained in anti-pornography issues. I actually ended up writing Washington State's anti-pornography laws a couple years later, which went to the Supreme Court. The Supreme Court struck down one word of my pornography law and left the rest intact.

That group also got me involved in the ERA litigation. Congress extended the length of time for the ratification of the ERA. I represented four Washington state legislators challenging the constitutionality of that extension of time. That case was ultimately consolidated with another case brought by the Arizona and Idaho state legislatures.

When I was involved with that case, I heard about the *Moral Majority* getting started and I went to Washington D.C. in 1980. I talked with the executive director of the Moral Majority (about a job) for five minutes. He found out I was a lawyer and a Baptist and that was good enough. He told me I could start the Moral Majority chapter in my state, which ended up being the largest state chapter in the country. In terms of the boots on the ground working on government issues, our operation was bigger than the one in Washington D.C.

In the course of doing that, I got to know Tim LaHaye a little bit, and he and his wife offered me a job as the national field director of *Concerned Women of America*. Eventually in 1983 they put me in charge of the Washington D.C. office. About that time our family started homeschooling. I started HSLDA and ran it as a volunteer, meaning I got paid nothing for about three years."

Other than the LaHayes, who were instrumental in starting CWA, who else has Farris worked closely with on political causes?

"I've worked with just about everybody you can think of in the conservative Christian community; James Dobson, Chuck Colson, Donald Wildmon, Tony Perkins, Gary Bauer, D. James Kennedy, Phyllis Schlafly, and Paul Weyrich. The list gets pretty long."

In the early days of the Christian Conservative movement, how was it possible to get people from such a diverse swath of theological thought to come together in the political arena?

"There was a general understanding that while our faith in Jesus Christ motivated each of us to action. We were uniting for political purposes and we weren't trying to create a church or a theological institution, and we would agree to disagree in another forum on eschatology, for example. So we agreed where we agreed and we lived in unity where we could live in unity.

It was a general belief that we were pretty united on what needed to be said to the country on political issues and what should be done in general terms. There would be strategic differences on what's the right priority and tactic, but the first consolidating idea was it was time for American Christians to speak up and sitting silently was no longer acceptable—that was the key unifying theme in the beginning.

Then we began to unify around particular issues such as pro-life. We did reach solidarity of opinion on the abortion issue pretty quickly. I became prolife personally in 1975 when my wife and I went through our first Lamaze class. It was pretty obvious if it was a baby you didn't kill it. It's as simple as that. I didn't know the science. I didn't know the theology—I knew nothing.

There were unifying factors about prolife, and there was a unifying belief that the moral decline of the country with pornography, homosexuality and other things of that sort were really harmful to the country. We had to stand up and do something about it."

Farris mentioned eschatology (study of the end times) as an area where the leaders of the movement agreed to disagree. However, if one's eschatology drives your thinking that can cause disagreement about how you can or should proceed tactically in the political arena.

Let's look at just one example. One person's eschatology might say that the world will get progressively worse no matter what we do, and Satan is essentially a co-equal of God's until Christ returns. Another person's eschatology may claim that the kingdoms of this world belong to Christ right now in human history. How do those two people come to an agreement on how best to engage the political process?

After all, one person goes in expecting defeat and the other person goes in expecting victory. Wouldn't that change their perspectives on whether to be more principled or pragmatic? Wouldn't a Christian's premise of who is reigning at the moment, and how or when history's ultimate conclusion happens, impact the tactics that a Christian in politics is inclined to engage in?

"The application of that question I've spent the most time addressing over the course of time, has been the viewpoint that no matter what we do, the world's going to get worse and then Jesus is going to come back. I've had people say to me words to that affect, and that since the world is horrible that means Jesus is coming back soon. I am a believer in pre-millennial, pre-tribulation rapture eschatology. What Tim LaHaye believes, that's what I believe. Yet Tim was here working on the issues just like I was, and sometimes even more so. He and Beverly were my mentors in many ways.

There was an article written back in the early 1980s called the 'Intellectual Schizophrenic: the Moral Majority,' raising just the issue you just raised. The answer I give is out of Scripture. I turn to the parable of the persistent widow in Luke and say, 'Jesus says she was commended for demanding justice in the face of injustice.' When he returns, will he find faith on the earth?

The lesson I took from that is, the kind of faith that Jesus wanted us to be exhibiting when he returns is that we're actively opposing injustice and not sitting on the sidelines, and hunkering down, and waiting for his return. He wants to see faith—real faith—and the example that he gave us is the persistent widow. We're to pray, we're to persist, and we're to fight back against the forces of injustice in our society. That's the eschatological answer that I would give and the Scriptural basis for it."

Steve recalled listening to a Christian conservative radio host who once urged listeners to call their congressmen and encourage them to take a righteous stand on a piece of legislation. After spending some time exhorting the audience to take action, the host then proceeded to remind the audience that "since we know this is the Laodicean age of the church, things will just continue to get worse."

In other words, this host had just discouraged listeners' political participation right after asking for it. Even though the words were contradictory the overall message was clear: as the Borg would say in a Star Trek movie "resistance is futile."

How can you consistently and successfully enlist people to participate in a cause they don't believe they'll win? Isn't that a little bit like trying to drive a car by applying the gas and the brakes at the exact same time? If that host's dim eschatological viewpoint on the future of human history represents the dominant perspective in American Christendom at the moment, could that help us understand why the results of our political efforts for the past generation have been so disappointing?

"I don't think we define victory, I think we define faithfulness, and if the Lord is pleased to give us victory, it's going to be because we're faithful. So, the results are His, the faithfulness is ours.

This verse has been so well used it's become almost trite to quote it: 'if my people, who are called by my name, will humble themselves and pray and seek my face and turn from their wicked ways—that's the part we like to leave out—then I will hear from heaven, and I will forgive their sin and will heal their land.' There's another passage: 'come, let us reason together. Though your sins are like scarlet, they shall be white as snow; thought they are red as crimson, they shall be like wool.' The sins being written about there are the sins of a nation.

We have no idea if we're seeing the end of the age, or if we're seeing threads of the end of America. We ought not to mix those things up. People have thought for hundreds or thousands of years that Jesus' return is right around the corner and we just don't know. I walked past a bench in Colorado Springs the other day and it said that Jesus will return on May 11, 2011. Right after I saw that I thought, that's one day that we can definitely mark off."

What about people who justify their political compromises because of their eschatology? What about the Christian political activist who says that since things get worse no matter what we do, it's better to compromise on the prolife issue and save some of those babies? After all, they reason, we know we won't be able to save them all. In other words, is a Christian allowed to behave in politics as if God is not truly sovereign?

"I believe that we should be operating in a way that allows us to win, and that we should not engage in the doctrine of preemptive surrender. We win when we're being found faithful, and that's kind of the spiritual framework that we have to be working in, but our minds function better at times when we think of it human terms, too.

For example, if we want to stop same sex marriage, which I urged a group of leaders to do in the mid-1990s, then we've got have tactics that really are consistent to trying to stop same sex marriage that will really work at the end of the day. If we're telling the American public let's stop same sex marriage and here's what we're going to do to stop it, the here's what we're going to do part needs to do what we say, and it's actually got to stop same sex marriage. The Defense of Marriage Act was never intended to stop same sex marriage. It was intended to slow it down a bit. It was intended to advance federalism principles relative to same sex marriage. It was never an agenda for victory.

I don't mind interim steps like that, if they're correctly explained to the American public that this is an interim step. That this is what we're doing today, and then we're going to do this, and here's the battle plan to stop same sex marriage. I don't believe in over promising and under-delivering. I believe if we're only going to take a partial step, we tell people this is a partial step."

Farris believes that the speculation the Rapture is coming soon lacks Biblical reinforcement. He also understands that even if he's wrong, that doesn't give Christians an excuse not to stand on principle.

"That we are the last generation, I don't think you can justify from Scripture. Even if we are, we're supposed to be found faithful under the persistent widow that makes that clear. So, we have to be persistent, we have to be trying for victory, and we have to be faithful in all that we do.

I'm building a college to train people to be effective 50, 75, 100 years from now, and I'm trying to build the college in a way that 200 years from now it will still be a faithful institution training Christian leaders. I'm getting to the age that I don't dare buy green bananas, and so I think we've still got to assume that this is a long term, multi-generational fight.

Maybe I have a little bit of an advantage because I've been paying attention to eschatology since 1958, and I've known people since 1958 who said, 'Well, I don't know exactly when it's going to be, but it's got to be within the next five years (Christ returns).'

After you hear that about 15 times, you start thinking you know what, the Bible really means it when it says no one knows the day or the hour—it really does mean that. Jesus could come before we get off this phone call. There's nothing stopping him. If that's God's pleasure, boom, now. On the other hand, it could be 200, 500 years from now, and I have no way of knowing. I'm going to live my life as if Jesus is not coming back for a long, long time."

Farris has had a passion for Christian education for over a quarter century. Overall, how does he believe the Church of Jesus Christ in America has dealt with the discipleship of its children during that time?

"I think that the church as a whole has failed dramatically to understand the importance of a Christian education, a really truly Christian education. You can read it in a lot of different ways. You can read Barna statistics. There's a new book written by this Princeton woman seminary professor who's an ordained Methodist minister. All my liberalism bells go off when I read her pedigree, but she nailed it on the head in her book called *Almost Christian,* that we are training this generation to believe in something that calls itself Christian but it robs Christianity of every vital component of it. It is feel-goodism, therapeutic and has very little to do with the Gospel of Jesus Christ. She just nails it.

Farris draws an example from his own life to illustrate his point.

"I'll tell you a story that illustrates what I think has been the general rule on this issue. Around 1982, I taught an adult Sunday school class at Westwood Baptist in Olympia, Washington. There were at least 125 adults in the class and I taught on different subjects involving secular humanism in the culture for 13 weeks. I deliberately saved education for the last class.

Every week these people were 'let's go get them,' and they were right there with me. I got to humanism in education and started presenting the idea that a school system that systematically excluded the knowledge of God reaps the consequences listed in Romans 1, where if you fail to retain the knowledge of God, God turns you over to depraved mind to do that which must not be done. Man alive, you would've thought it was a different class of people. It was all secular reasoning, and they claimed we had to be in the public schools to be salt and light.

That verse is so out of context. My response is the specific commands control the general commands. There are specific commands in the Scripture as to how we should educate our kids. The idea that we get out of those specific commands because of salt and light is a misuse of Scripture, so we're off into the secular world. There were two associate superintendents of schools in the class, there were principals, and there were public school teachers. Almost everyone had their kids in public schools. The dominant majority of born again Christians have their kids in public schools yet today."

Why does Farris believe there is so much spiritual blindness on the part of the average American Christian where government education is concerned?

"In large part it's kind of a default drive, their parents did it and so on. But the real reason is because they don't look in the Bible and make their decisions by what the Bible says. If I could have one wish for the Christian community, it would be they would read the Bible, figure out what it says about educating children and follow it.

People in secular education think the knowledge of God is not worthwhile. That's what it's about, and I don't know how Christians think they can get past Scripture. They have excuses and justifications (for utilizing government schools) but there is no Scriptural reasoning. I don't pretend to be the substitute for the Holy Spirit in their lives, but I would challenge them to go look in the Bible and figure out how they should live and educate their kids. This is one of the biggest decisions they'll ever make, and they ought not to make it by default or by some secular reasoning."

Next, Farris assessed the last generation of Christian Conservative political involvement. Given the gigantic growth in government, the humanistic bent in the culture, and the growth in power of bureaucrats, judges, and other unelected officials over the course of that time, was anything truly righteous accomplished?

"The right of parents to direct their children's upbringing and education is better than it has been. I think that the principle reason that is true, is the people that have been fighting for that have been faithful in God's economy, and sovereign timing of everything. Because of that, He's laid a blessing on that and said that one I'm going to bless."

Why does Farris believe God hasn't "laid a blessing" in other areas of political engagement like life, marriage, the rule of the law, and the economy?

"I have some ideas on this, particularly as it relates to abortion. I believe that God's not going to bless the prolife movement until His people turn from their wicked ways and seek God's face on this. That is, do we really believe that children are a blessing from the Lord? As long as the Christian church as a whole is silent on the issue of birth control, what we're doing is saying that children are not a blessing from the Lord. I think that robs us of any spiritual power, and that's a big issue.

The other thing is on why did we lose same sex marriage? We lost the same sex marriage battle because the leaders weren't willing to battle it at a time where we could've won. We got to the time that we needed to battle it, and there was a compromise at a big level within our leadership. God would simply not bless them wanting to put civil unions into the Constitution. That's what happened is that they attempted to stop same sex marriage by putting civil unions into the Constitution."

Was Farris a witness to this?

"The facts are this, after George W. Bush became president, the federal marriage amendment was drafted by Robbie George at Princeton, and we had two levels of meetings of (Religious Right) leaders—drafting and political. The drafting meeting was dominated by lawyers including me. I was sitting right next to Robbie George in the meeting.

I asked Robbie, 'do you intend by this language to ban civil unions?' and he said 'yes.'

I said, 'explain to me how this language bans civil unions,' and he went through this long convoluted explanation.

I said 'Robbie, unless you and I and three other people just like us are on the Supreme Court, this will never be construed to be that way. If we're going to ban civil unions, let's just say so.'

He didn't have a problem with that. So, I worked to get language that would make (banning civil unions) explicit because my theory was I don't care what you call it, if same sex partners end up as legal spouses it's still marriage. We proffered language that would accomplish that purpose.

We then went to the political committee of the Arlington group, which is a coalition of social conservative organizations, a who's who of the Religious Right. We went to the steering committee and at that meeting there were 25 people there voting. I made my pitch to ban civil unions and Richard Land carried the argument for the other side."

That statement demanded clarification. Was Farris saying that the president of the Ethics and Religious Liberty Commission for the Southern Baptist Convention, Richard Land, argued *for* civil unions?

"His pitch was that he didn't want civil unions, but he thought it was politically necessary to do so and allow the states to decide whether they wanted civil unions or not. I argued against it and the vote was taken. My side won 22-3.

Within 48 hours, we'd been ratted out. Other key leaders in that meeting went to members of Congress and made a deal with them to do the compromise language. A handful of us, like Bill Bennett, quit and we said 'God's not going to bless this. We're not going to try to amend the Constitution to put civil unions in the Constitution so we're done.'

It went down in defeat because it was compromised from the get go."

Was this sellout over the issue of marriage symbolic of the underlying reasons the movement wasn't more successful in his opinion? Could it be that Christian conservative leaders had in fact set out to define the terms of surrender before the battles that defined their effort despite all the money it raised and candidates it helped elect?

"I think it's a fair criticism. I would say that we've compromised way too long. We've been satisfied with tickets to the state dinner instead of actual policy implementation. We've bought into the idea way too often that says let's deal with the economic issues first and then we'll deal with the social issues. That started in Reagan's administration.

Ronald Reagan was a great president, but his administration bought into that idea that we'd deal with the economic issues first and then deal with the moral ones. However, Daniel 4:27 tells us renounce your sins by doing what is right, by being kind to the oppressed, and *then* your prosperity will continue.

We continuously elected people to office who patted us on the head and said I'm with you, but when it came to prioritizing things once those people got into office, we were never the priority. We didn't know how to effectively rally against that to prevent that from happening. We've allowed ourselves to be used in the electoral process."

As the founder of a university, and one of the trailblazers on home schooling, it's obvious that Farris has a passion for discipling the next generation. If he were to disciple his students on how to vote in an election where the candidates are each flawed in their political philosophy what would he say?

"It depends on whether they're violating a law of God, or some principal of government like federalism. Federalism is something I really believe in, but it's not the same as the law of God. If somebody is a little squishy on federalism, I don't like it, but I don't think I violate God's standards if I help somebody that can have a better view on federalism. But if someone's wrong on killing babies, I'm not going to help them. I'm not going to vote for them. I won't participate with them. If the price of entering the Republican Party becomes you've got to sit your views on abortion aside, we're not going to work on that.

I won't help somebody who is not correct on the core issues, and right now the two easily understandable core issues to identify that are easy to figure out are life and marriage. If a Republican is wrong on those two things, I'm going to run the other way. I'm not going to help them.

I don't know if this would actually work out. I'm going to have to listen to the Lord, but in terms of my own, human response to the circumstances, if someone like Mitt Romney, who is pro abortion and pro homosexual, is the Republican presidential nominee, I intend to at least try to get the nomination of the Constitution Party and run against him. I will not stand by and let someone like that be the only choice the American public has."

Farris considers the issue of embryonic stem cell research to be a prolife issue. So then, how does he justify supporting Senator John McCain for president in 2008, considering he's an outspoken advocate of taxpayer-funded destruction of human life at its most nascent stage?[96]

"First of all, we need to make sure that gets circulated because I didn't know that about McCain. I feel embarrassed that I didn't know that, but that's not consistent with being prolife. It's just not. In my position I should've known that—there's no excuse. There might have been a lot of Christians that didn't know that."

What lessons would Farris suggest the next generation of Christian political activism learn from the previous one?

"There's no substitute for personal faithfulness to God and His Word. People who enter the fray and think that they can work off of principles they've learned in the past as opposed to a dynamic living relationship with the Son of God, there's no substitute for that. We constantly need to be checking ourselves to see if we're being faithful to the Lord, doing what He wants us to do, and not listening to people, listening to the newspaper, but listening to what the Holy Spirit has to say to us.

There's no substitute for a dynamic faith in God. We talk relationship all the time and we act like it's some kind of static set of principles. Of course there are binding things from the Word of God, but it's not static, it's alive and powerful. I think we need to be wary of secularizing what we do. We need to say what does the Bible say? We need to diligently read the Word of God and apply it to political issues."

Farris concluded by saying accountability for leaders is vital if the next generation of the movement is going to turn things around.

"I don't want to be in a position to judge anybody else, so let me judge myself. You have to have a certain ego to be able to take on the world. The world will attack you, other people will attack you, and you'll be mistreated. Being a leader is no fun, easy thing. It is hard.

On the other hand, if you do not have real accountability, you get too full of yourself and you'll make really stupid mistakes and you will mislead people. The thing that I have been blessed with in my long-term ministry at HSLDA is I have a real board that will tell me no. That is the truth. It's as if God tells us that we've got to have accountability—iron has to sharpen iron.

If you don't have people in your life that will tell you no there's something amiss. You will not be blessed. You will not be successful in the long run. You'll lead people astray. I'm very grateful for our board who have had the guts to tell me no and confront me when I'm wrong. Keep holding me accountable. You know, that's not always pleasant, but it is right. I think that it would be fair for anyone that's going to get deeply involved in something, to say to the leadership tell me about your accountability structure, how does it work, when's the last time someone got told no?"

Gary Glenn

Interviewed by Gregg—May, 2011

Gary Glenn is one of those scrappy guys you want on your team when things heat up. Google his name, however, and you'll find that those on the cultural left can't stand him.

Glenn has earned a reputation for his relentless opposition to any public policy he believes threatens the institution of the family and is contrary to Biblical teaching. His opponents have taken notice of his consistent tenacity. Type in his name to your favorite online search engine, and it's liable to produce leftists describing Glenn as "creep of the week" or "an enemy of the state."

Those are criticisms, by the way, that Glenn is quite proud of considering the source.

While he is credited with making a real impact through his efforts with the National Right to Work organization, for the most-part Glenn's reputation was earned through his role as president of the Michigan chapter of the *American Family Association (AFA.)* AFA is one of the largest Christian Conservative organizations in the movement, and also one of the most despised by the cultural left. Glenn has decades of political experience as a former local public servant, congressional candidate, and now as an activist.

Unlike leaders in many of the movement's most well-known organizations, Glenn is not shy about going against the grain and speaking his mind about his contemporaries. Case in point: he began his interview with co-author Gregg Jackson by discussing how the Religious Right was to blame for a left-leaning Republican like John McCain winning the GOP presidential nomination in 2008.

"McCain was one of just six Republican U.S. Senators who voted against a marriage amendment to the U.S. Constitution, so that's just one example of why he was such a disappointing choice. No wonder we lost as badly as we did in 2008. One word describes how we ended up with McCain: incompetence. That's incompetence of conservative leaders. *World Magazine* had an article in which Michael Farris and Paul Weyrich agreed that many conservative leaders had blown it. So did *Charisma Magazine.* Dick Bott, senior president of Bott Radio Network, said that 'evangelical voters overlooked candidates' liberal positions and by doing so they ironically set back Christian causes instead of advancing them.' In the end, most conservative Christian leaders let down those Christian voters."

Glenn says that lately there's been more talk about the lack of leadership in the Religious Right than there have been pleas to close ranks and rally around it.

"I read another article from *World Magazine* and the author said 'I have grave doubts whether these leaders will anytime soon be able to offer credible credentials for positive endorsements of almost any kind.' That's from a *Christian* publication. There was a *World Net Daily* story written by Janet Folger lamenting the void of pro-family leadership in the movement. Those are just some of the words from our friends.

To pour salt in the wound, *Time Magazine* said the 2008 nomination process 'has exposed some of those leaders once and for all as emperors with no clothes and exposed what little clout, judgment, or principles they have. They have a much less lofty agenda. They just like their seat at the table, they don't like to lose, and they don't seem to realize that by signing on with a frontrunner they were following and not leading—demonstrating weakness not strength. What this plot twist has really exposed is that the shepherds have no sheep, and you get the sense that rank and file evangelicals are just as sick of their own leaders as they are of the political arena in general.'"

Glenn said that by meeting with Christian Conservative leaders he was privy to information that unfortunately confirms the sense the movement has lost its moorings.

"I was in these meetings over the course of two or three years leading up to the 2008 presidential nomination process. It certainly was an eye opening experience. Sometimes like an Alice in Wonderland 'through the looking glass' experience, because I was hearing and seeing things that I simply couldn't believe. It took me a while to believe I was actually seeing it.

Things were coming to a boiling point among Christian pro-family activists. I mean, it was to the point where these disagreements weren't going to be kept off the record. People were going to start talking and I know that a lot of us came out of that process absolutely intent on not allowing it to happen again. We were shocked and caught off guard the first time by what we witnessed. But we're no longer naïve, no longer shockable, and we left that experience with the intent that this time around we were not going to stand by and allow that same kind of incompetence to happen again (in 2012)."

These meetings leading up to the 2008 GOP presidential nomination process that Glenn was referring to were a part of an organization called The Arlington Group, which is a veritable who's who of national Christian Conservative leaders. This elite group was formed several years ago with the hope that Christian leaders could come together transparently for the sake of unity, but according to Glenn just the opposite happened in the time leading up to those first presidential primaries. Glenn said Christians deserve to know the truth about what went on in these meetings.

"The Arlington Group broke down into two camps fairly early in the 2008 presidential nomination process. One said we should find the Godliest candidate we can, recognizing that none of them are perfect, we're all human beings, and we're all sinners saved by grace. But we ought to find the candidate whose positions on the issues, whose public policy record is closest to the values that we tell all these millions of Americans are paramount to our worldview. This camp thought we should find the candidate whose track record is the most consistent on the hills we say we're willing to die on. In other words, not just the candidates who say that they're champions of family values while they have a history in elective office of promoting abortion on demand and the homosexual agenda, like Mitt Romney. Let's lead.

The other half broke into a camp that said let's look around and see who we think is viable, even if their record or stand on the issues is suspect on those issues that we tell our constituents that are paramount to us. Let's pick that person and get on the bandwagon of who we think is going to win. In other words, just like any other special interest group in Washington, put your finger up in the air, wet it, and see which way the wind is blowing.

This division went about 50-50 as it turned out. The ones who were saying let's find the candidate who most matched our principles fell largely into a camp of people who turned out and supported Mike Huckabee. The other group who had their finger in the air went for Fred Thompson, possibly Mitt Romney, and even to John McCain."

Glenn said that in the fall of 2007 a meeting of the Arlington Group was held with the intention of seeing if those in attendance could finally coalesce behind one candidate to avoid a more moderate or socially liberal Republican from attaining the nomination.

"This is where it really got bizarre. After the Values Voter Summit there was a meeting in September of 2007. After all this debating the expectation of everyone in the room was that we were going to actually come to a conclusion in supporting a particular candidate. Everyone in the room, regardless of which candidate they supported, anticipated that if that vote ever took place that Mike Huckabee would get that support. Gary Bauer was holding the microphone and running the meeting, and from our perspective did everything possible to make sure no such vote occurred because everyone assumed they knew what the outcome was going to be.

Gary Bauer was running the meeting, and he told us we would not be allowed to discuss the candidates' records or where they stood on the issues pro-family activists are committed to. That was the rule he laid down. This was mind boggling. We were actually being told we couldn't discuss where a candidate stood on life or marriage in the meeting of an organization like that. Janet Folger, now Janet Porter, objected. There was a 45-minute debate about whether that rule should be honored. I didn't participate in the debate. Janet was upset with me afterwards. I didn't speak out because I had no intention of honoring the rule even if they'd approved it.

I think the rule was instituted despite Janet's objection and I paid no attention to it anyway."

Glenn said he ignored Bauer's attempt to limit the debate, and openly discussed Romney's liberal record in Massachusetts in great detail with his colleagues.

"I did discuss Mitt Romney's long record of indignantly declaring himself not to be a pro-life candidate when he was running for governor and his opposition to a marriage protection amendment to the state constitution in Massachusetts. I recounted it in great detail. There were probably few politicians in America who more aggressively promoted the notion of abortion on demand and the homosexual agenda than Mitt Romney.

I shared the fact that after his pro-life conversion he signed into law Romneycare, the model for Obama care, which has the $50 copay for abortion on demand with the bulk of the cost paid for by the taxpayers. He now claims he's pro-life even though in the 2002 gubernatorial debate he said he's not a pro-life candidate. So he asks us to believe at age 58, after running for U.S. Senate and governor, that he suddenly saw the light, changed his core values and is now a great champion of family values?"

Glenn offered two specific examples of Christian Conservative leaders either supporting or covering for Romney that particularly irked him.

"Here you had Romney with that kind of record, and then you had Tony Perkins (of the *Family Research Council*) appear on a website in a video in which he said that Romney's positions were 'solidly conservative' across the board. This is the president of one of the most powerful pro-family organizations in America telling this to his constituency that trusts him to tell the truth. Then you had Dr. Richard Land of the Southern Baptist Convention telling people that Romney would make a good presidential or vice-presidential candidate despite that record.

A lot of us came out of that process in 2008 intent on telling the truth in the 2012 cycle, and not only about the candidates, but about any pro-family leader who failed to tell the truth as well. It is not necessarily an easy thing to do. It's something we wish we didn't have to do, but the shock has worn off. I, for one, as well as a lot of other pro-family leaders, am not going to sit back and watch it happen again in 2012."

In the minds of many, *Focus on the Family* and its founder, James Dobson, is the titular head of the Religious Right. Yet Glenn says neither Dobson nor other representatives from *Focus* played much of a leadership role in the midst of this schism within the Arlington Group.

"I have grown up an admirer of Dobson. I wanted to believe that he didn't know about Mitt Romney's record. Yet I've talked to people that said that they told him face to face and he was aware of it. There's a problem going on in Colorado Springs that goes farther than the question of Mitt Romney. Perhaps you can simply say *Focus on the Family* seems that they've been more molded by the culture than they now have any impact on the culture.

Let me give you another example.

The first time President Obama got a chance to nominate a member of the United States Supreme Court, not one but two spokesmen for *Focus on the Family* said that it should not concern Christians whatsoever if Obama were to nominate an openly homosexual nominee—which is pretty shocking. Let me read you the exact quote, 'Our concern at the Supreme Court is judicial philosophy. Sexual orientation only becomes an issue if it effects their judging. Sexual orientation should never come up. It's not even pertinent to the equation. The issue is not their sexual orientation, it is whether they are a good judge or not.'

I called on Focus to take back that statement and after a year they finally did. At least they backed off on the moral surrender. When *Focus on the Family* is telling Christians we shouldn't be concerned if President Obama nominates an openly homosexual nominee to the United States Supreme Court that has to come as a shock to a lot of people. And the *Family Research Council* essentially said the same thing."

Glenn believes this sort of double-mindedness has created instability within the Christian Conservative movement, as well as a disconnect between its leaders and those they're supposedly leading. Glenn says the grassroots no longer trusts its leadership, and leaders like him need to commit to restoring that trust.

"Millions of people look to us for leadership. They trust us because they believe that we will tell them the truth, and that we will adhere to the Biblical values we say that we are all about. We should do what they trust us to do. When any one of us doesn't, they should no longer look to us as counsel, or endorsements, or suggestions.

We should be faithful to those positions of defending prenatal life, to defending marriage between a man and a woman, to opposing that insidious homosexual agenda that attempts to undermine how God defines the family, and we should tell people the truth about political candidates. I think we should also tell when one of us doesn't tell the truth about these candidates."

Is there a reason that Glenn believes some in the Christian pro-family movement haven't told the truth about candidates like Romney?

"Mitt Romney has been a friend to the pro-family movement in regards to his checkbook. Of course, his family used to donate to Planned Parenthood. But when he decided he needed to be a conservative to run for President of the United States, he and his underlings got out their checkbooks and wrote checks to various pro family groups, some of which used to be critical of him, and suddenly we're saying he's a pro-life, pro-family champion."

Glenn says contrary to what some Christian pro-family leaders contend, Romney is anything but a "pro-family champion."

"Romney in 1994, as a candidate for the U.S. Senate against Ted Kennedy, said he would be more effective at promoting gay rights than Kennedy would. He endorsed Barney Frank and Ted Kennedy's federal gay rights legislation, which establishes special protective class status on the basis of homosexual behavior and cross dressing.

Then there's Catholic Charities being told they have to process adoptions to homosexual couples. Romney endorsed taxpayer-funded same sex benefits for the homosexual partners of government employees. He opposed the marriage protection amendment to the state constitution that was proposed by pro family groups *before* the State Supreme Court issued its illegitimate ruling regarding homosexual marriage. He's responsible for having issued the executive orders that actually implemented so called homosexual marriage in Massachusetts. It was Romney who issued the executive order that state marriage licenses be amended to no longer say husband and wife and instead to say Partner A and Partner B. Romney personally issued marriage licenses for homosexual couples.

Across the board on pro-family issue after issue, Romney was a guy who aggressively promoted the homosexual agenda, and was endorsed by homosexual activists. Yet, Dr. Richard Land of the Southern Baptist Convention, to whom millions of Southern Baptists look to for leadership, said Romney would be an excellent candidate for president or vice president. Tony Perkins of *Family Research Council* said on the internet in a video that Romney's positions were solidly conservative across the board. James Dobson said that he couldn't endorse Mike Huckabee until Romney had left the campaign trail because they were two equally pro-family candidates. Huckabee championed the marriage protection amendment to the Arkansas Constitution, and was one of the most pro-life governors in America, and Dobson equated his record with Romney's."

Glenn believes that unless other Christian pro-family leaders, such as himself, speak out about what they claim is Romney's real record, the Republican Party will nominate a candidate for president in 2012 that is just as liberal as John McCain was in 2008—if not more so.

"Once again we find ourselves front and center confronting the possibility that the Republican Party might nominate a candidate for president with a record of signing taxpayer funded abortions into law, individual health care mandates, and promoting the homosexual agenda. You know, if Romney is president he'll be the honorary chairman of the Boy Scouts of America. You think the homosexual activist groups won't go back and pull up the video where Romney says 'I believe people should be able to participate in scouting no matter what their sexual orientation?'

We find ourselves again facing the prospect that it will be the 'conservative' Republican Party that will nominate a man who thinks states should pass gay rights laws that pose the single greatest threat to religious freedom in America today. Now, some of us, having come through that process in 2008 and seeing people that millions of Christians look to for leadership whitewash and misrepresent his record, are committed to not remaining silent again in 2012. We're committed to the truth, and to tell the truth to those that look to us for leadership and trust our counsel and judgment."

Glenn says the whitewashing of the records of big-name Republicans isn't unique to Romney.

"It goes beyond Romney. For example, before (Indiana Governor) Mitch Daniels announced he wasn't going to run for president he was being trumpeted by the media and by establishment Republicans as the guy that would come in and be able to beat Obama. There were even Christian pro-family bloggers saying here's the case for Mitch

Daniels. He did sign a bill to defund Planned Parenthood, but when he was running as a candidate for governor, he actually adopted a policy for his own campaign in which he said he would not fail to hire campaign staff based on their sexual orientation or gender identity.

If you're not aware of what gender identity is talking about, Barney Frank—the openly homosexual Massachusetts Democrat—initially refused to put it in his federal gay rights legislation because it's so radical it calls for things like communal showers in the work place, so that people with penises could shower with women. Daniels actually made that a matter of his campaign organization's philosophy.

When he became Governor of Indiana, by executive order, he actually made it a matter of formal policy the state would not discriminate on the basis of cross-dressing, sexual identity dysfunction and confusion, psycho sexual confusion, men who claim that they're women and want to wear a dress to work, use the women's restroom and shower, etc., etc. There was even a report from the homosexual activist group in Indiana that Daniels' campaign had made a contribution to one of the transgender activists groups."

Does Glenn believe the double-mindedness and dysfunction he's witnessed within the Christian Conservative movement is the result of a lack of a Biblical worldview, or the corrupting influence of partisan politics?

"The answer to your question is that it is disturbing to even ask the question, isn't it? I go back to that meeting we previously discussed when we were actually told when discussing the presidential candidates that we would not be allowed to talk about their records. More specifically, we would not be allowed to talk about Mitt Romney promoting abortion on demand and the homosexual agenda.

That was shocking. The shock has worn off and a lot of us have come out of that 2008 cycle intent that we would not stand by and allow it to happen again.

Just one other example, the *Family Research Council* website had what was purported four years ago to be a candidate survey. It included a promise to veto any repeal of the ban on homosexuals in the military. If you looked at it under Mitt Romney it said that Romney had promised to veto any such repeal. But that was absolutely false, and Romney never said any such thing. If you clicked on the supposedly documenting newspaper article that was listed right there on the website, it took you to a news article in which Romney did not disavow his prior endorsement of gays in the military, but said simply that this was not the time to change the policy since we were involved in a war.

How do you go from that to telling Christians, who go to the FRC website believing they can trust what's on it is factual, that Mitt Romney has pledged to veto any attempt to repeal the federal law? He's never done any such thing."

Finally, Glenn lays out his pithy solution to restoring the movement to its Biblical foundation and heritage.

"Faithfulness is the key. Millions of Americans trust us to tell the truth and to be faithful to the agenda that we say we're all about. That's what we've got to get back to."

Joe Glover

Interviewed by Gregg—February, 2011

For the past 14 years, Joe Glover has directed *The Family Policy Network*, one of the largest and most influential Christian pro-family organizations in the country.

Glover, and other representatives of his organization, promote Biblical morality in interviews with newspapers, magazines and on major television networks. The influence of *The Family Policy Network* is felt both in the U.S. and throughout the world.

Glover agreed to be interviewed about his involvement in the Christian pro-family movement, its successes and failures, and what he believes is necessary to avoid failure in the future. To him, this movement is meant to bring the virtues found in Scripture to the halls of government. Unfortunately, he has seen many people get into politics because of their faith, only to abandon Biblical principles in exchange for money, political power, and notoriety.

Although involved in politics from a young age, Glover's journey into pro-family activism began in earnest while he was working in ministry. After studying business and divinity at Liberty University and Southeastern Baptist Theological Seminary respectively, Glover began preaching at a military outreach near Washington, D.C. While in that position, in the mid-1990's, he also began attending meetings with other conservatives and members of Congress on Capitol Hill. It was during this time that he became alarmed because so many matters of righteousness being dealt with were not being reported to Christians across the country.

For that reason, he started *Family Policy Network* with a mission of "informing Christians and confronting the culture on the important moral issues of the day." Later, he started the communications consulting company MoreInformation.NET so he could work to teach, train and equip other Christians to be "salt" and "light."

According to Glover, providing information to Christians on the major social and moral issues of the day involved obstacles which, ironically enough, emanated predominantly from other conservative Christian pro-family organizations, rather than from the liberal-left. Over time, Glover realized there were too many pro-family organizations that were "checking their Christian beliefs at the door."

"People use this euphemism of thinking Biblically but speaking secularly, so when they get to the public square their positions are based on civil arguments that are absent of any Biblical reference," Glover said. "My concern as a Christian activist in the public square is the last thing on earth we wanted to do was to check our Christian beliefs at the door, and to try to somehow manipulate the political process with man's wisdom in order to accomplish God's aims. The fact of the matter is the one resource that we have as Christians (that) we're promised will not return void, is God's Word itself. Why on earth would we want to check that at the door when walking into the civic arena to make our best arguments for what God wants for our lives?

Over the last 14 years our goal changed a little. We started out naïvely believing that we could simply inform Christians across the country, and give them action items on things that they could do to impact public policy, and that would be good enough for them to take the ball and run with it. But what we found is we often have to compete with other Christian organizations that are providing information that is erroneous or nuanced about immorality and/or compromises in the public square, and often those groups providing misinformation are better-funded and have more clout, so to speak, in Christian circles.

It's been quite frustrating to fight for Biblical righteousness, only to be undercut by misinformation from other, supposedly Christian groups. Many times, the misinformation from those groups was nothing more than an attempt to help the Republican establishment, or perhaps to broker some sort of ungodly compromise."

Glover then went into more detail.

"The first example I would give was the *Christian Coalition* which now is, for all practical purposes, a defunct organization. When they were in their heyday, they were working under the guise of providing information to Christians so that they could then vote with proper knowledge of various candidates on issues like right to life and the traditional family. But what we saw was that the *Christian Coalition* was manipulating the information that they would provide the churchgoers in order to get the outcome they wanted at the ballot box.

I'll give you just one instance to demonstrate this, which was with Kay Bailey Hutchison in Texas. She was, and has been all along, a pro-choice politician. She openly says that she favors 'a woman's right to choose.' She supported the Senate resolution endorsing *Roe v. Wade*, although she did vote for the partial-birth abortion ban, but that didn't stop any abortions, which is another story we could get into. But Kay Bailey Hutchison was listed as a pro-life politician in the *Christian Coalition* voter guides in Texas when she ran for re-election to the U.S. Senate. And that's just absolutely false information."

Glover believes this example of the *Christian Coalition's* distorting Hutchison's record to fool Christians into voting for her is, sadly, not an isolated incident but rather a trend.

"I would say it's shocking to see how often these supposedly great Christian organizations provide such information, but it really isn't shocking any longer. It happens on such a regular basis that it's commonplace. The problem is that the average Christian is really unaware to what degree they've been duped by these organizations, and I often tell people, 'you cannot look at what organizations tell you about candidates.' And I'll even say check what our organization says against the facts, and that's why we try to footnote as much as we can when we make a claim about a politician.

We want to make sure that you can see the evidence for what we're saying in the document that we're disseminating because you really have to, as the Scriptures say, test the spirits and you have to check to see what the evidence is. That's because there's just so much desire to see the so-called 'lesser of two evils' elected by some of these so-called Christian leaders that they'll do anything, including manipulating people to vote for politicians that could care less about the right to life or traditional values."

Glover says the temptation to follow a "lesser of two evils" strategy is plentiful.

"I shudder when I ponder such a thing because I wonder at what point along the way I've compromised. I wonder at what point along the way my flesh has drawn me in to what is clearly sin and desiring to be lauded and praised and appreciated by this world—by men— rather than God.

The fact of the matter is, even those compromisers I am speaking about may possess imputed righteousness because of the blood of Christ. So those leaders, although compromising, are headed to heaven just as sure as I am. There's level ground at the foot of the cross, and the fact is I'm just as likely to do evil as the next Christian is."

Glover says this temptation is rampant because many believe that effectiveness in our political system is based on access and relationships rather than Biblical convictions.

"One of the things we struggle with is we want to be liked. The more you're involved in politics across the country, and even at your local level, the more people come calling and begin to sing your praises and to tell you, 'boy you really had an impact on this process,' or that 'you're really something.'

When I was going to the meetings on Capitol Hill, I found myself being wooed at times. I'll never forget there were certain people that came to me and put their arm around me—literally put their arm around my neck—and said 'let's take a walk I want to talk to you about what you're doing, I really think it's important.'

I began to feel this warm feeling of significance. I felt it, but I'm telling you something wasn't quite right about those situations. I had Godly friends who pointed out to me this may be the wonderful thing you think it is, or it may actually be the devil wanting to compromise the very thing that God wants you to do."

About a year and a half into his time in Washington, D.C., Glover realized the best thing he could do was get out.

"We moved about three hours away from Washington, which may not be far enough, but we wanted to be close enough to be able to be in DC when we needed to. We wanted to be far enough away not to be infected by the culture. I recall now having conversations with people where I would begin statements by saying, 'Well you've got to understand how things work in Washington,' not just thinking about the political process but about the culture too. So the first answer is, and I hate to say it, it's the sinfulness of man. It's the struggle that we all have this side of eternity."

Beyond a culture of compromise, Glover says money has also had a corrupting influence.

"The money flows to those things that are Christian-based but that have more of an establishment Republican appeal to them. The bottom line is that the mechanics of fundraising—everything from vendors, to economies of scale, to the direct-mail process, and all of those kinds of things—are impossible to manage without putting them into a sort of 'machine mode' to run it all. Those machines are rarely impacted as they should be by truly righteous concerns, but instead by whatever is going to bring the money through the door.

Unfortunately, money plays such a significant component in getting a message out for these organizations that it really does often put those organizations in a bind where they don't feel the freedom to say and do the things that they should."

We shared with Glover a statement Dr. James Dobson made in his farewell speech to the *Focus on the Family* staff in 2009:

"We are awash in evil, and the battle is still to be waged. We are right now in the most discouraging period of that long conflict. Humanly speaking, we can say we have lost all those battles."

We asked Glover if he agreed with Dobson. In spite of all the hundreds of millions of dollars raised and spent by leading pro-family organizations, has the Christian Right lost every major social and moral battle of our time?

"First of all (Dobson) wasn't the first to say it. Paul Weyrich (cofounder of the Heritage Foundation, Free Congress Foundation, and the Moral Majority) was the first. He wrote about it to 116 people that he considered allies and friends in the conservative movement. In his letter, he called for a meeting of conservative leaders to discuss how we could insulate ourselves from the harm that would be coming as a result of losing the culture war. I was one of those who received Paul's letter, and I agreed with his perspective and the reason for wanting to meet.

A few weeks later, I hosted a luncheon where my guest speaker took it upon himself to rip Paul's letter to shreds. He said Weyrich was suggesting we should 'throw in the towel,' and that it wasn't too late for the conservative cause. I was shocked and dismayed because I agreed with Weyrich that we had lost every major policy battle thus far, and I knew he was right to look for ways to protect our families and institutions in the years ahead. Unfortunately, Paul was vilified by many others, too. But he was right, nonetheless.

What Weyrich was suggesting that we do was try to insulate our families and our businesses, and even ourselves as individuals, against the onslaught of the cultural decline, in the same way that homeschoolers had found ways to do with regard to the education establishment and education bureaucracy throughout the country.

So I agreed with what he said, and I agree with what Dr. Dobson said, that we've lost all the major public policy battles. What I would say to Dr. Dobson, and to others in our movement, is we haven't actually lost a thing! God is still on the throne in Heaven and God is still sovereign over all of creation, including the White House, the U.S. Congress, the U.S. Senate, every state legislature, on down to every local governing body throughout this entire world. Everything that we could know to be true from God's Word fifty years ago, we still know to be true today. Nothing is lost if God is sovereign, which in fact, He is!"

Glover therefore believes Christians have lost the public policy debates because they've become too immersed in the political process, and abandoned the greater cause of advancing the Christian gospel. Too often they engage in perpetuating politics rather than promoting righteousness in the public square.

"We lost after spending truckloads of cash, over decades and decades, on what I would call pragmatic ways of making an impact on the public square with Christian views. Why go into the public square and simply argue that we need to define marriage correctly, while at the same time saying we're not going to tell another person that it's wrong to engage in same-sex sodomy? Why would we do that?

Well, that's exactly what *Focus on the Family* has done. *Focus on the Family* has even argued that we should provide marriage benefits to homosexual couples as long as we don't say it's on the basis of their homosexuality. *Focus on the Family* supports this legislation, and they call it 'reciprocal beneficiary legislation.'

They promoted it in at least two states this year, and they've done it in the past, where they actually are arguing for a capitulation of this idea that marriage between a man and woman should be enshrined in the law as the ideal, should be put up on a pedestal, should be promoted by the civil authorities, and it should be the exclusive union the government rewards and promotes in order to further stabilize and benefit all in society. They've given up that particular perch, and instead ceded that ground significantly and said, 'no we just want the word 'marriage' to have meaning.' So they've defined a word that they want to protect, but they're not protecting the institution of the family.

Even to churches, they've argued in their 'Love Won Out' conferences that a preacher should refrain from preaching Leviticus 18 because it will offend! Well, if you're going to have that kind of ungodly compromise then you're not going to be victorious."

To Glover, it is clear that Christians are losing the battle for the social and moral high ground because Christians continue to ignore their greatest weapon.

"We've lost our way when we no longer find the entire canon of Scripture is (sufficient) in addressing what's wrong with sin. And we've lost our way if we think we can go into the political arena and get some significant meaningful impact from our godly views when we're not willing to discuss them from a godly perspective, visa vi from Scripture itself.

So why have we lost? I believe we've lost because we've given up our best asset, which is the Word of God itself. We won't stand in the public square and say the words, 'thus sayeth the Lord,' as opposed to 'this is my opinion,' or 'this is what I can prove empirically,' or 'this is how I feel.' God has laid down for us a pattern and a plan for our lives, and if we follow it we find blessing. If we disobey these same commands, we do so to our own peril."

Glover also says too many Christians are more concerned with pleasing the masses than obeying God.

"I have been in meetings with elected officials that are supposedly very conservative on social issues and they'll say things like, 'we realize this form of this legislation would do absolutely nothing, but it would be a meaningful piece of legislation I could trump to my supporters back home to say that we're with you on these family type issues'. None of these (people-pleasing) concerns have any merit in Heaven. There's not going to be a Republican chairman waiting for us in Heaven to say 'well done thou good and faithful servant.'

Even us as Christians, we have difficulty sometimes determining what's pulling us in one way or the other. The fact of the matter is that the one thing that can clear that up is the Word of God itself. So, cling to Jesus, cling to the cross regardless of whether you are an individual voter, or even if you are the President of the United States."

What about those who say it's "divisive" to criticize Christian leaders or "un-Christian" to hold them accountable? Does Glover believe there is a Biblical justification for exposing compromise and corruption within the leadership of the conservative and Christian Right movement?

"Well, Ephesians 5:11 makes it clear we're to have no fellowship with the unfruitful works of darkness, but rather reprove them or expose them. What's interesting is that Ephesians 5:11 says 'the unfruitful works of darkness.' Well the pro-family movement has been unfruitful. Paul Weyrich told us. James Dobson told us. It's been unfruitful because it has sought to move from a position of promoting Biblical righteousness to a place of human pragmatism in order to try to accomplish something meaningful and significant, and it can't be done. That's something that should be exposed."

What kind of darkness does Glover believe should be exposed?

"I'll give you this as an example. Dr. Rick Scarborough, who is the president of *Vision America*, hosts a weekly conference call for Christian leaders from across the country called, 'Stop Obama.' In 2010, one of Scarborough's calls featured Sen. David Vitter of Louisiana, talking about how to bring 'values voters' to the polls.

The problem, though, was the media had repeatedly named David Vitter as a client of a prostitution ring in a scandalous court case in Washington, DC. According to reports, Vitter was even known to have had a 'diaper fetish.' It was an extremely shameful, immoral thing he had done. He offered a public apology for his behavior, but frankly, this is not something that puts the Christian Right in a good light, when ministry leaders who are trying have a meaningful dialogue in the public square are using people who have been caught up in prostitution to make their best arguments for how to manipulate Christians to get to the polls. It's really unimaginable, the degree to which people are willing to set aside (Biblical) principles.

I spoke directly with Dr. Scarborough about this and asked him, 'please don't do this.' You don't want Christian leaders on your conference call to be citing David Vitter as some sort of a moral authority, especially when David Vitter was one of those who called for Bill Clinton to resign for his immorality, and here David Vitter is involved in his own. Forgiveness and restoration are Biblical, but giving (Vitter) a place of preeminence in the pro-family movement is absolutely not."

Glover then cited another example; former Senator George Allen from Virginia who, at the time of this writing, is preparing to seek re-election to the seat he lost in 2008.

"(Allen) actually stated, on the record, if it appeared that abortion was in the best interest of his own daughter he would support that decision, and yet I've heard a number of people refer to him as pro-life. Most disconcerting is what *The Family Foundation*, a prominent pro-family group many Christians trust in Virginia, has been doing. They have been taking George Allen around the Commonwealth, allowing him to speak at their steak dinners in advance of his working toward a reelection bid. They're helping to prop him up, and this is the guy that after promising pro-family activists in 2000 that he would not support 'hate crimes' legislation for homosexuals, voted for hate crime legislation for homosexuals.

The homosexual activists in Washington called George Allen's office the gayest place on Capitol Hill. He had open homosexuals working as his chief of staff, as his chief spokesman, and as his chief counsel. People like homosexual activist Mike Rogers, who runs *PageOneQ* and *The Raw Story* blogs, which 'outs' a lot of gay Republicans, actually said that there were more homosexuals in George Allen's office than in any other place on Capitol Hill.

So here's a Christian conservative group helping to prop up an elected official who doesn't believe in the right to life, even for his own grandchildren, and who willingly supported the gay agenda. As Morton Blackwell of *The Leadership Institute* likes to say, 'personnel is policy.' In other words, if you hire liberal people you're going to get liberal policies."

Glover believes the next generation of Christian political activists needs to learn from the previous one's greatest mistake, which he believes was to place more faith in their access to politicians, than in their faith in a sovereign God.

"We don't need a king, we need a Savior and God is our King. He's on the throne in heaven, and He's sovereign over all of creation. If we really believe that, then we should let not our hearts be troubled. God is going to take care of His own. There's no question. It is God who protects the remnant, but neither do we need to abandon the public square.

To paraphrase a famous quote, 'If you find politics to be a cesspool and then abandon it because it is a cesspool, then that is immoral.' Christians should invade those cesspools with the Gospel. We should not turn Biblical arguments into pragmatic, empirical ones, but rather the Word of God should be the first words out of our mouths. We should actually quote the Bible.

Actually, I see that change taking place. You're going to see that kind of thing taking hold in a lot of different places in Christendom over the next few years."

Buddy Hanson

Interviewed by Steve—October, 2010

———•••••———

After conducting several interviews for this book assessing where the Christian Conservative movement went wrong over the last generation, it became time to interview someone about how best to make it right in the next one.

Buddy Hanson left Corporate America to make that his life's mission.

As the president of the *Grace and Law Christian Policy Network*, Hanson uses the skills he honed as a college baseball coach to galvanize Christian leaders who desire to employ a Biblical worldview as the framework for their calling. If you're going to read one book after reading this one, we suggest Hanson's book, *The Christian Prince.*

A Bible-based response to Machiavelli's much-celebrated yet loathsome masterpiece *The Prince*, Hanson illuminates the road less traveled in modern American politics. In contrast to Machiavelli's humanistic assertion that the best leadership is that which glorifies the leader, Hanson makes the case that the best leadership is that which glorifies the Almighty, and emulates the principles in His Word.

Hanson began our discussion by bemoaning how much of Machiavelli's anti-Biblical principles have seeped into the contemporary collective consciousness among believer and unbeliever alike in America.

"Jesus says that the non-Christians are wiser in their generation than we are, and Machiavelli is the epitome of that. He got it right, even though he was 180 degrees off in his worldview. He figured out how to manipulate people and how to appeal to their interests, and so Christians don't realize that some of these tactics they're used to hearing about and living with are non-Christian. Or maybe they want to believe in them because it's easy, it appeals to their base desires, and they want to believe it instead of trying to live according to the truths that they profess to believe."

Buddy Hanson   125

Hanson discussed the difference between political conservatives and liberals in their stated moral convictions, and in their philosophy of governance. For example, the two political movements have dramatically different moral philosophies, with conservatives embracing the moral tenants of Christian orthodoxy in recent generations, which is why Christians have tended to vote conservative.

However, when it comes to the philosophy of governance (or leadership) there doesn't appear to be much—if any—difference between conservatives and liberals. That's because while they each believe dramatically different things about the nature of morality, they also each systematically share the same application of their beliefs—they both agree that the law evolves based on human opinion/traditions, and they both agree in the preeminence of power centralized in the ruling class (whether they be in Washington, D.C. or your state capitol).

Hanson believes this is why the size of government grows and liberty is lost, and America's moral foundation erodes, regardless of whether Democrats or Republicans are in power. One side may just act more swiftly to enable evil—defined by any belief, action, principle that is in opposition to God and His Word—than the other.

"Moralistic people who may not be Christians like this middle ground political approach, but for Christians this isn't an option. My concern is that the church hasn't taught how to live the Christian life. They just like to say, 'God loves you and has a wonderful plan for your life.' I've caused a lot of unrest in people when I say other than going to Heaven, what's the wonderful plan? Most Christians are speechless at that question and don't have a clue. The Bible does, though, and it's all right there.

What I respond to people in those situations when I'm giving my talks is look, the definitive distinction between Christianity and all the other religions is that we have an objective religion. All religions say they're true, but there's subjectiveness about it. In other words, either Christ rose again as objective historical fact or he didn't.

We have the Bible, which encompasses all four areas of government: individual government, family government, church government, and civil government—which is the one we're talking about here. These are the four aspects of human civilization through which God wants to make His plan come about on Earth as it is in Heaven, as Jesus tells us to pray for."

Hanson contrasted Christian political engagement over the last generation with the Bible's teaching on the subject.

"The good news is, we've encouraged our brothers and sisters to engage the culture rather than sitting at home and keeping our beliefs inside the four walls of our homes or our churches. We've done that, but that's where it stops, because the church has given us no context. We're running around busying ourselves on various issues that sometimes are the peripheral issues, but they're not the core issues, so the problems never get solved. However, it makes us feel good at the end of the day and we say man, I'm tired so I must have done something."

Hanson believes there are "core issues" Christians with a Biblical worldview must address beyond the sanctity of life and marriage. He believes the Bible must be applied to all issues, and not just those typically relegated to the Christian Conservative movement.

"We should apply Biblical principles to the economy. For example, in Leviticus it teaches us to have 'just weights and balances.' We had that in America until 1913, when Congress figured out that it was easier to spend money if they could simply print it rather than have it based upon a fixed value."

Hanson believes the Bible has much to say about economic philosophy.

"The Bible is capitalistic and promotes self-government. Paul taught that whoever will not work should not eat, and the Bible teaches that it's the role of the church to care for the poor and needy, not the state. The Constitutional Convention did not specifically produce a Christian Constitution per se, but the collective Christian worldview of the time caused them to include nothing about a welfare state."

Hanson also believes the Bible addresses the current immigration crisis.

"In the Old Testament immigrants—or aliens, or sojourners as the Bible calls them at times—were allowed among the Israelites, and they could enjoy all of the civil protections, but they couldn't take part in civic and religious responsibilities for several generations. This was so they could learn to observe the lifestyle and ethics of the Israelites, or what we today call assimilation.

The idea that aliens or sojourners would not only be allowed to live in the land, but also to continue living as they did in their pagan countries simply isn't Biblical. There is diversity in the Bible, but it's diversity in unity by various peoples in various places living simultaneously as the Lord has commanded, regardless of their cultural preferences, not the balkanized diversity we celebrate today where everyone does as he or she sees fit.

It is true the Bible commands us to give compassion to the alien, but the alien is also commanded to assimilate into a lifestyle in accordance with God's Word, and not take advantage of that compassion. The Constitution gives us a glimpse of this teaching by requiring our President to be a natural-born American, or at least it required that until Barack Obama moved into the White House."

Hanson also believes the Bible is clear on when war is morally allowed.

"Romans 13 teaches that civil rulers are 'God's ministers' and are supposed to protect us from invasion, keep the peace and provide justice by ruling in accordance with God's revealed commandments and case laws. Let alone how much our Founding Fathers clearly despised foreign entanglements, there is also no mention made of being the world's policeman in the Bible, therefore I'm not certain when the last time was that we truly fought a 'just war' as traditional Christian orthodoxy on the subject has defined it."

Why has Christian political activism focused so much on sanctity of life and sanctity of marriage? While those are clearly the preeminent issues that define much of the civilized order, they're also clearly not the only issues. Hanson believes there's a reason Christians have either not been willing or able to apply the Bible to those other issues.

"The reason fellow Christians have jumped on to the life and marriage issues is that these are obvious, but also because the church has not systematically taught members how to live-out their profession of faith. I'm afraid that the vast majority of Christians—if they are truly Christians, instead of merely well-intentioned, law-abiding moralistic conservatives—believe that being a Christian means that they substitute some 'good' Biblical behaviors, for some 'bad' non-Biblical behaviors, instead of attempting to completely transform their lifestyles. The 'good guy' pastors are careful to preach accurate sermons, but without relating the truths to the cares and concerns of their members. The result is that we know a lot about God, but know little about being a Christian.

No other vocation I know of, except the church, stops with *informing* people about their services. They all *instruct* people how to use their products and services, or how to sell them, or how to play their game. Pastors apparently imagine that it's all about God's 'Xs & Os,' but as any sports coach will tell you, it's about the 'Jimmys and Joes,' and our 'Jimmys and Joes' don't know how to play this game."

Hanson said the lack of laying a Biblical foundation, and then following it up with a real-world application, has hindered Christian political activism.

"Does God tell us what we can do in certain situations? Does God give us concepts to use, and is the church preaching on them? I'm trying to put the content in there because the church is not giving the application—even the good guys out there. There's a lot of bad guys, but the good guys seem to stop at presenting a correct sermon, making sure that they didn't take anything out of context and so people sit there and enjoy it and say I've learned something. By the time they get home they've forgotten it, because there's nothing they can incorporate into their lifestyle come Monday morning. That's where we've fallen down. We don't know *how* to do things."

Hanson said he's asked several pastors over the years why the church isn't teaching people how to engage the culture?

"The response I get from them is the Holy Spirit will teach people. I respond it will *convict* people to do things, not teach them how to do it—that's the preacher's job!"

Hanson turned to his background as a college sports coach to explain why he believes it's vital for the church to instruct Christians in this way.

"What if a coach said to his players, 'you have been gifted with great hand-eye coordination, you've come in running fast and throwing hard, but I'm not going to tell you how to prepare yourself for the upcoming opponent because your gifts can just take care of that?' How long would you put up with the coaches if they did that? Well, we'd fire them.

We're all hard-wired the same way when we learn things, so why don't you build into your sermon explicit things (like a coach would)? You don't have to just teach a political sermon, but when you're talking about something in your sermon you can say this is how this relates to issues in the news and then people will get it. There is no such thing then as a religious realm and a real life realm in our lives. There is just one realm. God created a universe not a biverse with two different ethical systems.

I have a little coin I give out to people and on one side it says, 'Only God's Word works' and on the other side it says, 'Man's Word only fails.' God's Word is truth and it applies everywhere. It's completely sufficient for all aspects of our lives.

I think it's one of Satan's most effective tactics of deceiving us is that he knows he can't come in and say God's Word is not true. But, how effective is it if he can convince us to keep it to ourselves and not impact culture with it? God created a purposeful universe, it's cause and effect. From the get go, Adam and Eve are told if you don't do this one thing, everything's going to be great, but if you do it we're going to have problems—its cause and effect."

Speaking of cause and effect, does Hanson believe something within the church caused Christians to be rendered rather ineffective in the civil government?

"I used to look back to the 1930s with the Germans and often wondered how they could've put up with a Hitler. Then it hit me. Germany was basically Christian, and 90% of the German Christians in the 1930s were Lutherans. I knew about Martin Luther's 'two kingdom' view, and that's what we're really talking about by a different name—the kingdom of the church and the kingdom of the state. So when a Hitler was rising through the ranks, they said 'that's political stuff' (kingdom of the state) and it doesn't apply to us (kingdom of the church). It's in an easy sell for Satan to convince us to not dirty our hands in the everyday things of life and to delegate it to someone else, in this specific issue to the politicians. That's a scary thought."

Hanson believes Christians who buy into what he believes is a flawed theological application end up acting like liberals who believe in a faulty form of the separation of church and state.

"We have to get out of that mode of separating religious life and 'real life.' God has given the church specific commands to implement, and He's given the state specific commands. He's given parents specific commands. He's given individuals specific commands. The trick is not to usurp the authority of either one of those. Let the church do its thing, let the state do its thing, let parents do their thing, and let individuals do their thing. That's how God has set up His divinely ordained plan for the world.

In America, we're kind of running on the fumes of the Founders. The Founders put our civil government and the laws in place because they were basing them specifically on commandments five through 10 in the Ten Commandments, which tells us how to deal with each other. It would be funny if it wasn't sad, but whenever I see a court-room scene above or behind the judge that says 'In God We Trust' like that is superior to the judge. As if to say everything we do in this courtroom is in submission to God, even the judge who is its highest official. I wonder, you know, who that God is because we're not really operating according to God's laws today, and I think maybe the god is like Adam and Eve's god. It's us, and we're operating by our rules, and the god we trust in is really man instead of God. How did that sign get on there? That got up there for a reason, and we've forgotten all that right now."

Hanson also believes tax policy has effectively muted churches.

"The 501 C-3 incorporation of churches was begun by LBJ when he was running for senator in Texas. The First Amendment declares that churches are automatically tax exempt, so this legislation is unnecessary. But by churches incorporating to the state, they have to play by the state's rules, and therefore cannot preach the whole counsel of God's Word because they are afraid that their 'tax-exempt status' would be revoked. The bottom line is that the churches fear the state more than they fear God."

Can Hanson give us an idea of how differently things would look in America if we returned to what we were when the church was the dominant cultural influence in the country?

"I'm going to say some things, and people are going to say that will never work, so I'll preface it by saying this is the way it was in America 120 years ago, or even a generation ago. The civil government would be much smaller because the total of our taxes would be less than 10%. That was the case up to the early 1900s, and the reason for that was because God only requires 10%, so to give the state more than we give to God is to value the state more than God. That concept has flown out the window. Talk about personal liberty, how much more personal liberty would you have if the total taxes reduced down to less than 10%, and then there would be included in that property tax because the earth belongs to the Lord not to the state.

There are all sorts of things that we could go back to, like the death penalty for pedophiles. What do we do now? We run around and say that you can't live within a certain number of feet from a playground. Well, good night. We're trying to be smarter than God and that's not working. I could give some other examples and people would say, 'Hanson, you're out there,' but I'm not saying we're going to do this in the next year or two, ten or fifteen because we didn't get to where we are overnight, but those are goals we need to start working towards if we're serious about it.

In many regards, it would look like what America originally looked like, with the populace self-governing themselves instead of paying for the civil government to provide various services. Originally, the local civil governments were the most important, with state government second and national government barely on the radar screen. We should also remember that the personal income tax and Social Security are 20th century inventions, along with a fiat monetary standard. When our money was based upon gold it was impossible for Congress to fund programs by printing more paper money, which de-values our savings plus drives up the cost of everything we purchase."

In Hanson's book *The Christian Prince* he contrasts a Biblical worldview of governance with Machiavelli's humanistic masterpiece. What are the lines that Hanson believes a Christian statesman can't cross over?

"I would say you can't deviate from your state or federal constitution, that in and of itself would be a magnificent accomplishment if we could start by doing that. And then asking ourselves how does this piece of proposed legislation conform to the truth that I confess to believe in? If it doesn't, then I shouldn't support it, and if it does then I should support it. Those would be the two big triggers. When I lobby legislators, and I only lobby the ones that call themselves Christians, I'm diplomatic about it but I ask does this bill conform to what you confess to believe?

This is really not as overwhelming as you might think. Years ago I wrote a commentary on the Ten Commandments. I've discovered in my research that the Ten Commandments are a skeletal outline of the entire Bible. After they are given to Moses there's no concept in the entire Bible that is different from those. All the rest of the Bible does is add flesh to that skeletal outline. So keep a little card next to you with the Ten Commandments on it and say, does this decision that I'm about to make violate any of those Commandments? If it does I can't do it. We can say all we want that we don't want corrupt politicians who kill, lie, cheat or steal, but as long as we base those things on our common sense and pragmatism the definition of those things are going to change. But if we say because God says it that's what we're looking for, then that gives us a line in the ethical sand that we can't cross over."

Finally, Hanson suggests a six-point plan for how Christians can be more effective in the next generation of engagement.

"First, let's not be overwhelmed at our situation and remember that there is not one non-Christian going around causing all of this trouble, there's millions of them. But there's also millions of us, so if we'll get off our couches and begin living as though God's Word is truly sufficient for all areas of our lifestyle, we can make a difference.

Second, think about all the non-Christians have accomplished without God, and then think about what we can accomplish with Him. Third, identify our spiritual gifts. This may sound difficult but in reality they are those areas to which we are drawn. If God did not interest us in a particular topic, He wouldn't have given us the ability and wisdom to deal accurately with it. Fourth, attend worship service and small group studies with the intention of learning how these truths can make me a more consistent servant of Jesus. Fifth, pray, pray, pray, and pray some more. Sixth, remember that non-Christians are cogs in God's wheel for the earth, and we are the hub: we win; they lose!

Remember the words Martin Luther once wrote in his journal: 'Whatever I do will be done, not by the prudence of men, but by the counsel of God. If the work be of God, who shall stop it? If it be not, who can forward it? Not my will, nor theirs, nor ours; but Thy will, O holy Father, which art in heaven.'"

Brannon Howse

Interviewed by Gregg—February, 2009

———•••••———

Brannon Howse is the president and founder of the *American Family Policy Institute*. He is also the founder and President of *Worldview Weekend*, which is one of the largest Christian worldview conference series in the nation.

Howse is also the author of nine books, which mainly focus on contemporary political and social issues through a Biblical worldview. He hosts a radio show titled "Christian Worldview This Week," that is heard on more than 225 radio stations each weekend. These various platforms have afforded Howse an intimate familiarity with the Christian Conservative movement in America. In recent years, he has become one of the most outspoken critics of many of the leading conservative and Christian pro-family leaders and organizations.

Howse's criticisms stem from his controversial contention that most Christian political leaders lack an authentic Biblical worldview. As a result, Howse believes that liberals like Barack Obama are "just a symptom" of the underlying problem plaguing our nation, which he believes to be inherently spiritual.

"We've got a code blue crisis in the church and in the culture. The church today reflects the culture, not the other way around. We all are a little schizophrenic in our worldview in that we say one thing and do another. That's just the sinful human condition, but most people in the church today have a serious worldview crisis. They don't think any differently than the world and in most cases their stats are worse when it comes to things like divorce, how they handle their money, bankruptcy and so many other issues."

Howse believes one of the biggest reasons professing Christians are not living lives in stark contrast to non-believers is because too many of the people in American churches aren't really Christians.

"One, we have so many people in the church today that think they're Christians and they're not, but they're really false converts. I was a false convert for many years. I was raised in a Christian home, went to church, and went to a Christian school, but those things neglected to explain to me what it really meant to be a Christian, and what it really means to have a heart of repentance.

Having a heart of repentance doesn't mean you're not going to sin or that you aren't going to mess up, but you live a life of obedience more often than you live a life of disobedience. Godly sorrow produces repentance that leads to salvation, but worldly sorrow leads to death. Godly sorrow is turning from your sin and going in the opposite direction, not continuing in a pattern of willful disobedience over and over while saying, 'I can say a magical prayer and go and say that again next weekend.' That's not repentance, that's just flat out rebellion.

Then we have those that are Christians, but don't know why they believe what they do. They may know what they believe, but they don't know why, and can't defend those essential Christian doctrines."

Howse views America having a president like Barack Obama, whose governing philosophy is in many ways contrary to traditional Biblical morality, as a sign of divine judgment for our lack of faithfulness.

"I believe that getting a wicked leader is consistent with the ways that God judges a nation. If you look at the template that God used to judge Israel, it's the same as He uses to judge every nation in history.

George Mason, one of the Founding Fathers, said that God judges nations in this life because they don't go on to the next one. Therefore, God judges national sins with national calamities, and I believe we're going through a national calamity right now. I've read the Bible to the end and we win, and Romans 8:18 tells us the sufferings of this present time are not worthy to compare to the glory that shall be revealed in us. Nonetheless, I hate to be the bearer of bad news and doom and gloom, but we're presently in a financial crisis right now that is really a worldview crisis."

Howse claims that the major reason for the financial crisis in America is that we have rejected a Christian worldview for economics.

"We get leaders that reflect the culture, and Obama is a reflection of the culture. In the church today only 4% of adults have a Biblical worldview, and 91% of young people in the evangelical churches don't believe in absolute moral truth –meaning there's truth for all people, all times, all places. There are 2400 verses dealing with money in the Bible, so when a culture doesn't have a Biblical worldview on economics you get the problems we have today."

Howse sees a rise in socialist (big government) economic policy as a side effect of what he describes as "cultural Marxism."

"Obama is a cultural Marxist, and we've been fighting cultural Marxism in America since 1933, when it was brought here by some German intellectuals and they implemented what we now know as political correctness. Political correctness is a masking term for the real agenda which is cultural Marxism. Whether it's feminism, 'tolerance,' or 'diversity' which is really perversity, you name the education philosophy that's being taught and you call it political correctness, but it's really cultural Marxism.

The ultimate goal of cultural Marxism is to change the worldview of a culture, and you get it in such a position where Christianity is destroyed, and chaos ensues. Once you've created chaos, you grow the size of government to handle the contrived chaos, and eventually you move away from cultural Marxism to traditional Marxism, and that's where we're at right now."

Or as one of President Obama's closest former advisors once infamously said, "Never let a good crisis go to waste."[97]

Next, Howse commented on an article that he authored shortly after the Super Tuesday Republican Presidential Primaries in February 2008. The article was entitled, "WHEN HILLARY AND OBAMA WIN THE WHITE HOUSE, YOU CAN THANK PRO-FAMILY LEADERS FOR NOT BEING LEADERS." In that article, Howse had the following to say to five of the most prominent Christian Right leaders in America:

"Note to self, in the future ignore whatever Gary Bauer says. (Bauer served as Reagan's Under Secretary of Education, President of the Family Research Council, and ran for President of the United States in 2000.)

Hey Gary, if you had encouraged Romney to get out of the race and had you done some soul searching and backed a 100% pro-life, pro-

*family candidate instead of a flip-flopping Romney, we would have
seen Governor Huckabee do even better than he did on Super Tuesday. The bottom line is the pro-family voters showed more leadership,
commitment and sense then some of our pro-family leaders. Look at
the incredible results Huckabee achieved on Super Tuesday with little
money and without the support from pro-family leaders such as James
Dobson, Gary Bauer, Jay Sekulow, Tony Perkins and Pat Robertson.
Imagine what Governor Huckabee could have done if Gary Bauer,
Jay Sekulow and Tony Perkins were not in the camp, by word or deed,
of Johnny-Come-Lately-"pro-family"-Romney. What if Pat Robertson
had not been fawning all over pro-abortion, pro-same-sex marriage,
anti-Second Amendment Mayor Giuliani?"*

In the same article, Howse had this to say about James Dobson (founder
of *Focus on the Family*):

*"Imagine if Dr. Dobson would have spent less time telling us who he
could not vote for and instead told us why he could support Governor
Huckabee with his 100% pro-life, pro-family track record. Dr. Dobson
has clearly revealed that he is tired and did not have the 'want to' when
it came to this presidential fight. Funny how Dr. Dobson said this of Fred
Thompson just a few months ago. Every presidential election is the most
important in today's world and Dr. Dobson refused to jump in with both
feet and back Governor Huckabee (whom Dobson ultimately endorsed).
First Dr. Dobson told us he could not support Fred Thompson, and then
he said he could not support Giuliani, and I agreed with him on Giuliani. Then Dr. Dobson told us he could not support McCain. Really?
Well, there is a news flash. However, by not supporting Huckabee and
by putting out a statement on Super Tuesday that he could not support
McCain many felt he was sending the message that he was comfortable
with Romney."*

Howse concluded:

*"The bottom line is we need new pro-family, pro-life leaders. I do want
to thank Bauer, Sekulow, Perkins, Dobson and Robertson for their service to our country and the pro-family, pro-life movement. You have
accomplished many good things and I thank you. However, your time
has now passed and you have failed a huge test and thus I must no
longer follow your lead or trust your instincts. If others can still follow*

you then I believe they may do so at the peril of our cause. From now on I will take your advice, counsel, and opinion with a grain of salt because of your incompetent leadership and lack of discernment during the presidential race of 2008. Your decisions seem to have largely been based upon pragmatism; which is really just another way of saying the end justifies the means."

What prompted Howse's scathing rebuke of many of the top Christian Right leaders in America?

"One of the things that is killing our country is pragmatism as in the ends justifies the means. Too many of these leaders think winning, and having access, is the most important thing. Quite frankly, I just don't go to a lot of the conventions these guys have, the meetings these guys have, because I went to them years ago and they're just guys standing around trying to be more important than the next guy. The reality is that most of these guys are missing the boat. If you were to walk up to a lot of these guys, some of the biggest pro-family people in the country, and start having a Biblical worldview conversation with them you'd go over their heads really fast."

Howse believes the lack of a Biblical worldview has lead to a lack of discernment among too many Christians involved in political and cultural issues.

"The problem is, we've divided our worldview between the secular and the sacred, or here's what the state does and here's what the church does. That's exactly what caused Hitler to rise to power, because the church was absolutely impotent and had bought into the idea of the secular and the sacred. I'm sad to say that even many of our Christian pro-family leaders are so consumed with public policy they've neglected a Biblical worldview, and they're more interested in access and winning than they are holding up to the standard of righteousness. If you lift up the standard of righteousness, I believe the people will follow that, and I believe that we'll get leaders that will aspire to that, but we've dumbed down the standard."

Howse believes that when Christians in politics fail to hold firm to a Biblical definition of right and wrong, they end up contradicting the very values they claim to esteem the most. As a result, it's the Christians in politics who are paving the way for even worse candidates to emerge in the future.

"What do you think happens when (Pat Robertson) endorses a Rudy Giuliani type of guy, or (Gary Bauer) endorses a John McCain type of guy? We end up destroying our own standard. After we do that, what do you think we're going to get next time around?

If President George W. Bush had been a Ronald Reagan conservative, had followed the original intent of the Constitution, had not been into globalism and trashing our national sovereignty, and giving up the free market to save the free market like what he said—which is just weird in itself—we would not have had McCain as a nominee (in 2008)—we would've had another Ronald Reagan candidate. When the pro-family leaders endorse the lowest common denominator, we get the lowest common denominator for the candidate next go-around, and you're going to lose because the base won't turn out for that."

Howse believes that large-scale Christian political activism has evolved from a movement to an industry.

"This is my opinion, but from what I hear from numerous people that are in places that know, this has become about money, which is the mother's milk of politics. All of these groups need money to keep going, and a lot of them are in debt. A guy like a Mitt Romney has money, and his machine has money too. I'm told that money was spread around, and some people's debt was taken care of, and others were given huge sums of cash."

Howse fears that win-at-all-costs Christians haven't learned from the lessons of 2008, and he fears they're poised to repeat it in 2012.

"I believe the little guy out here is sick and tired of socialist party R and socialist party D. The Republicans are socialists, and the current administration are neo-Marxists and cultural Marxists, and they're moving us from cultural Marxism to traditional Marxism, and nationalizing everything. Their goal is to destroy Christianity and create chaos.

Obama gets to be the guy that's at the tail end of Bush, who was starting to move us in this direction with giving up free market principles. Now Obama gets to come in and finish it. Some of the Republicans are trying to fight it, but many of them, like McCain and others, don't get it because they've bought into statism, and that's really what we're doing here—the idea that the answers to everything come from the state."

Howse thinks too many Christian Conservatives have accepted the Left's premise that government can solve our problems.

"Many of our pro-family leaders think that. They think that the answer comes from the state. The liberals think the solution is big government. Conservatives think the solution is smaller government. Yes, I'm for smaller government. We could go to a smaller government, but if we have not had everything based on a Biblical worldview and on the principles of God, it doesn't matter how small your government is, you'll still have a godless government. Eventually, that small, godless government will become a big, godless government. Unless your house is built on a firm foundation, you're on shifting sand."

Howse believes for America to remain the world's greatest super power, it will have to return to its foundation again.

"The solution always is to come back to the Bible, it's always the foundation. Even *Time* Magazine admitted in the 1980s that the Bible is our founding document. It's hard to believe that they admitted that in an article, but they did.

Our form of government is a constitutional republic not a democracy. Democracy is what the Founding Fathers despised. They said it was the 'devil's own.' We're a constitutional republic. William Blackstone, a scholar to the Founding Fathers, said a constitutional republic means we do not contradict the law of the divine. If the divine has ruled on it, we don't rule against Him. For instance, with abortion we will always be wrong because the Divine has said 'Do Not Murder.'

If we get rid of the Ten Commandments, we're denying the foundation of our country."

Peter LaBarbera

Interviewed by Steve—September, 2010

———◆·◆·◆———

Few have fought as tenaciously over the years to halt America's dark embrace of moral depravity than Peter LaBarbera of *Americans for Truth*. Unlike many, who experienced salvation prior to their political involvement, LaBarbera was a fresh-faced graduate from the University of Michigan, working his first major journalism job covering communism in Central America for *The Washington Times,* when he was converted to Christianity.

"I was travelling down there with my wife, and reported on the election in which the Marxist regime lost, and all the liberal media expected the Sandinistas to win. I came back and got involved with my new faith, and pro-family politics, because the communism battle was waning.

I went to work for *Concerned Women for America* and later the *Family Research Council.* I started working on the homosexual issue and saw there was a lot of information that was not getting out so I formed a publication called *Lambda Report,* which reports on the actual homosexual agenda using homosexual sources."

The interview with LaBarbera took place in the fall of 2010, just after an eventful summer that saw several high-profile conservative organizations and celebrities publicly capitulate to the homosexual agenda.

"I've been doing this for 20 years now, and I decided to go full-time and fight on this issue because we're tremendously outgunned. I'll tell you now, it's really something to behold 20 years later to see prominent conservatives leaving that issue as if it's no longer a moral issue—as if things have changed. It's really troubling to me."

LaBarbera said a galvanizing moment for him was Ken Mehlman's public admission that he is a homosexual. The former top aide to President

George W. Bush, and former head of the Republican National Committee, even disclosed that while he was a member of the GOP establishment he worked from the inside to sabotage people like LaBarbera. Those who were trying to use the Republican Party as a means to fight for righteousness in America were actually paying Mehlman to undermine their efforts from within.

"The homosexuals tried to out Mehlman years ago, and I have to say they have a pretty good record on these things, and a lot of these guys who they say are homosexuals actually are. One of the main concerns we have with secret homosexuals in the Republican Party is they are susceptible to bribery. They can also work mischief behind the scenes where they often do things that are antithetical to what they claim to stand for. They say they're conservative but they're actually fighting us behind the scenes. We've actually got candidates now all across the country that many people suspect are involved in homosexual behavior, and yet the media just allows this to happen.

For example, there was a guy here in Illinois, Mark Kirk, running for U.S. Senate that the homosexual activists are basically claiming is a homosexual on a website. Somehow this is allowed to fester, and it's because the media loves a gay Republican. It's their favorite kind of Republican, one that actually works against pro-family values.

Mehlman should never have been appointed. When the rumors started surfacing, he should have been kicked out right there. Even worse, look at what RNC Chairman Michael Steele said about Mehlman announcing in public he's a homosexual. Steele said, 'I am happy for Ken. His announcement, which is often a very difficult decision, which is only compounded when done on the public stage, reaffirms for me why we are friends and why I respect him personally and professionally.' That's Michael Steele. That's the head of our Republican Party."

The RNC is the body which governs the political party that has spent a generation profiting at the ballot box from the hard work of the Christian Conservatives that dominate the ranks of its grassroots base. If two recent heads of the Republican National Committee have no problem with that which God spells out in His Word as an abomination, should Christians still consider this "our" Republican Party?

"I think your question is a great one. And the answer is no, because I'm coming to the conclusion that being an active Republican, working with such leaders, is getting to the point where it's bad for your faith.

Here's why I say that.

You get good people, who do have strong values, and they rise up and they get to the top of the Republican Party, say a congressman or a senator of a state. Then, they find out that the culture at the top has been infiltrated by homosexual activists. Of course, the Bible says that if you advocate for sin, you're as guilty as if you were practicing the sin yourself.

So you find out that at the top of the Republican Party is this culture of decadence, where they're actually affirming homosexuality, and then you have the choice: am I going to back the Republican Party's values or am I going to stick with my Biblical values?

Too many people start to bend toward the Republican values because they can find all sorts of justifications like we're better than the Democrats, in the long run we have to make some compromises, or you can't make an omelet without breaking a few eggs, etc. They use it to justify this bending towards actually affirming immorality, which is actually what's going on in the Republican Party."

How would LaBarbera, as a 20-year veteran of the culture war, define his own relationship with the Republican Party today?

"There's been a lot of corruption, and this idea that the Republican Party is the savior of America is, I think, increasingly in doubt. I've come to the conclusion the Republican Party needs a serious third party challenge. I guess the problem is that the system is so rigged for the two parties that it's very, very difficult. They need competition, that's for sure."

Obviously a political party, like any organization, is only as righteous as the people who inhabit it. Does LaBarbera believe Christians themselves carry any blame for the Republican Party's apparent willingness to abandon its Judeo-Christian mores?

"I guess we've started to make worldly compromises with this justification in the back of our minds that we're serving God. We make these worldly compromises, and we forget about the Bible. There are many, many problems with the (Christian Conservative movement)."

Such as?

"One of them is a fear of the Republican Party. There is a sense that the Republican Party uses Christians, and they do. They need their votes, they want their votes, they know they're passionate about issues, and they do use them. The problem is, I think, facilitated by the way some religious conservative leaders allow themselves to be used.

I made the pledge to myself, and before God, that I wanted to be a Christian first and a Republican second. I've always said I don't think God shines on Republican homosexuality or Republican-supported abortion anymore than the Democratic variety. Yet, these leaders see the Republican Party as the last, best hope for America, and I think that colors their thinking.

For instance, it really shocked me to the bone that nobody was making a big deal out of the fact that Mitt Romney came right out on *Meet the Press* during the 2008 presidential election and said his position on the Employment Non-Discrimination Act, which is the federal sexual orientation law.

That's incredible to me, because if you don't understand the harm of homosexual legislation in Massachusetts, you just don't get it and you are pro-homosexual. Massachusetts is one of the worst states for pro-homosexual, pro-transgender activism in the schools. There was even a 'Fist-gate' episode and perversion was pushed to underage kids at a state sponsored event in Boston. If Mitt Romney doesn't get the effect of pro-homosexual laws on a culture and young people in Massachusetts, he doesn't get it anywhere. Pro-family leaders were still backing Romney after he said this and had this pro-homosexual record."

LaBarbera said these issues of the movement's leaders compromising its core convictions "goes really, really deep."

"I first came to Illinois to run the *Illinois Family Institute*, and when I was there I was part of the *Focus on the Family* national network. *Focus on the Family* started to walk the line that the issue was really marriage and it wasn't homosexuality. From there it goes to, 'it's a worthy goal of our movement just to protect the word marriage.'

In other words, we'll allow civil unions. I'm not saying they said this explicitly, but I remember sitting across from Glenn Stanton, who is one of the big marriage policy guys at *Focus on the Family* and a good guy. He sat across the table from me and said 'I do think just defending the word marriage is a valid goal.' Well, once you start watering down what victory is, then it begins to become easier selling out on a number of levels.

Recently a spokesperson for *Focus on the Family* said they wouldn't have a problem with a homosexual Supreme Court justice. We challenged that and Tom Minnery, to his credit, put out a statement where they went back on it. You wonder how these things happen. If we, as a movement, do not have a problem with a homosexual Supreme Court judge, aren't we saying that we agree with the world that homosexuality is kind of a natural or a positive identity and it's not really about changeable, sinful behavior? These compromises keep coming."

Outside of the Republican Party's flirtation with homosexuality, how does LaBarbera believe the church itself is handling the issue?

"We just had something here that we call the Truth Academy, where we brought in experts, and we discussed the homosexual issue in a comprehensive three day conference. We had Rob Gagnon, who's probably the leading authority on the Bible and homosexuality. He made the point that homosexual behavior is still an abomination which is detestable in God's sight, and nothing has changed.

The way to be Biblical on homosexuality is to treat it like any other egregious sexual sin. We don't go around calling someone who is against incest an 'incestphobe' right? So why do we keep talking about being a homophobe? Why do we use words that are not even real words, and are certainly not Biblical? Are we 'pedaphobes' because we oppose pedophilia? It's ridiculous.

We stop thinking Biblically and then we start rationalizing. To me and anyone else that believes the Bible, the worldview is that homosexuality remains a detestable practice. It's not the basis for a healthy identity. You don't go around saying you have adultery practicing friends, so why would we go around saying we have gay friends? We change things because the world is changed and we change with it, and we sometimes try to con ourselves into thinking that we're still following God.

Even as we're out there promoting these Biblical worldview projects in churches across the country, we're not really acting as if homosexuality is an abomination. And now we see that the church is pulling out of the realm of the culture war and doesn't even want to engage anymore. Then you've got the Emergent Church coming along, where we've got one guy here in Chicago that says we need to declare a moratorium on preaching against homosexuality in churches. It's a matter of bending to the world, and on this issue at this moment the so-called gay agenda is at the top of Satan's agenda as the vanguard for destroying morality here in the United States."

Why should the average person reading this right now care about "destroying morality here in the United States?"

"As a Christian I do care about other people. I've met about 40 former homosexuals. I know people can leave that lifestyle. They normally do it through Christ, by the way. Born again Christians are the most successful former homosexuals.

If something is Biblically true, there are often other reasons it's true. Homosexuality promoted in a culture has a cascading effect that will result from legalizing homosexual so-called marriage. You will have homosexuality taught in schools. You will have young boys taught that one day they can grow up and marry another man. You will have private businesses, say owned by a Christian or an Orthodox Jew, which will be forced to subsidize relationships that they believe are wrong or deviant, which is un-American.

We're supposed to have freedom in this country to not just hold our beliefs, but also to act on our beliefs. What the Left wants to do is say you can have your belief in your home, maybe, with your family, or maybe huddled in your church walls, but the moment you try to be public about it in the public square, we're going to make it illegal for you to act on your belief that homosexual behavior is wrong."

LaBarbera mentioned "other reasons" beyond what the Bible says about a subject such as homosexuality that reinforces what the Bible says. Are there "other reasons" to be concerned about the culture embracing homosexuality beyond just what the Bible has to say about it?

"Oh absolutely, there is an incredibly disproportionate rate of disease among men who have sex with men, as the Center for Disease Control calls it," LaBarbera said. "Men who have sex with men have these astronomical rates of sexually transmitted disease including HIV. Almost half of all new HIV cases are men that have sex with men, and syphilis has a similarly high rate. You can go down the rate of these diseases and they're higher among men who have sex with men. That's because the behavior is unnatural. You see higher rates of domestic abuse among lesbians and homosexuals. You see all sorts of dysfunction because it remains wrong. What's changed is the culture, but the behavior remains as dangerous and wrong as it was 1000 years ago."

Polls show the next generation is more pro-life than the previous one, but certainly more tolerant of homosexual behavior as well. Is LaBarbera concerned that his particular aspect of the culture war is already lost on the next generation?

"I think what the young people are looking for is integrity. They're not going to find it when they see people backing candidates that have compromised just because they're Republicans. Again, here in Illinois we have (Senator) Mark Kirk who could not even vote for a bill to ban partial birth abortion. I don't care if he's a Republican. I don't care if he's a Democrat. I don't care if he's Green Party. That's wrong.

I have to say there is a sort of incestuousness within the Religious Right. What I mean by that is even when people know something wrong is happening, they have a tendency to say we can't really criticize. Or, it's a Matthew 18 situation so we can't talk about it—even if the infraction is very public. Even if you have public pro-family organizations doing things that are wrong or unbiblical publically, we feel we can't highlight that. I think that's wrong, especially when it's a public situation.

I think we have to start listening to new people, and go to voices at maybe some of the smaller groups that are not as compromised. I think one of the problems is big money. Let's face it, this is a huge business. What I think we're going to have to have is a remnant of people who are Biblically faithful and are willing to face persecution, including the internal persecution that comes from telling the truth within the pro-family movement. I think there's a remnant of truth tellers, and those are the people that the grass roots have to listen to because you can't always trust the institutionalized groups."

LaBarbera says the list of conservative capitulators to the homosexual agenda is a long and distinguished one.

"Why doesn't Sean Hannity talk about this issue more? Sean will do the easiest stuff, like some atrocity in an elementary school, but he won't have a former homosexual on. What about Bill O'Reilly? He's supposed to be no-spin, but he has almost totally sold out on this issue. Glenn Beck says that homosexual marriage is not a national issue. Is he ignorant of what's going on across the country? The writer Kathleen Parker is another one. Now she's making fun of Christian Conservatives. Everyone is getting on the bus because they're sensing that the Republican Party, and secular conservatives and libertarians, are giving up on the homosexual issue."

Going forward, how would LaBarbera suggest Christians determine who has sold out and who has held firm?

"I think we're going to be able to separate the men from the boys on this homosexual issue and here's why; it's becoming quite clear that not only the Republicans but the leading conservatives want to ditch it as an issue. So are the pro-family groups going to stick with the truth on this issue, or are they going to begin to compromise in order to appease their Republican interests? Anyone that goes Republican at the expense of truth should not be followed."

Richard Land

Interviewed by Steve—October, 2009

————

Dr. Richard Land, who holds degrees from both Princeton and Oxford, has been the head of the Ethics and Religious Liberty Commission for the largest Protestant denomination in the United States since 1988. During that time, he has represented the political interests of the Southern Baptist Convention at the highest levels of government. His influence has at times even reached all the way to the White House. Named by *Time Magazine* as one of America's most influential evangelicals in 2005, Land is also an author and the host of two nationally-syndicated radio broadcasts.

The Land interview took place just as opposition to President Obama's healthcare and cap-and-trade proposals was mobilizing across the country. He began the conversation by saying that despite wishful thinking masquerading as analysis and reporting by the mainstream media, the movement known as the Religious Right was anything but dead.

"I have a message for all of those who were saying that the social conservatives or the Religious Right were dead, and that a stake had been driven through our heart by Obama. Mark Twain put it best: the accounts of our death have been greatly exaggerated, and we're back."

Land pointed to recent polling data, like one showing the majority of Americans describing themselves as "pro-life" for the first time, as examples for his optimism.

"Just look at the president's approval ratings which are now lower than the number of people who voted for him. A majority of people also disapprove of his health care proposal. I think you can see it in the energy with which the opposition is making its voice known at the town hall and the Tea Parties. I must tell you that I underestimated the ability of Nancy Pelosi and Harry Reid and Barack Obama to energize social conservatives."

While it was clear conservatives and/or Christians were galvanized by the administration's large leap to the left, it wasn't clear if the Republican Party establishment would embrace its base again or not. Numerous media reports cited the tension between the emerging Tea Party movement and the GOP establishment. In 2009, the head of the Republican Governor's Association and potential 2012 presidential candidate, Mississippi Governor Haley Barbour, gave a speech to the Iowa Republican Party. During his remarks to party activists in the first in the nation caucus state, Barbour said the following:

> *"There are tens of millions of pro-choice Republicans that are just as good of Republicans as I am, and they need to be welcomed. Now that's the way our party's supposed to be. We have pro-life Republicans voting for pro-choice Republicans, and pro-choice Republicans voting for pro-life Republicans, and that you don't have to agree with Haley Barbour on everything to be a good Republican. Now that's what unity is about, and don't think that's giving up your principles. It's not giving up your principles."*

So, after hearing Barbour's remarks, and speaking as the head of the Ethics and Religious Liberty Commission for the Southern Baptist Convention, does Land believe that Christians can in good conscience vote for politicians who advocate murder provided they agree with them on other matters?

> "No, I don't agree. Haley is a consummate politician. I'm not a politician, I'm a social conservative and I am an advocate for the pro-life cause.
>
> Now if I'm faced with a choice between voting for a pro-choice Republican and voting for a Democrat whose pro-choice I'm going to just vote for somebody else. I'm not going to vote for a pro-choice Republican, and I would say to those pro-choice Republicans you've got a choice. You can either put up with me and my views on life, or you can put up with Mr. Obama and his views on taxing your money.
>
> Look, if the pro-choice Republicans want to ride on the Republican bus fine, but they don't get to drive, and they don't get to navigate, it's just that simple."

After making it clear that life is one of his non-negotiable issues, Land explained that he has other areas where he will not compromise.

"I couldn't vote for a racist. I couldn't vote for a bigot. I couldn't vote for an anti-Semite. I couldn't vote for someone in favor of same-sex marriage. I couldn't vote for someone who was anti-Israel, and I would be very troubled about voting for someone who had broken their marriage vows and particularly had broken them repeatedly. Now if you're going to be divorced, the best answer you can have is the one that Ronald Reagan had, which is he didn't want the divorce because his wife dumped him. The second best answer I guess is the one John McCain had in the Saddleback forum when he said the greatest regret of his life was the failure of his first marriage. He made it pretty clear that he was the reason for the failure of that first marriage, so you know I can probably forgive someone who said what McCain said, and who had been married for 30 years or more to his second wife. But I got to say in relation to a Newt Gingrich two ex-wives is one ex-wife too many.

Harry Truman said it best when he said that he would never knowingly hire a man to work for him who cheated on his wife. When he was asked why, he said if a man will lie to his wife he'll lie to me, and if a man will break his oath of marriage he'll break his oath of office as well. It's pretty hard to argue with Harry's logic."

Since Land addressed presidential politics, particularly by ruling out supporting Gingrich, who was widely expected to announce a White House run at the time of the interview, it seemed a good opportunity to get his take on other prospective candidates for 2012—some of whom decided against running as this book was being published.

"I think you have to look at (Louisiana Governor) Bobby Jindal, who is a very bright man, and if he can survive the cesspool that is the politics of his state, I think he is a candidate for the future. Bobby is one of those guys you better take a look at because he's got the right genetic code.

If there were to be another terrorist attack on the United States of any significance between now and the primaries, then I think (former Florida Governor) Jeb Bush is back and hot because the penalty that goes with the Bush name right now will immediately be done away with. People will say you know for seven years his brother kept us safe, and if there were to be another major terrorist attack a Jeb Bush-General Petraeus ticket wouldn't be bad.

Mike Huckabee is a great campaigner, who gives a great speech, and is a rock solid social conservative. I've known Mike since 1981 when we were both young men, and Mike proved the last time around that he's a viable candidate. I think what really hurt him last time was could he win? Clearly he's eliminated that issue. I think that he needs to articulate his foreign policy a little more clearly because there were some who I think took offense at his attacks or critique of the Bush foreign policy, and I think he needs to lay out his economic message more forcefully because there were some who thought that he was not as conservative as they would like for him to have been on economic issues, but I think Mike is going to be a very formidable candidate.

Sarah Palin has charisma, the one thing you cannot coach, and she's got it in spades. I mean if you've ever been around any of her rallies, she's got it like Reagan had it. It's hard to quantify how that would come out in the primaries. I think Rush Limbaugh has a point when he says if you want to know who the liberals fear look at who they're attacking. Well, they're attacking Sarah Palin with everything they've got, like they're trying to strangle this baby in the cradle before she gets too big, so I think personally that she's going to be a formidable candidate. I think she needs some coaching on the things that can be coached. I think she ought to be getting some regular help with foreign policy and things like that."

What about former Massachusetts Governor Mitt Romney, whom many in the media believe to be the frontrunner?

"I think that it should bother people who are thinking about Mitt as the front-runner that he didn't do better than he did last time. You know, the American people have a funny way of deciding for them-selves who they like. Back in the day Texas Governor and Secretary of the Treasury John Connolly changed parties and ran for president. I thought he would be a great president, and he spent a lot of money and got one delegate. The American people just didn't like him. So I suppose Mitt could catch fire. I thought he successfully addressed the Mormon issue in his speech at the Bush Library in College Sta-tion, but my lingering doubt is why didn't he do better last time? You look at him and he's got the looks. He's got the family. He's a good speaker. You wonder what's not connecting here, but he didn't make the connection."

Appearing on C-SPAN in 2007, Land said the following about Romney:

"Mitt is a very attractive person in many ways, and I think that if Mitt Romney were the nominee there wouldn't be a third-party candidacy because Mitt is pro-life. Mitt Romney would be a perfectly acceptable candidate to most pro-life voters."[98]

When asked if he still stood by those comments, given Romney's decades-long support for infanticide, and his relatively shaky pro-life "conversion" that just so happened to coincide with his presidential aspirations, Land gave an unexpected answer.

"Against Barack Obama yeah. I had an opportunity that a lot of people haven't had, and that is to sit down and talk with (Romney) personally about this issue, and you know he convinced me. His mother was a pro-abortion activist, and he convinced me that starting with the discussions with the Harvard folks and their callousness towards the embryo, he began to rethink the issue and that he became a believer in the pro-life position."

Did Land also think it's typical of someone having undergone a pro-life conversion to be against a Human Life Amendment to the U.S. Constitution, like Romney is?[99] Would he also say it's typical for that person to sign into law government healthcare with $50 taxpayer-funded abortions like Romney did?[100]

"I wouldn't do it and I'm pro-life. I think the fact that he was such a recent convert to the pro-life position, people thought well you know this guy just changed his mind because he wants to get the Republican nomination, in the same way as we had people who used to be pro-life who became pro-choice because they wanted to get the Democratic nomination like Al Gore, Bill Clinton, and Dick Gephardt just to name a few. If you spend $40 million and you didn't connect, I have to wonder if you're going to connect the next time."

So then, as the head of the Southern Baptist Convention's Ethics and Religious Liberty Commission, does Land believe that a politician who signs into law taxpayer-funded abortions can still claim to be pro-life, or should he be considered a supporter of abortion?

"I would not describe Romney as that. In light of the fact that I know him, I would say that he's a confused pro-lifer, and I'd take an unconfused pro-lifer over a confused pro-lifer, but I'd take a confused pro-lifer over a radical pro-abortion advocate. Barack Obama is the most radically pro-abortion president in the history of the United States. He's never met an abortion he couldn't live with."

More specifically, what is Land saying the standard for being pro-life should be? Is being less pro-abortion than the "most radically pro-abortion president in the history of the United States" the standard, or is there a better one the head of the Southern Baptist Convention's Ethics and Religious Liberty Commission could point to? Could Dr. Land explain how believers can stand before Christ one day and give an account for casting a vote in support of a "confused pro-lifer" over a pro-abortion advocate, and do so in good conscience? Could he even give a definition of what a "confused pro-lifer" is?

"If you're dealing with a confused pro-lifer versus a radical pro-abortion advocate, I think it would be a misnomer to describe that as a discussion of the lesser of two evils. Voting for someone who's a confused pro-lifer, over someone who's a radical pro-abortion advocate, is not is not a pro-abortion vote."

Would Land be willing to stand before Christ one day and defend this standard?

"Sure," he said.

This led the interview to a deeper philosophical discussion about how Christians should approach voting in the first place. Land explained whom he believes ultimately determines our leaders based on his reading of the Bible.

"We do," Land said. "The LORD let Israel make a lot of poor choices."

But did Israel choose its kings or did God?

"He picked the king," Land said.

Is it possible, that if God allowed morally compromised leaders to become king it was because they reflected the moral condition of the people? In other words, does a holy God give us the leaders we deserve?

"I think that happens. I think if He's going to give us choices, He has to allow us to live with the consequences of our poor choices and our sin. I think that Bill Clinton was a judgment of God upon the United States, and I think Barack Obama is the judgment of God on the United States."

Does God's judgment only reveal itself through morally compromised Democrats, or does He judge us with morally compromised Republicans as well? For example, John McCain was in favor of the controversial TARP,[101] actively worked to thwart the Federal Marriage Amendment as a U.S. Senator,[102] and is also a proponent of taxpayer-funded embryonic stem cell research.[103] Does Land believe it's a sign of God's judgment when the party that has institutionalized at least some righteousness into its party platform nominates someone for the highest office in the land that repudiates it?

"No, I don't think so. I think it's a sign of not letting the perfect be the enemy of the good."

We're not sure where "not letting the perfect be the enemy of the good" is at in the Bible, but we do know the Bible teaches that there is no authority on earth except that which God allows.[104] In light of that fact, should Christians vote in a way that honors God's sovereignty regardless of the outcome, or should Christians use their vote as if they're determining the outcome?

"If you want to run a third party candidate who is 100% pure, and help defeat an 80% pure candidate that lets a 10% pure candidate win, then you're going to have to answer that question to Jesus. Your pursuit of purity, as you see it, in a fallen and sinful world helps defeat the 80% pure candidate."

Is there a standard for "80% pure" in the Bible? Does the Bible say Christians aren't supposed to pursue purity? For example, Would Dr. Land vote for a Republican who was in favor of murdering babies that were conceived via rape or incest?

"Well, yeah and let me tell you why. If I came around a bend in the road and I saw a school bus that had just gone into the river, would I save none of the children because I couldn't save all of them, or would I try to save the 95% that I can save?"

As the discussion with Dr. Land continued, the head of the Ethics and Religious Liberty Commission for America's largest evangelical denomination offered almost no Scripture to back up his arguments. He was either unprepared to offer Scripture to support his positions, or aware that supporting Scripture does not exist.

Whichever the case may be, this consistent lack of Biblical application and reference from such an esteemed figure in evangelicalism was disturbing. Land's inability to support his positions with Scripture seems to support Brannon Howse's controversial contention in a previous chapter—that very few Conservative Christian leaders actually have a Biblical worldview. It should come as no surprise that Howse has been a frequent critic of Dr. Land.

For example, Dr. Land's school bus analogy is a utilitarian argument, and perhaps even a good one, but similar language is found nowhere in the Bible. Therefore, doesn't Land see that analogy as somewhat flawed because by voting for less pro-abortion candidates don't we give them permission to kill some babies so that you may save most of them?

"No, that's not true, you're being unnecessarily hostile, and if I might say so somewhat offensive."

We asked again about supporting candidates who are in favor of murdering babies conceived via rape and incest. As was noted during the Coulter interview, co-author Steve Deace's family history contains tragic stories of children conceived in less than ideal fashion, including his mother-in-law who survived three illegal abortion attempts in the 1950s. Had Planned Parenthood or "confused pro-lifers" had their way back in those days, Steve's entire family line – including the three children he and his wife share today – would never have been born.

Does that specific example change Land's perspective on voting for candidates who are pro-abortion in some cases at all? It was telling to listen as Land avoided the premise of this question in his response.

"The point is that if you could get a law passed that would eliminate all abortions except to save the physical life of the mother, and cases of rape and incest, you would eliminate 98 1/2% of all the abortions that are taking place in the United States today. If I'm a Senator or Congressman, then I'm going to come back and try to get rape and incest later, and my analogy does hold, because if I can save 98.5% of the children on that bus am I not to jump into the river and start saving them because I can't save the one and a half percent?

I think (your example) is a hypothetical that I'm not prepared to answer because that's above my pay grade, and if I may say so frankly it's above yours. All we can do is seek to do right as God gives us the light to see, and you know God knows that my heart is to save babies. I believe that it would be selfish of me to say unless I can get all of what I want I'm going allow 98.5% of the babies to continue to be killed. There's a reason why the a majority of Americans are now pro-life and there's a reason why we're winning this argument with the American people, and it's because we have focused on saving babies and doing the best we can to save babies. We're winning the argument it's taken a long time but it took the abolitionists longer."

It's interesting to note that Dr. Land used the same "that's above my pay grade" verbiage Barack Obama was rightly criticized by many pro-lifers for using at the 2008 Saddleback presidential forum when Rick Warren asked him when a baby deserves human rights.

It was unclear during the interview how Steve's firsthand, personal example from his family could be considered "hypothetical" by Land. What was also unclear during the interview is if the so-called "pro-life with exceptions" politicians Land has advocated have ever even tried to put forth legislation banning the "98%" of abortions Land keeps touting. In fact, we couldn't come up with a single example in our own research.

On the contrary, more often than not, our research found these so-called "pro-life with exceptions" politicians Dr. Land is fond of usually don't try to ban any abortions at all. The track record of the "pro-life with exceptions" politicians is one of trying to regulate the abortion industry through largely symbolic and meaningless bills that include waiting periods or statistical reporting. The bills these abortion regulators proudly parade as their claim to fame, like banning abortions when a fetus feels pain or has a heart-beat, relies on the abortionist to determine when that threshold is met.

That's right. In order to save babies with these compromise measures you have to rely on the honesty and integrity of those who are so shameless and soul-less they murder babies for a living. You'll excuse us if we're not all that optimistic about the abortionist holding up his end of the bargain.

Not to mention these toothless efforts usually precede a vote for budgets that fill Planned Parenthood's coffers with taxpayer money as well.

"If we had a ban on all abortions, and we made a compromise to allow rape and incest, that's one more that's an immoral decision cause you're allowing something to take place that is going to allow more abortions to take place than are currently taking place," Land confusingly said. "But when you have wholesale abortion up to and including almost partial-birth in most states, if you have an opportunity to pass a law that would ban most abortions and you turned it down because you couldn't get the rest, I believe you would be morally culpable for the ones you allowed to be slaughtered. I would rather not have that on my conscience."

So then, Land is in favor of voting for politicians that would have allowed Steve's mother's-in-law to be murdered? Would a globally recognized Christian leader really promote politicians that support policy that would have caused his wife and children to never have been born? Is that Biblical? Is there *any* amount of murder a Christian is allowed to support? Doesn't the Bible teach about a God who defies humanistic pragmatism to leave 99 behind to find the one, lost sheep? How would the head of the Ethics and Religious Liberty Commission at America's preeminent evangelical denomination answer such questions?

"When I was interviewed for my job, I was asked the question if my 15-year-old daughter were raped would I want her to have an abortion. I said no, I wouldn't. You're asking me to choose between my daughter and my grandchild, and I can't make that choice. My grandchild deserves to have the right to live."

That eloquent answer, which seemed to contradict what he said previously, prompted a different, although related, line of questions. Could Land point to any Biblical examples of "the lesser of two evils" being approved of or advocated by God? His answer did not include chapter and verse.

"Look, I'm a Christian ethicist, and I try to apply my ethical principles in doing the greatest good, for the greatest number, by compromising legally and not morally."

What does that mean? Again, the obvious question was could the head of the Ethics and Religious Liberty Commission of the Southern Baptist Convention—America's largest Protestant denomination—provide any Biblical examples advocating for or approving of his favored "lesser of two evils" philosophy?

"There are a lot of things that are legal that are not moral like adultery," Land said. "God wants a pro-life America, and God wants us to have a country where every baby is welcomed into life as President George W. Bush said. But in a democracy you have to change hearts and minds and sometimes that takes a long time, and as the Apostle Paul says, you have to be all things to all men that you might therefore win some, and we have to be very wise, and sometimes the simplest answer is not the right answer."

With the time allotted for the interview with Dr. Land ran out long before the possible questions did—questions like is Land aware we don't live in a democracy but a constitutional republic? Nevertheless, he was very gracious with his time and answered some tough questions, which we appreciated. However, at the conclusion of the interview, lingering questions remained.

How many babies is a politician allowed to kill and still be considered pro-life?

Can a movement ultimately be successful if it's willing to surrender the moral high ground of its cause from the outset? In other words, by saying up front that we won't stand in the way of killing certain babies, aren't pro-lifers essentially arguing the pro-choice position? Has the pro-life leadership actually been saying that sometimes a woman does have a choice to murder her child or not, we just don't want as many choices as Planned Parenthood does?

The interview ended without Land explaining if the Scriptures allow Christians to make the sort of pragmatic political calculations with God's Law against things like murder that Land was philosophically advocating. Land seemed either unable or unwilling to answer that question definitively.

Finally, Land mentioned President Bush's axiom about America being a country where every baby is welcomed into life. Given more time, it would have been interesting to ask why that same President Bush opposed South Dakota's abortion ban proposal because it didn't exempt certain abortions? Wouldn't upholding God's absolute standard against

murder effectively "welcome every baby into life?" Instead, South Dako-
tans weren't willing to kill the babies that Bush thought it was okay to kill,
so Bush essentially said keep killing them all.

These questions will come up again later during our interview with
Tom Minnery of *Focus on the Family.*

It is important to note that, while it didn't come up during our interview, Land is the only Christian leader interviewed for this book who
maintains membership on the Council on Foreign Relations,[105] whose glo-
balist goals, activities, and objectives[106] would seem to be at odds at times
with Biblical principles and a Christ-centered worldview.

John Lofton

Interviewed by Steve and Gregg—June, 2010

John Lofton is the rare man who has seen the conservative movement, and the so-called Religious Right, from the inside as an unbeliever first and then as a Bible-believing Christian.

Lofton became a Christian in 1980, the year Ronald Reagan became President of the United States. Prior to that, Lofton had worked at the National Republican Congressional Committee (NRCC), the Republican National Committee (RNC), and was the editor of the Republican Party's National Weekly Newsletter. Lofton also worked for former Senate Majority Leader Bob Dole, and then President George H. W. Bush when they were chairmen, respectively, of the RNC. In addition to writing a right-of-center nationally syndicated newspaper column, Lofton had also served as editor of numerous conservative publications including the American Conservative Union's *Battle Line* publication, and conservative publishing giant Richard Viguerie's *Conservative Digest Magazine*.

Similar to St. Paul once describing himself as the "Hebrew of Hebrews," it could be said that at one time in his life Lofton was a Republican's Republican.

"I ran around with all of these big names in the conservative movement in that time. From 1964 to 1980, I ate and drank and slept and breathed conservative politics. To paraphrase Scripture, I lived and moved and had my being in conservative politics. I was achieving some degree of prominence and notoriety, getting speaking dates, and being on national TV shows like *Good Morning America*, *Oprah*, and *Donahue*. My column was appearing in many papers and things were going fine, except I was headed for Hell."

So after working to advance the conservative movement most of his adult life, what compelled Lofton to begin reassessing his priorities at just the time the movement was finally about to go mainstream with the emergence of Reagan? The self-described "recovering Republican," who is now editor of *TheAmericanView.com*, credits (or blames depending on your perspective) a spiritual awakening.

"I knew I was a Christian at that time, (1980) but I had no idea exactly what that meant. Then a longtime friend of mine, M. Stanton Evans, gave me a book titled *The Politics of Pornography* written by Dr. R.J. Rushdoony. I'd never heard of him but I read the book. Long story short, I read it and it showed me that God had something to do with everything. God is sovereign, and the Lord is the Lord of everything, and that means the Lord of politics.

This was a shock to me, because almost all of those big name conservative leaders I ran around with and knew all claimed to be some kind of Christian. What shocked me, and struck me, was that in the hundreds of meetings that we had held over the years, all of our manifestos, our platform drafting sessions, late night bull sessions, exploring every possibility of what to do or not to do, none of these people who claimed to be Christians ever even slightly mentioned what Christ or the Bible had to do with what we were doing. Then it began to dawn on me that this conservative movement was operationally de facto atheistic in the political realm. I'm not talking about whether its leaders would go to Heaven or not if they dropped dead.

I'm not talking about their salvation, I'm talking operationally in all their political plans they were atheist. They were secular humanist conservatives and that's all we were."

Lofton said this realization compelled him to also consider that regardless of how well-intentioned such efforts seemed to be, they would not be successful because as the Bible says, apart from Christ we "can do nothing."[107]

"We were implicitly seeking a salvation of our country through politics, politics that was 'conservative' to be sure, but still it was only politics. After I was saved, I attempted at many times in these meetings to inject God or Christ or the Bible into the plans, or just raise the issue, and I was looked at as if I had lost my mind. That's why in my judgment, to put it in a nutshell, the 'conservative movement' had failed, and it should have failed. Again, I'm not talking about any individual persons' salvation, but the movement was for decades, and still is, in the political realm godless."

Lofton wrote a column for *The Washington Times* from 1982-1989 in which he said he attempted to make this point several times before it was too late for the movement.

"I wrote often about how nothing could be saved or become prosperous—a person or a nation—apart from God, apart from Christ. I was even quoting the Bible, and also even trying historically to show the foundation of our country, where blessings and prosperity and all the things that we were supposedly trying to achieve came from. How can you possibly just leave God out of the whole equation and expect to succeed?

I remember when Paul Weyrich wrote a column and declared the culture war officially over and that we had lost, and he was promoting something called 'cultural conservatism.' When I read that manifesto, as when I read so many of these new kinds of plans, it was godless. It had no God, no Bible, and no Christ—nothing.

Weyrich and I exchanged columns about this in the paper, and it was just eerie that those who claimed to be Christians really, when it came to politics, hadn't a Christian thought in their head. As if that wasn't bad enough, they were actually hostile to raising the issue. In other words they had totally bought into this separation of God and government. They had bought into this whole compartmentalization idea that this is religion and it's ok for the church and the home, but you're some kind of theocrat if you mix the two. I quickly learned from other Christians that theocrat was a bad word."

Lofton said he was often chided by fellow conservatives for attempting to utilize the Bible as the guideline for the movement's efforts. Most of the time the scolding came from those claiming to be Christians.

"We're not talking, John, about a theocracy I would often by told. And I would say, 'why aren't we? Theocracy simply means Godly rule. What's wrong with Godly rule?'

And then, very quickly, whoever you were trying to talk to would stop talking and start to gesticulate or make grunting sounds waving you off like you're just a one trick pony.

In fact there was a reader of my column in *The Washington Times* who said that he had called up columnist Richard Cohen at *The Washington Post* and was trying to arrange a debate because we had written about several things that were different. Cohen told this person he would never debate me because, 'John is always dragging God into everything.' And I thought, well isn't that big of me since God is the creator of everything and He is the Lord over everything. What does that mean to drag God into everything?"

Lofton believes that because it refused to build its foundation upon the rock from the beginning, the Religious Right/conservative movement was doomed to failure.

"My understanding is that the modern conservative movement was stillborn, it was dead on arrival, because it was godless on arrival. If you go back and read something like the Sharon Statement, that was supposed to be one of the big documents of the conservative movement and actually met at Bill Buckley's home, you can see generally speaking it was godless. If you go back and look at bound copies of *Modern Age* and *The New Individualist Review,* they would actually include a couple of articles which would raise the questions of whether or not you could be a conservative and not believe in God. Some defended that position and some denied that position, but the point being that early on in the movement there were tiny cracks in the cement.

So, the people who formed the modern conservative movement did not have a Biblical philosophy of government. Even at the time of our official founding, deterioration was already settling in. If you read *The Federalist Papers* there's no talk of Biblical government. Patrick Henry was one of the key anti-federalists and they were the ones who were, relatively speaking, really the Christian faction, and they opposed the Constitution in part because it gave short shrift to the Christian religion.

Similarly, 'modern conservatism' never claimed to be Christian. However, if you think about it, what are they then conserving?

Of course, today after two terms of George W. Bush, we know that what they were conserving was liberalism! I was thinking, if I ever wrote a book it would have the title 'Vain Imaginings,' which is a reference to Psalm 2. There is nothing vainer than the idea that we can restore a nation, rebuild our once great country, and leave Christ out. That's the whole conservative movement in a nutshell. It's been apart from Christ. I can't say it's accomplished nothing. Oh that it had accomplished nothing! It gave us George W. Bush, who greased the skids for all the stuff that Barack Obama is doing."

Lofton believes that because the conservative movement was never built on a solid foundation, it was left without a standard by which to hold itself accountable. Since it was never accountable, even to its own stances on the issues, hypocrisy was almost certain to become the norm.

"The conservative movement has never had a canon or even a fixed standard. You can be an unbeliever and be in the conservative movement. You can be a homosexual and be in the conservative movement.

There's no fire to really hold the feet of conservatives to, but there is a fire if you're a Christian. When most of the leaders of the modern conservative movement claim to be Christian, and don't behave like Christians or have any kind of a Biblical worldview of government, that explains to me in a nutshell why it's been a failure."

Lofton's solution to the compromised and ineffective conservative and Christian Right movement in America is straight-forward. He suggests that it stop focusing its efforts on what can be done only in human terms, and start focusing on what God commands us to do.

"Unless the Lord builds the house the people labor in vain. The Lord has not built the modern conservative movement or the Religious Right. That is why both have failed. Scripture says that when we please God, He makes our enemies at peace with us. God is our Department of Homeland Security. We have an audience of one! When Christians wherever they are—talk show hosts, fathers, writers, etc.—obey God, that's what makes your nation prosper."

Lofton even believes the tactics of the past generation started from a flawed premise.

"You don't necessarily have to go off and join an organization like a party. You don't have to necessarily do that. What, if anything, should a Christian do if a Christian is to be involved in politics? In other words, don't start with the presupposition that we have to all be involved in politics, or as Dr. James Dobson said we have a God-given responsibility to vote. What is he talking about?

First of all, there's no voting in the Bible so that's just ridiculous. So, in a way, you could also say forget conservative-liberal, forget red state-blue state. Secular conservatism will not, has not, and will never defeat secular liberalism, because to God they are two atheistic peas in the pod. He does not care about either one. Politics will not save us."

Lofton says history shows that salvation through politics alone has been a miserable failure whenever it is tried.

"There's a book written in the 1940s by Charles Norris Cochrane called *Christianity and Classical Culture,* which used to be a standard historical work read in college, but it was too Christian so it was dumped long ago. Cochrane says that the ancient Greco-Roman period failed because it attempted to establish peace, freedom, and security through politics, through the fortune of a new leader, or through the fortunes of a new party. I couldn't underline that enough because that's exactly what the modern conservative movement has attempted. And we see how it ended up. It ended up not merely a failure but giving us George W. Bush who, until Obama, gave us the most lawless, ungodly, unconstitutional, debt-ridden government in our history."

Lofton believes the Religious Right, operating within the framework of the modern conservative movement, was also a failure.

"I think I can say that they were all the blind leading the blind. Nobody had to be misled into downplaying the God/Bible/Christ aspect of politics, because no one talked about it. I mean *no one* talked about it, so they came into the thing misled. The root of being misled is Biblical illiteracy.

It was Mark Noll who wrote a book years ago called *The Scandal of the Evangelical Mind,* the scandal being that they had no mind, or they had no mind of Christ. Like Esau, the modern conservative movement—most members of which claim to be Christians—sold their Christian birthright for a mess of partisan political pottage, to be Republican Party cheerleaders. You don't have to mislead people that are misled already."

One topic that Lofton is very outspoken about is a hot-button debate in Christian political circles, which is the question of whether or not Christians can vote for unbelievers.

"What does God call unbelievers? He calls them wicked. He calls them evil. In John 8:44, following when Jesus talks to the group that said He wasn't God, Jesus says to them, 'Your father is the devil.' Wow!

So, if you're saying that it's okay for a Christian to vote for an unbeliever, what you're saying is its okay for a Christian to vote for a child of the devil, or an evil or wicked person. Mark DeMoss and I tangled because I answered some post that he'd put somewhere, and he was hugely offended that I would say that you have to vote only for believers. He was hugely offended by that. He never answered all the Scripture I had about God having qualifications for those who hold His civil government offices.

I remember Ralph Reed (former Executive Director of the *Christian Coalition*) in an interview saying he'd much rather vote for an unbeliever that was right on the political issues, than for a Christian who didn't know the political issues. I'll never forget he also said, 'We're open to atheists and to other unbelievers in the Christian Coalition.' You've probably heard of that bogus Martin Luther quote, 'I'd rather have a wise Turk rule me than a stupid Christian.' Gene Veith of Patrick Henry College has written a lengthy article that totally debunks that Luther quote. It is bogus."

Lofton says contrary to many other Christians that are concerned about the destructive path our nation seems to be on, he sees this as a "joyous time."

"This is a joyous time for Christians, because we are seeing before our very eyes in the nightly news and in the newspapers, God smashing and grinding to rubble all these inventions that have been brought against Him. Like all these plans that have been cooked up by both political parties, and people who call themselves Christians who totally omit Him."

Over the years Lofton has tussled with many of the biggest names in the conservative movement/Religious Right. These revealing and unflattering interviews once prompted Religious Right heavyweight, the late Paul Weyrich, to confront Lofton. Weyrich was angry because Lofton had unrelentingly pursued William Bennett in a lengthy interview, and argued with him from his Christian/Biblical perspective. Bennett at the time was Reagan's Secretary of Education, and later became the celebrated author of *The Book of Virtues.*

"I did this killer interview with Bill Bennett, considered one of the intellectual giants of the conservative movement, in *The Washington Times* that went on for five pages in the paper. During the interview, Bennett told me that my problem was that I'm still campaigning and people like him are now governing. I responded 'no Bill, God is always the one doing the governing.'

When the paper published the interview, Weyrich called me up and was viciously yelling and screaming at me. 'Why are you always attacking our people?' he asked. I said, 'Paul if you're talking about Christians as our people, it's because halfway through a lot of my interviews I discover they're not our people.'"

Over the years, much of the philosophy that has been embraced by most Christians in politics isn't Biblical Christianity at all according to Lofton, but instead is a philosophy called syncretism. That is the belief that ideas, even those that are seemingly or clearly distinct from another, can be fused together to form a consensus.

"I think really there are only two worldviews our Lord speaks of, and that is you're for Christ or you're against Christ. An adulterated gospel is no gospel. It's a different gospel. This sort of gospel takes a little bit of everything, like some wing of bat, eye of newt, and a dash of this and puts in a pot, stirs it together and whatever comes out is referred to 'thus sayeth the LORD.'

What I am talking about here is a very serious matter with eternal consequences, or Christ denial in the political realm. I don't know anything in the Scriptures more fearful than the idea of Christ saying about anybody: 'I don't know him, he's not with Me, he's not one of ours—next case.' This should be such an anguishing matter. It should also be something that makes us angry to hear the name of our Lord plastered on some of these groups that don't have a Christian thought in their head and don't talk about Christ."

Lofton recalled one example from the early 1990s to make his point.

"There was a *Focus on the Family* article by Tom Minnery, Chuck

Colson, and Gary Bauer, that was supposed to tell Christians how to be more effective in politics. The article had with it a cartoon of a guy hitting someone in the face with a Bible, and the headline was 'Don't Swing that Bible.'

The gist of the article was don't quote the Scripture and instead, when in Rome do as the Romans. What's ironic is that when the first Christians were in Rome they didn't do as the Romans, and they were murdered for it. Anything that tells us to leave the sword of truth, the Word of God, in its sheath, is in effect saying do not put on the full armor of God. Rather, charge onto the battlefield naked with no armor of God.

The modern conservative movement and its leaders did not swing the Bible and they lost. So now, they are like the fish god Dagon—face down in the dirt and they deserve it. How many books and articles have I read about the Republican Party being captured by the Religious Right? No! No! It was the Religious Right that was captured by the Republican Party!"

Lofton believes the Religious Right has no future with its present view of politics and government.

"This sinful, erroneous view of the Religious Right is rooted either in unbelief and/or Biblical illiteracy. When Christians stopped judging everything Biblically, everything started sliding into Hell. But we must judge everything Biblically, and that includes politics and government.

Christ is Lord over all! And our Lord commands us to judge with righteous judgment and not on the basis of appearance, but we are commanded to judge. We will all stand before the Lord to give an account for every idle word out of our mouth. Yes, we'll disagree about things, but if you go through the Bible one of the interesting things it says is we, as Christians, are to be of one faith, one baptism, and in one accord on the essentials."

Lofton anecdotally summed up what's happened in the past generation.

"I've been told a million times, 'You have your view and I'll have mine.' I say, 'I have a better idea, why don't we have God's view?'

I always ask those that disagree with me if they're a Christian so that we can go to the Scriptures to settle our dispute. I'll never forget one lady I asked that of who angrily answered me through gritted teeth, 'Yes, I am a Christian, but what difference does that make?' There's your epitaph for Western Civilization."

Tom Minnery

Interviewed by Steve—March, 2009

For more than 20 years, Tom Minnery has overseen the political arm of *Focus on the Family* as its senior vice president for government and public policy. He was one of the founding board members of the *Alliance Defense Fund*, and is also a former senior editor for *Christianity Today* magazine. He is the author of the book *Why You Can't Stay Silent: A Biblical Mandate to Shape Our Culture.*

Formerly Dr. James Dobson's right-hand-man, Minnery's lofty perch within what is considered the largest and most influential pro-family organization in the United States affords him the luxury of being one of the leading Christian conservative strategists and activists there is. The list of those better connected or better informed within the movement than Minnery is microscopic. The interview with Minnery occurred just days after Dobson's retirement as chairman of *Focus on the Family* was announced.

The media at the time described Dobson's retirement as sudden and abrupt. Did Minnery see it that way?

"Dr. Dobson absolutely determined to do things the right way, and part of that includes finishing well. He started the process six years ago by inviting someone else to be the CEO of *Focus on the Family*, and he gave up that title and remained as chairman of the board. A former official in the Reagan administration, and someone who's been on our Board of Directors, stepped in to be the CEO and he set about looking for someone to take over for him because he was not a long-termer. He found Jim Daly, one of our long-time employees who had grown up in several areas of the ministry. Jim has a wide background with *Focus on the Family* and was a natural.

Dr. Dobson understands that Jim Daly is fully competent, but might do some things differently. Dr. Dobson has come to the realization that you can't have two cooks in the kitchen. That's why I'm so thankful that Dr. Dobson is still healthy and will be part of the process here by being the voice on the radio program at least for the foreseeable future, and still will be writing his letters to constituents so we will still see him around here and his influence will still be felt."

In the wake of Dobson's retirement, the conversation turned towards the luminary's legacy. Minnery commented on several statements Dobson had made over the years, beginning with this pledge he gave at a rally in 1990:

"Finally, I want to give a pledge to you on a political level, and I'm speaking for myself not Focus on the Family, which is a non-political organization. I can just tell you that I am determined, that for the rest of my life, however long God let's me live on this earth, I will never cast one vote for any man or woman who would kill one innocent baby!"[108]

That bold pledge was then reaffirmed by comments Dobson made to the national media regarding the 2008 presidential race:

"And there are two (Republican candidates) that I've indicated now that I absolutely cannot under any circumstances vote for. One of them is Rudy Giuliani and the other is John McCain, for different reasons. Giuliani is not pro-life and McCain sometimes is. He's in favor of embryonic stem cell research and so I'm not sure where he comes down on some of the issues but neither is acceptable to me and I've said so and that's what all the flack is about. You know that I'm a patriot. I love my country and I'm deeply concerned about it right now and the fact that I would even consider not casting a vote for presidential candidate…I certainly will vote for all the other issues and people on the ballot, but the fact that I would not vote for the president if it comes down to Obama and Clinton versus McCain…I can't in good conscience be a party to putting any of them in power because I believe they'll do irreparable harm to our country."[109]

Eventually Dobson did endorse John McCain for president. The endorsement came despite the fact McCain continued to hold the same position on experimenting with human life through embryonic stem cell research that Barack Obama did. McCain received the Dobson endorsement even though he was opposed to a Human Life Amendment to the U.S. Constitution just like Barack Obama was, and McCain fought for years to have the Republican Party platform call for allowing babies to be murdered in certain situations. So did Minnery see the 2008 endorsement of McCain as a violation of Dobson's heroic 1990 pledge?

"Well, in a sense he did, but let's go back to that 1990 statement and that is Dr. Dobson's emotional, principled position. He made that statement shortly after we formally got into the world of public policy in 1988, but we both have seen over the years that there are a number of politicians who will be pro-life for 99% of unborn life, but they will not oppose abortion in cases of rape and incest which have about 1% of all abortions. So the question comes is 99% good enough for a politician or because he is not going to go for that 1% is he insufficient, and if we don't vote for that 99% then we allow the other guy who's probably an out and out liberal who will vote for abortion in all 100% of cases to be elected?

Suppose you pass an orphanage, and the place is on fire and there are 100 kids in there needing to be saved, and the firemen come and says we need help can you run in there and grab some kids? You say, well am I not able to get all of them out, but you can get about 99 of them out yet one might die. You say that's not sufficient and then you turn your back and walk on."

This analogy seems less like something you'd find in the Bible and more like those utilitarian ethics test given in secular schools, where they give students a list of 10 passengers on a small rescue craft that can only hold five of them. After reading the bios of each passenger, the students are then asked to select five passengers to throw overboard to keep the craft afloat, presumably because they're not as worthy of saving.

Not to mention that in America we have a "government by the consent of the governed." That means that by voting for a politician who is willing to murder any baby you are giving him *permission,* via your consent as a voter, to do so as your representative. Isn't it hypocritical for a Christian to on one hand to say that the unalienable (or God-given) right to life is his non-negotiable, and then turn right around and vote for political candidates who violate it just because they're presumably not as much of a transgressor against the law of Almighty God than their opponent?

"It's not hypocrisy it's the reality of politics," Minnery said. "The issue is how many can be saved? Obviously we will not stop working on this until every last child is protected in the womb, and given the right to life at the time of birth, but we're in a deep well. We can't jump out of that well in one leap, as you seem to be suggesting. We have to claw our way slowly out of this well by educating, convincing more and more people, and slowly we are winning that one. More and more surveys show that predominantly people are pro-life. They're not pro-life 100% but they're getting there. They understand the evil of abortion and so we are making progress toward our goal."

Is Minnery aware of a Biblical mandate or precedent that supports his so-called "lesser of two evils" argument? Does the Bible even define what that is? If the Bible doesn't define what that is, or advocate this philosophy anywhere, is it something Christians should be pursuing in the civic arena at all?

"Are you advocating that Christians ought not to be involved in government? Your position suggests that unless they feel good about it 100%, Christians should not get in there and not fight to protect as many babies as you can. You want to feel good about your position, but you'll do absolutely nothing at all to advance it."

Aside from the fact that Minnery made his comments on a three-hour daily talk show hosted by someone widely known for publicly applying his faith to political engagement, and broadcast on one of the legendary 50,000-watt radio stations in the United States, he seemed to be implying that the corruption in politics is beyond the redeeming power of Christ or the influence of His followers. On the contrary, Steve, who is described by other media outlets as a "Christian talk host," engages his Christian faith publicly over the airwaves as he discusses the news of the day.

Additionally, Gregg wrote a political best-seller entitled *Conservative Comebacks to Liberal Lies*. So Minnery's accusation that the question advocates Christians abandon politics doesn't hold water. Instead, we are Christians who are driven into the political arena because of our faith, as is Minnery.

That said, if Minnery is convinced that Christians were engaging the culture and politics in a way that honored Christ over the past generation, how could he explain the sobering numbers featured in the introduction to this book? In summary, the statistics show the government is bigger than ever, government schools are more anti-Christian than ever, the judiciary is more rebellious against God's Law than ever, and America is the least Biblically literate she's ever been.

In other words, where are the fruits of our labors?

"If you summarize the first seven verses of Romans 13, it says honor the governing authorities. The government is of the people, by the people, and for the people. We are the people in this outworking of Christianity here in the U.S. under this government. We are the citizens, and we must go in there and do the dirty work to try to improve things.

Everybody says I won't be involved in politics because it is dirty, I say it's dirty because Christian people have not been involved in politics. We have neglected the right to life issue for so long. Answer this question: if you have a politician here who will be pro-life except for rape and incest he is 99% pro-life, and you have another politician who is 100% in favor of all abortions what would you do?"

Minnery's challenge makes sense if you only consider numbers, but it proves more problematic when you understand each of those numbers is a real human soul. Herein lies the problem, can the pro-life movement prove ultimately successful if it adopts the philosophy, language, and tactics of those with no regard for human life, and no reverence for the Creator of life in the first place?

To put a finer point on it, who are we as pro-lifers to say it's okay to murder even 1% of that which God has created? Aren't we essentially committing the same sin the pro-abortionists are committing by determining who is worthy of life, and who is not if we do so, albeit less egregiously? Doesn't James say "whoever keeps the whole law and yet stumbles at just one point is guilty of breaking all of it?"[110]

Pastor Bob Deever, the Senior Pastor at Grace West in Iowa, where co-author Steve and his family are members, discussed this very dilemma in a sermon once. He did so by challenging the congregation and telling them that if they think it's okay to vote for someone that will murder some babies, then go ahead and volunteer their own children to be that some.

The church was silent as they considered the solemnity of this challenge.

As has been mentioned, co-author Steve Deace's wife's family has a history of children conceived in less-than-ideal circumstances and illegal abortion attempts. It is from the perspective of sitting under the teaching of a God-fearing pastor, and enjoying a life surrounded by those who would not exist had today's political pragmatism prevailed in bygone eras, that Steve urged Minnery to answer the challenge.

Is Minnery okay with allowing members of Steve's family to be murdered if they are part of that 1%, including Steve's own children? Would Minnery so easily disregard some human life to save others when he actually put a name and a face on those lives being disregarded?

That's what made Dr. Dobson's aforementioned 1990 pledge so courageous and prophetic. It affirms that God's Law provides no caveats for murder, nor any subsections or escape clauses filled with fine print that allows it in certain situations. Dobson understood that God did not say, "thou shall not kill, unless it's a Republican killing the kid and not a Democrat." Therefore, why not just stick to what Dr. Dobson originally pledged, which was the most righteous and Biblical standard?

What have we won since 1990 that we would've lost had *Focus on the Family* done so?

Could it be argued we might have won more since 1990 than we have if only a ministry with the resources and influence of *Focus on the Family* honored this pledge?

"That is well said, but you ducked my question. What would you do in that particular election where you have somebody who's 99% pro-life on the other side versus someone who's 100% pro-abortion?"

Is the premise of Minnery's question even Biblical? After failing to provide a single Biblical support for the philosophy he's advocating, let alone a single example of a politician he's backed that has actually attempted or accomplished what he's advocating, Minnery clung to his analogy.

Minnery's analogy is strikingly similar to the argument used in an earlier chapter by a leader in the Southern Baptist Church, Dr. Richard Land. Still, even if they combined the two arguments and talked about a bus load of orphans on fire in a river, as Christians they ought to be able to support the analogy with Scripture. Instead of using *Sola Scriptura* to make their arguments, Land and Minnery instead used pragmatic or utilitarian philosophical what ifs.

"Wait a minute, you've got the mandate of Romans 13 to respect the governing authorities by being involved so what would you do?"

Minnery was obviously trying to turn the tables, which is a respected debate tactic, but it doesn't address the fact his premise is Biblically flawed. Nowhere does the Bible allow God's people to break God's Law because the state compels it. Quite the contrary, numerous examples from Daniel to Christ himself point to quite the opposite.

"Render therefore to Caesar the things that are Caesar's, and to God the things that are God's."[111] Ultimately that which is God's is our obedience to and worship of Him alone, not to Caesar. Thus, if it's a choice between Christ and Caesar, then it's really no choice at all for the Christian. The blood of martyrs, which was spilled for failing to worship Caesars down through the centuries and into the present time, tragically testifies to this.

Nevertheless, God has allowed us to live in a country where we are permitted to vote as Minnery points out, albeit in a convoluted way. So what is a Christian to do in the scenario Minnery described, which is an all too familiar occurrence in recent elections? It seems to really come down to two choices, but not the catch-22 Minnery is describing which is really choosing among two law-breakers.

Perhaps the choice is really between "the lesser of two evils" approach Minnery is advocating, and the wisdom of Founding Father John Quincy Adams who once said, "Duty is ours; results are God's."[112]

"I think the answer is obvious. Conform the culture to the Word of God, but then the question is, can you sit back and just expect it by answered prayer? How much more evil would it be had not courageous Christians been in the trenches working to save every life possible? There are untold thousands of babies' lives that have been saved simply because states have worked themselves toward a pro-life position by requiring 24-hour waiting periods, by requiring parental consent; this is the hard work of righteousness. You have to work toward your principle."

There seems to be a lot of focus on the work we do and how we are to do it, but what is it that we expect God to do? What role does the Bible say He has in choosing our leaders? How would Minnery say we can be sure the work we're doing is faithful to Him in the first place?

"Dr. Dobson, as you know, has been at the head of the National Prayer Movement, and for more than a decade oceans of prayer have gone to heaven, waves upon waves have crashed against the gates, seeking righteous candidates. We're doing all of that all the time. There was a lot of prayer, for example, offered in California by a very vital prayer movement prior to Proposition 8 passing and preserving God's definition of marriage, but I have to tell you if prayer was the only thing that campaign would not have been successful. He has not sent us the miracles that we feel we need in the political process."

Could the reason God has yet to bless this movement in such a powerful way, and it's largely had to fight, scratch, and claw for small or symbolic victories for decades, be because this movement is defined by pragmatism and political partisanship? Could it be that the need to scrap and fight in a human sense is the natural result of a movement that doesn't first seek after His kingdom and His righteousness?

"Just so people know; you did not let me know the nature of this interview when you called. I thought that you wanted to do what you said, which was to talk about the legacy of Dr. Dobson."

Isn't that exactly what we're talking about?

"I can answer these questions, but you've got me on a grill here and I was totally uninformed about the nature of this interview, and don't appreciate you springing this on me like this."

Didn't Minnery believe that who Dr. Dobson and *Focus on the Family* supports, and what it says, is a part of the Dobson legacy?

"That was a ruse, I mean this was an ambush interview! I'm happy to talk about Dr. Dobson's great influence in the pro-life movement over the years, and the fact that he's beloved by nearly all pro-life leaders for his courageous leadership. We've been going round and round and we're not getting anywhere."

Could it be that part of the reason we're in a "deep well" is because of our own actions over the years that are contradictory to a Biblical worldview? If Minnery felt ambushed, perhaps he could point to something that was said which was untrue.

"We have a difference of opinion. If you believe that we can jump out of a deep hole in one jump go ahead."

Maybe Minnery should instead consider the wisdom of the old saying, "When you find yourself stuck in a hole—stop digging."

Judge Roy Moore

Interviewed by Gregg—February, 2011

———

Judge Roy Moore has lived the American dream.

From humble beginnings, he received an appointment to the U.S. Military Academy at West Point. From there he served his country as a captain in Vietnam. After returning home he became a lawyer, eventually becoming a prosecutor, then a circuit court judge, and ultimately was elected Chief Justice of the Alabama Supreme Court.

It is during his tenure as Chief Justice that he became a national cause celeb for his defiance of a federal court order directing him to take down a Ten Commandments monument he, as Chief Justice, had erected in the Alabama Judicial Building. The story of the controversy that ensued, and the way it led to Moore's removal from office, is the most vivid contemporary real-world case study of the central premise of this book.

That's because Judge Roy Moore is an eyewitnesses to the stark reality that in the end, it's not the secular humanist liberals who are the most opposed to governing by God's standard—it's some of the so-called "Christian leaders."

Prior to erecting the two-ton granite Ten Commandments monument in the Alabama Judicial Building, Judge Moore had already put up a small Ten Commandments plaque in his court room as a circuit court judge in 1992. As a result of this flagrant display of the foundation from which our laws originate, Judge Moore was sued by the American Civil Liberties Union. Moore said that by doing so he was simply following federal precedent.

"At that time, it was a matter of faith in God and logic that if the United States Congress could open with prayer, and the United States Supreme Court could open with a salutation to God, then certainly acknowledging God's Law wouldn't be incorrect, but I knew there might be problems. As I began the battle in federal court, and state court in the early 1990s, I began to learn about our history. I began to learn about the First Amendment to the United States Constitution."

It was Moore's understanding of the First Amendment's freedom of religion clause ("Congress shall make no law respecting the establishment of religion nor prohibiting the free exercise thereof") that would put him at odds with not only leading liberal-left legal organizations such as the ACLU and the Southern Poverty Law Center, but more significantly leading Christian and conservative legal organizations and politicians, including the born-again President of the United States, George W. Bush.

"When I put up a monument at the Supreme Court of Alabama as Chief Justice, which I was entitled to do, that was not only a matter of faith, it was a matter of law. I don't want to think that I took an action out of my own personal beliefs; this was not only out of my personal beliefs, but as a matter of law. The United States Constitution, our history, our law, our logic, does not forbid the acknowledgment of God. To say that it does is absolute hypocrisy and foolishness.

Our law actually mandates an acknowledgment of God. You see, the *Declaration of Independence*, what began as our Organic Law, in its first sentence says we're entitled to exist by the 'Laws of Nature and of Nature's God.' That's not just a pretty phrase that Thomas Jefferson put in there. That was a reference to William Blackstone's laws, which was a real, divine law out of the Holy Scriptures."

Moore believes he was only acting upon the belief that many other conservatives and Christians publicly claim to have. However, once a federal judge ordered him to do something that violated his conscience by removing the Ten Commandments, Moore quickly learned that actions speak louder than words.

"As I started trying to convince others, I saw politicians that would take advantage of the Christian perspective and say that they supported me, but that support stopped when it came down to a federal court order that told me to do something that the law allowed me to do under the First Amendment. To obey that court order would have also violated my freedom of conscience. Actually the federal judge had no authority to give me such an order anyway."

Moore went on to explain why Federal Judge Myron Thompson, who issued the court order, had no constitutional authority to do so.

"Our Constitution of Alabama acknowledges God in its preamble, and every constitution of every state in some way acknowledges God. The United States Constitution, in the First Amendment, talks about freedom of religion. The definition of religion given by James Madison who offered the amendment, given by Joseph Storey who wrote the commentary on the Constitution, given by the United States Supreme Court in *U.S. v. Reynolds* in 1878, and included in the attachment to *Everson v. Board of Education* in February of 1947, defines religion as 'the duties which we owe to the Creator and the matter of discharging it.'

In other words, if you put that definition to the First Amendment, its Congress shall make no law respecting the establishment of the duties which we owe to the Creator and the manner discharging it. Without acknowledgment of the Creator and duties we owe to Him, there would be no first part of the First Amendment.

This federal judge, when he said I had to take down the monument because it recognized a particular god, was completely out of line. He overturned not only the law of Alabama, but the First Amendment, and the United States Supreme Court in two cases that recognized that our freedom of conscience comes from God. He overturned even that, and essentially said you could not recognize who God was."

The media at the time made Moore's story to be about just a monument, but it was about something far more monumental than that.

"Now for people that think it was about a monument, it was not, it was about whether or not I, as a Chief Justice of the Supreme Court of Alabama, could recognize that God existed in my official capacity. The federal judge said 'while the Chief Justice is free to keep whatever religious beliefs he chooses, the state may not acknowledge the sovereignty of the Judeo-Christian God, and attribute to that God our religious freedom.'

Anybody would certainly recognize there's a hypocrisy that exists when the United States Supreme Court can open with 'God save the United States and this honorable court.' That's their opening salutation. In fact, that opens every federal district court in this land.

Yet they say through the federal court that you can't acknowledge a sovereign God?

There's a great hypocrisy going on when our law regarding the Pledge of Allegiance puts 'under God' in the pledge, when the National Anthem says things about God. Most people never hear the third stanza of the national anthem, if they did they'd realize that not only the law says we can acknowledge God, but our country is indebted to God for our existence:

'oh thus be it ever when free men shall stand, between their loved homes and the war's desolation, blest with victory and peace may the heaven-rescued land, praise the Power that hath made and preserved us a nation. Then conquer me must, when our cause is just, and this be our motto, in God is our trust.'"

Moore believes the ruling wasn't just a question of personal faith, but rather of the law itself.

"It was about whether or not a public official could sincerely, genuinely acknowledge that a sovereign God and higher law exists. This battle has been going on for many, many years, and is going on today as vigorously as it was going on back in 2003. We stood up for the law of our country, and the Constitution of the United States, and the Constitution of the State of Alabama, which I was sworn to uphold."

In his book *So Help Me God*, Moore compares America today to ancient Judah which, according to Moore, "was a nation that called upon God's name, but refused to recognize his sovereignty or abide by his law." Moore quoted the Old Testament prophet, Isaiah.

"Isaiah 48:1 says 'Hear now this oh house of Jacob, which are called by the name of Israel and come forth out of the waters of Judah which swear by the name of the Lord and make mention of the God of Israel but not in truth or in righteousness.'

The reason I quote that, and I often do in various speeches, is because in the days of Judah the same things were going on. They swore by the name of the Lord. Do we not swear by the name of the Lord in our oaths? And make mention of the God of Israel? And in our national anthem, we talk about the God of Israel. We're talking about that God. And throughout our references to God, it's about the

God of the Holy Scriptures. Are we not doing the same thing, but not in truth or in righteousness? In other words, they (who swear by the name of the Lord not in truth or righteousness) are hypocrites."

Most of the leading Christian pro-family groups, legal organizations, and politicians claim to stand for religious liberty. If ever there were a perfect "religious liberty" case for these organizations and politicians to defend, it seems as though Moore's cases would have been perfectly suited. Yet, aside from the late D. James Kennedy at *Coral Ridge Ministries*, Dr. James Dobson (formerly of *Focus on the Family*), and former U.N. Ambassador Alan Keyes, amazingly and tragically no other leading Christians or conservative legal or religious organizations came to Moore's defense at the time.

During our conversation with Moore, we cited an e-mail from former *Concerned Women of America* President Sandy Rios in which she said:

"You may remember (Moore) had been elected chief justice by something like 84% of the Alabama vote. The night before a pastor's prayer breakfast in support of Justice Moore, Jay Sekulow and Richard Land made phone calls to pastors scheduled to attend and persuaded them to withdraw their support for him. The next morning only a handful came. They trusted Jay and they trusted Dr. Land as did other voters in Alabama and confusion and doubt set in."

Sekulow is the high-profile head of the American Center for Law and Justice. Richard Land, a member of the Council on Foreign Relations who is more widely known as head of the Ethics and Religious Liberty Commission for the Southern Baptist Convention. Why, in Moore's view, would two of the most prominent "Christian leaders," who claim to stand for religious liberty, actively seem to betray a man who took such a courageous and bold stand in defense of it?

"Well, I didn't believe it would happen, but I was naïve, To answer your question, I'm going to refer to the first chapter of Romans: 'when they knew God, they glorified Him not as God and neither were thankful, but became vain in their imaginations. Their foolish hearts were darkened professing themselves to be wise, they became fools and exchanged the glory of the incorruptible God to an image made like corruptible man. Even if they did not like to retain God in their knowledge, God gave them over to a reprobate mind to do those things which are not inconvenient.'

That answers your question from a Biblical standpoint. Sekulow, Land, and (Pat) Robertson don't put the sovereignty of God above the sovereignty of man. They put the sovereignty of man above the sovereignty of God. These religious leaders and people like Bill Pryor, who once defended the Ten Commandments in court when he was an attorney general, but wanted an appointment to the 11th circuit by the Bush White House, chose to prosecute rather than to defend."

Regarding his removal from office for standing up for the Word of God, Moore explained to us that neither the federal district judge nor the attorney general of Alabama had the authority to remove him.

"When you violate a court order, who is it that punishes you? It's the court that gives the order. A contempt hearing was set before the federal district judge. It was cancelled and of course I didn't object. But then it was transferred to an ethical tribunal which said that because I violated an order, it didn't matter whether the order was lawful or unlawful, I was to be removed from office.

So, we had gotten to the point where we recognize unlawful orders over your duty to the Constitution. That is exactly the opposite of what happened to Lt. Callie in the Vietnam War. I was involved in the Vietnam War and I remember the story. He massacred a great deal of people in MiLa. He was prosecuted and in the court martial it says that his commander authorized him. We don't believe he did, but even if he did, you aren't authorized under the Constitution to massacre people. There's a higher law.

Well, there's a higher law than a federal court order. It's the United States Constitution, and there's even a higher law than that and that's God's Law. It just so happens that the United States Constitution was written in conformity with God's Law. There was no dissonance to it. The First Amendment to the United States Constitution recognizes that God is the Creator God."

Moore said they ended up removing him on what amounted to a technicality.

"Basically, the federal judge didn't remove me from office. They cancelled the federal court case so I had no appeal to the Supreme Court on the lawfulness or unlawfulness of the order that he gave. I submit to you his order was completely unlawful, and it disagreed with the

United States Supreme Court. But you see the United States Supreme Court has a problem. They can't explain how they can open their sessions with a prayer and yet forbid school children from opening with prayer."

Wasn't President Bush both constitutionally bound, and morally obligated as a professed Christian, to do something in Moore's defense?

"I think he was obligated to uphold the Constitution of the United States, and the First Amendment doesn't forbid the acknowledgment of God. You're missing one critical point here. He was advised by Karl Rove, who mandated out of the Bush White House the movement of this monument.

It wasn't a Democrat governor in Alabama. It was a Republican. It wasn't a Democrat attorney general. It was a Republican. He came out of a Republican administration and the White House. So, even though I was a Republican when I ran as Chief Justice and still am, it wasn't a Democrat that removed me. It was out of a Republican administration.

I'm so disappointed in the Republicans. I'm more disappointed in Republicans than I am Democrats. I mean, Democrats you expect it. You know, but these Republicans they play a political game. It's like a game, get elected, fool the Christians, get up there and play the game to keep the power."

Moore explained to us that the reason so many leading Christian and conservative legal organizations such as *ACLJ, Pacific Legal, Liberty Council* and *Alliance Defense Fund* didn't come to his defense is because "they wanted to win in court, and they want to win the way the court says win, which is to basically to deny that there's a sovereign God, but they'll let you do it if you do it a certain way."

When Moore was told to take down the Ten Commandments monument, he explained to us that he was offered the opportunity to save his job and pension.

"A Senior Associate Justice came to me in my office and made me an offer. He said we've talked about this and we've agreed that if you transfer your authority to me, he would remove the monument and I could keep my job, 'be a hero and save face and people would understand.'

But I said that it's my job and my authority and I wouldn't sign the paper. I could've signed the paper and prohibited any removal from office. The federal district judge didn't remove me from office. It was a panel out of the state and they transferred out of his authority. The only way a judge can enforce his orders are through contempt, but I was never held in contempt. It was a state tribunal that removed me without questioning the lawfulness of the order. I understand that they wanted me out of the way because I would not bow down to the federal authority which was contradicting the United States Constitution. So they got their way, but I still think God is in control."

But what about modern notions of "separation of church and state?"

"Render to Caesar what is Caesar's and to God what is God's. Jesus wasn't saying that there were things that Caesar had that God had no authority over. He was saying that whatever Caesar had God gave him authority over, but He didn't give him authority over one thing. This one thing was so important to our Founding Fathers, so important to our history, and most Christians today don't know what that one thing that he would not submit to Caesar and that's our freedom to worship God in the manner in which we choose—that's called freedom of conscience. It's contained in the First Amendment. The First Amendment in its first part says that Congress shall make no law respecting the establishment of religion or prohibiting free exercise of religion. That definition of religion goes back to the duties that we owe to God and the manner of discharging those duties. That was outside of the government interference."

Moore says that when matters of conscience are no longer considered "outside of government interference" it ends up redefining our way of life in a way that is contrary to God's standards.

"When government starts saying you can't worship God, it assumes the position of god, and then begins to grant rights that only God can grant. Some of those 'rights' government grants include abortion, homosexuality, same sex marriage, and it goes on and on and on because they're creating rights in today's courts and not recognizing the ones given by God.

Instead, the whole role of government is to protect our God-given rights. How do I know that? Because it says so in the *Declaration of*

Independence, 'We hold these truths to be self-evident that all men are created equal and endowed by their Creator with certain inalienable rights among these are life, liberty and the pursuit of happiness.'

He went on to say 'that to secure these rights, governments are instituted among men deriving their just powers from the consent of the governed. That whenever any form of government becomes destructive in these ends, it is the right of the people to alter or abolish it and to institute new government laying its foundation on such principles and organizing its power in such form, as to them that shall see most likely to affect their safety and happiness.'"

Moore said the failure to understand the proper role of government as well as the condition of human nature, as our Founding Fathers did, has had dire consequences in our day in age.

"Today, we do not understand the role of government, that's why you see so many government officials going around assuming they can do things not in the Constitution, and quite frankly adverse to our law. Our forefathers understood that smaller government, separation of powers, checks and balances, and the principle of federalism, all existed because they distrusted the fallen nature of man.

George Washington said as he left office, that 'a just estimate of that love of power and the proneness to abuse it which predominates in the human heart is sufficient to satisfy us of the truth of this position.' Jefferson added 'let no more be heard of confidence in man, but bind him down from mischief by the chains of the Constitution.'"

Moore believes we cannot understand the proper role of government, and the fallen condition of human nature, without first acknowledging the ultimate sovereignty of God. Moore also said that failure to acknowledge the sovereignty of God has real world practical, political consequences.

"Disregard of God's laws does lead to mischief, even to the complete disregard of our own laws, as seen in the failure to enforce immigration laws and the President's recent suit against the State of Arizona for enforcing the law the federal government has ignored. When our government will not recognize the sovereignty of God it will disregard the restraints on power under the Constitution."

It's no surprise these foundational principles have been rejected by the American Left, because they must be rejected if the Left is to justify their schemes. On the other hand, as Moore's own story proves, all too often those on the Right who claim adherence to these foundational principles are just as quick to abandon them.

For example, one would expect an ACLU-trained lawyer to claim, as Supreme Court Justice Sonya Sotomayor once did, that law and public policy is really decided in the courts.[113] However, the Founding Fathers granted no such lawmaking authority to the courts in the express words enshrined in the United States Constitution.

So how does Moore explain why most of the leading Christian and conservative legal organizations perpetually cede the lie that the judiciary is the final arbiter of what is and what is not legal (i.e. supreme to the other two branches), as well as functionally supreme over God Himself?

"According to the Constitution it was never meant for the courts to make law, and courts don't make law. Everyone will say that they recognize that courts don't make law, but then fearfully they do not impeach these justices for ruling by foreign law, and by excluding the very mention of God which is in the chambers of the United States Congress. They allow judges to rule as they feel and that's what's going on all over the country when these judges are overturning things.

For example, our *Foundation for Moral Law* recently filed a brief in the case where the federal district judge out of Massachusetts said that the Defense of Marriage Act passed in 1996 by Congress was unconstitutional under the Fifth Amendment of the Constitution, which contained an equal protection provision. If you read the Fifth Amendment, there are no equal protection words in the Fifth Amendment whatsoever. That's in the Fourteenth Amendment. These judges don't even know what's contained in the Fifth Amendment.

We're living in a society where God doesn't give rights anymore because we don't acknowledge Him. Man can rule whatever he wants to if he has a black robe on. That's what I really object to. The oath of office doesn't say that we're sworn to uphold the Supreme Court of the United States, but rather the Constitution of the United States. It says that every judge, legislator and executive shall swear to uphold the Supreme Law of the Land.

The Constitution says that this Constitution, and the laws of the United States of America made pursuant thereof and all treaties made and which shall be made under the authority of the United States, are the Supreme Law of the Land. In other words, if courts go way off on a tangent and start interpreting a law in exact contradiction to its original purpose and meaning, the president should stand up and Congress should stand up and they should impeach these justices."

If what Moore is describing is the constitutional republic our Founding Fathers originally intended, then how come Christians aren't the first ones to assert these principles? Why won't Christian leaders lead, especially when it's their worldview and morals that this new form of judicial oligarchy is most threatening?

"Most Christian people in this country do not understand the Bill of Rights wasn't to give us rights; it was to protect us from the federal government taking those rights away. They act as if the United States Supreme Court can take away our religious freedom, and that's exactly what the court in my case did. Man wants to be as God, but when Jesus said render to Caesar the things of Caesar and to God the things of God, it doesn't mean Caesar has authority over everything but will leave the afterlife to God. That's not what Jesus meant."

There were a number of high profile marriage cases that were decided in Massachusetts, California and Iowa. In each case, the individual state supreme courts decided that laws limiting marriage to one man-one woman were discriminatory and unconstitutional. Following each court opinion, the governors of those states (two Republicans and one Democrat) began the alterations to, and issuance of, marriage licenses without a binding, enabling and accompanying statute as required by law. In fact, the 2011 Iowa Code still defines a legal marriage as one man, one woman despite the 2009 Iowa Supreme Court ruling.

All three governors (Mitt Romney, Arnold Schwarzenegger and Chet Culver) falsely claimed that they were merely "following the law," when in reality the law governing marriage had (and to this day has) not changed to accommodate same sex "marriage." Since the courts are not permitted to issue illegal and anti-constitutional court opinions changing the generally accepted definition of marriage, doesn't the real blame for the marriage licenses being illegally altered and issued therefore lie with the governors? Aren't they ultimately responsible for the enforcement of all the laws and statutes of the state in which they govern?

"I think these governors want to issue marriage licenses to same sex couples, and they're using the courts to get them to lie. I think they're bowing down to unlawful authority. Their job is to execute the law, not to obey unlawful orders (and opinions) and I think that's what they're doing.

I'm most familiar with the judges in Iowa because I spoke up there. After I spoke, a pastor got together with people and started to attack the justices of the Supreme Court who had voted in same sex marriage and overruled Iowa's DOMA law, which is the Defense of Marriage law.

I went back and spoke on television and radio about the unlawfulness of these orders and low and behold, three justices of the Iowa Supreme Court that were up for retention were removed from court for the first time in Iowa history. That's a very big thing, because it shows that when the people understand what's going on in these courts, they will remove these justices whether they were elected, appointed or whatever—they'll get them out."

Moore said a different level of accountability is needed for federal judges.

"Federal judges have lifetime tenure, so they're free to rule against the law and it's up to the legislative branch to impeach them and they should. If they would impeach one of these judges then they would stop rebelling against the Constitution. We've even got Supreme Court Justices of the United States openly stating in their opinions that they're following foreign law precedent now.

A good example was *Lawrence v. Texas* in 2003, when they overturned the precedent which was set in 1986 (*Bowers v. Hardwick*) that said there was no right in the Constitution to commit sodomy. Some 17 years later they found such a right, but they didn't find it in our Constitution. They found it in the laws of France, Germany and the United Kingdom.

The United States Congress should've impeached them when they ruled by laws which they weren't sworn to uphold. United States justices and people in our land aren't sworn to uphold the laws of France or Germany or the United Kingdom. They're sworn to uphold the Constitution of the United States, and they had already recognized there's no right to commit sodomy in the Constitution."

Should any executive who falsely claims that a court ordered him to enforce an opinion contrary to our Constitution be impeached and removed from office?

"I think those like Romney should have been impeached and removed from office because they're not following the Constitution. When judges do wrong things, it seems like the executives and legislatures so highly regard their position that they don't question it. Elected officials are not willing to impeach those who violate their oaths because they don't understand the Constitution of the United States. The Constitution of the United States basically exists to control the fallen nature of man. That's why you have three distinct branches with checks and balances and separation of powers. We often complain because laws are so slow. It was meant to be that way. They wanted to restrain the power of man, and they did it with various systems like federalism which allows for states' rights."

In 2010, Moore attempted to put these principles into practice as a candidate for governor in his home state of Alabama. He finished 4th in a tightly-contested GOP primary with 19%, which was nine points behind the winner. Does Moore believe his Ten Commandments controversy helped or hindered his campaign?

"I do not feel my involvement with the Ten Commandments case has ever adversely affected my campaigns for office. Those doors were shut in order to give me a greater voice on the stage of national politics where most Americans understand that we must continue to be 'One nation under God or we will be a nation gone under' as President Reagan so aptly stated."

In spite of everything that he has had to personally endure to stand for what he believes in, and often enduring abuse coming from those who market themselves as people who believe as he does, Moore remains sanguine.

"I think there's a lot of hope because there is a God. I think He's awakening the people. I think we're under a great awakening right now, and I think that people are coming to understand the Constitution of the United States, and a little bit better the history and the actions of these judges and presidents who ignore the law and just distort it according to their own individual predilection. I think people are awakening, and I will never give up on our country. I served this country and saw too many die in its defense. Some people very closely related to me at the United States Military Academy. I think of them often, and think of how we've turned our back on that which they were sworn to uphold. I vow never to do that."

As this book was being finalized Moore announced a presidential exploratory committee, leaving open the option he make seek the 2012 Republican presidential nomination.

Dr. Strangelaw: Or, How Christians Learned to Stop Worrying About Self-Government and Love Judicial Oligarchy

—•—

Imagine if you will that a time machine suddenly appeared, and allowed you to go back to visit September 17th, 1787.

You arrive at the Constitutional Convention in Philadelphia, just as its delegates were meeting to ratify the United States Constitution they had been working on for four months. You want to give this collection of flawed yet wise men a look into the future at the rule of law they were formally establishing. You tell them you come from over 200 years in the future, and the United States of America of your time has been recognized as the dominant power in the world for almost a century now.

You bring with you newspaper articles for them to read. The headlines tell about what is happening in the future nation they are forging this very day. They wouldn't understand much of the vernacular and context because the technology involved is so much more advanced than where things stand in their day. On the other hand, they would certainly understand the moral foundation (or lack thereof as the case may be) behind America's debt crisis, economic downturn, becoming the world's police force, and the size of government growing well beyond the 18 enumerated powers in the Constitution they are about to sign.

Astonished and dismayed they would surely be to see that the nation for which they pledged their lives, fortunes, and sacred honors had been so easily disregarded. With a heavy heart, you show them articles with the following headlines that have actually occurred in your lifetime:

- "Supreme Court makes abortion the law of the land."
- "Federal judge overturns state constitutional amendment defining marriage as one man, one woman."

- "Supremes uphold traditional interpretation of Second Amendment by a slim, 5-4, majority."
- "Supreme Court expands eminent domain powers of government at all levels."
- "Supreme Court relies on 'separation of church and state' clause in Constitution to make school prayer illegal."
- "Supreme Court cites foreign court precedent in striking down sodomy laws."

After reading these headlines these men we now know as our Founding Fathers would surely be simultaneously perplexed, troubled, frustrated, and saddened, because some of the same men gathered in Philadelphia that day were also there on July 4th, 1776—the day the *Declaration of Independence* was ratified by the Continental Congress.

Otherwise known as the Organic Law of this nation, *The Declaration of Independence* asserts, "We hold these truths to be self-evident, that all men are created equal, that they are endowed by their Creator with certain unalienable (or God-given) Rights, that among these are Life, Liberty and the pursuit of Happiness. That to secure these rights, Governments are instituted among Men, deriving their just powers from the consent of the governed."

In a nutshell, these are "the Laws of Nature and Nature's God" that Thomas Jefferson is referring to in his *Declaration of Independence*'s opening paragraph. He reminds us that men are created, or in other words that they are made by God. He asserts that their Creator (God) is alone the granter of rights fundamental to human existence, and names several such as life, liberty, and the pursuit of happiness. He punctuates these conclusions by saying that this is so obvious it's self evident restating the truth of Psalm 14:1 which says, "the fool says in his heart there is no God."[114]

Jefferson reminds us that governments are established to secure these God-given rights, and that God is "not a respecter of persons," so ultimately power flows from the people to the ruling class as opposed to the other way around.

To justify breaking away from the British Crown, Jefferson lists a series of "repeated injuries and usurpations" committed by the monarchy of his day that led to "the establishment of an absolute Tyranny." Many Americans believe that chief among them is "no taxation without representation." While that was certainly a battle-cry among our Founding Fathers, that particular usurpation is only listed once. However, several other times Jefferson refers to specific problems with the judiciary on his list.

In response to this, the Founding Fathers did several things.

They used half of the Bill of Rights (Amendments four through eight) to clearly define the legal rights of every U.S. citizen. They established a separation of powers, with three branches of government whose jurisdictions are clearly defined in the Constitution. Unlike the British system that had the judiciary system serving as a subsidiary of the executive branch (in their case the king), our judiciary would be given independence to provide a true system of checks and balances between the three branches.

However, it is interesting to note that the Constitution provides very limited means for the judiciary to place that check on the other two branches. It's given the fewest enumerated powers (3) of the three branches, the legislative branch is given the means to limit the jurisdiction of the judicial branch, and it's the only branch whose resources on the federal level (funding and appointments) are completely at the mercy of the other two branches.

It's obvious by these actions, that while our Founders felt their legal rights were usurped by a British judicial system serving at the mercy of a tyrannical monarch as opposed to acting independently in the best interests of its subjects, they were equally wary of replacing a monarchy with an oligarchy. As a result, they made that independent judiciary the weakest of the three branches in order to avoid having the people ultimately ruled by judges they did not elect—which goes against their concept of "government by the consent of the governed."

The Federalist Papers were distributed nationwide by several framers of the Constitution at the time of its ratification to explain why they did what they did. *Federalist 78* was written by Alexander Hamilton as a response to those known as anti-Federalists. The anti-Federalists were concerned that even a judicial branch with only three enumerated powers would still have the means to acquire much more in the future with judges insulated from the scrutiny of voters via lifetime appointments.

To soothe these justifiable fears, Hamilton wrote that the judiciary is "beyond comparison the weakest of three branches":

> *"The judiciary, on the contrary, has no influence over either the sword or the purse; no direction either of the strength or of the wealth of the society; and can take no active resolution whatever. It may truly be said to have neither force nor will, but merely judgment; and must ulti-*

mately depend upon the aid of the executive arm even for the efficacy of its judgments."

In that spirit let us return to your trip in the time machine and show our Founding Fathers what became of the republic they gave us. Let's gauge their reaction to the aforementioned headlines.

- How would they react to the idea that the branch they intended to be the weakest was now the strongest?
- How would they react to the idea that the branch they put at the mercy of the two elected directly by the people has now made the will of the people subservient to it?
- How would they react to the other two branches just blindly carrying out the will and whims of the branch that wasn't intended to have any?
- How would they react to judges no longer being confined to the "Laws of Nature and Nature's God" as the means for interpreting the Constitution?
- How would they react to the law evolving based on the unrestrained worldviews of judges?
- How would they react to courts granting men so-called rights that are not "endowed by their Creator?"
- How would they react to "we the people" being governed by rulers we didn't elect? Doesn't that sound awfully close to the sort of tyranny they were rebelling against in their day?

Throughout the course of this book we have interviewed those who have served on the front lines of America's culture war for the past generation. Each of them has cited various reasons for why the fight for righteousness in America went wrong. Yet if there is one transcendent factor that explains why our efforts in the civic realm have barely managed to even slow the decline of the republic, the loss of the rule of law is most assuredly it.

But don't just take our word for it, instead take His:

- "Keep my decrees and laws, for the man who obeys them will live by them. I am the LORD."[115]
- "Keep all my decrees and all my laws and follow them. I am the LORD."[116]

- "Follow my decrees and be careful to obey my laws, and you will live safely in the land."[117]
- "And what other nation is so great as to have such righteous decrees and laws as the body of laws I am setting before you today?"[118]
- "Be careful that you do not forget the LORD your God, failing to observe His commands, His laws, and His decrees that I am giving you this day."[119]
- "Cursed is the man who does not uphold the words of this law by carrying them out."[120]
- "The secret things belong to the LORD our God, but the things revealed belong to us and our children forever, that we may follow all the words of this law."[121]
- "You came down on Mount Sinai; you spoke to them from heaven. You gave them regulations and laws that are just and right, decrees and commands that are good."[122]
- "Blessed is the man who does not walk in with the counsel of the wicked or stand in the way of sinners or sit in the seat of mockers. But his delight is in the law of the LORD, and on His law he meditates day and night."[123]
- "The law of the LORD is perfect, refreshing the soul. The statutes of the LORD are trustworthy, making wise the simple."[124]
- "Your laws endure to this day, for all things serve you."[125]
- "Your righteousness is everlasting and your law is true."[126]
- "All your words are true; all your righteous laws are eternal."[127]
- "Woe to those who make unjust laws, to those who issue oppressive decrees."[128]
- "It pleased the LORD for the sake of his righteousness to make his law great and glorious."[129]
- "Hear, O earth: I am bringing disaster on this people, the fruit of their schemes, because they have not listened to my words and have rejected my law."[130]
- "My people are destroyed from lack of knowledge. Because you have rejected knowledge, I also reject you as my priests; because you have ignored the law of your God, I also will ignore your children."[131]
- "Do not think that I have come to abolish the Law or the Prophets; I have not come to abolish them but to fulfill them. I tell you the truth, until heaven and earth disappear, not the smallest letter, not the least stroke of a pen, will by any means disappear from the Law until everything is accomplished."[132]

- "For it is not those who hear the law who are righteous in God's sight, but it is those who obey the law who will be declared righteous."[133]
- "But the man who looks intently into the perfect law that gives freedom, and continues to do this, not forgetting what he has heard, but doing it—he will be blessed in what he does."[134]

So what is this law that the Word of God speaks so frequently of? Could it be that this is what our own laws should be based on? Were our laws ever based on it? What happens when there's a conflict between this law the Bible speaks of and the laws made by men? Which of these laws hold precedence? Are some laws higher than others? Can mankind "legalize" that which goes against "the Laws of Nature and Nature's God," and what are the consequences when it tries to? When our government officials swear an oath to defend the Constitution who are they swearing that oath to?

For answers we turned to three people who have spent their lives actively wrestling with these important questions.

Dr. Edwin Vieira holds four degrees from Harvard, and is in his fourth decade of practicing law. He's argued before the United States Supreme Court, and is the author of several books including, *How to Dethrone an Imperial Judiciary*. Judge Tom Parker is serving his second term as an Associate Justice on the State Supreme Court of Alabama, which elects its judges by popular vote. Attorney Michael Peroutka is a co-founder of *The Institute on the Constitution*. He once resigned from an appointment to the U.S. Department of Health and Human Services when he realized that none of the programs which he was working on were actually constitutional. In 2004 Peroutka was the Constitution Party's presidential nominee.

In conversations with all three there was a general consensus that since the late 19th century, the judiciary's view of the law has transitioned from the naturalistic standard laid out by our Founding Fathers to a more positivistic one. In other words, instead of the law being derived from a fixed standard, embedded in the creation by the Creator (i.e. "the Laws of Nature and Nature's God" or the Ten Commandments), the law is an evolving standard set forth by the human authoritarian body recognized as being in charge at that particular time (i.e. opinions and preferences of judges, majority rules, latest cultural trends, might makes right, postmodern ethics, etc.).

Like ancient Israel, America has become a land where we no longer recognize the King of Kings as the Supreme Ruler; therefore, everyone does what is right in his own eyes. Just as some denominations who have turned away from the narrow road that leads to eternal life fancy themselves tolerant by using statements like "God is still speaking" to justify their betrayal of the Bible, we have morphed the fixed standard of the Constitution into "a living, breathing document."

Once a people have unhinged themselves from accountability to their Creator, the next step is to essentially become accountable to nothing. After rebelling against Almighty God, it doesn't take long to become so shameless that you don't care about what your neighbor thinks, either. It's no coincidence that as the Bible has become less and less revered in the culture, our interpretation of the Constitution has drifted further and further away from what our Founders intended.

This is what John Adams feared when he said:

"We have no government armed with power capable of contending with human passions unbridled by morality and religion. Avarice, ambition, revenge, or gallantry, would break the strongest cords of our Constitution as a whale goes through a net. Our Constitution was made only for a moral and religious people. It is wholly inadequate to the government of any other."[135]

According to Peroutka, this indoctrination into what is usually known as legal positivism begins as soon as students enter law school.

"I took two semesters of Constitutional Law in law school, and we never once read from or directly quoted the Constitution itself in class. We read lots of people's opinions about what the Constitution supposedly says or means, but never the Constitution itself. After years of practicing law my brother and I became concerned because we had taken an oath before God to protect and defend the Constitution, and to live up to its provisions, and we didn't know anything about it. That's not really unusual, and I know that sounds very strange to most ears, but in modern law schools the Constitution and the principles for which it stands that undergird it are not taught."

Parker believes there has been a "clash of worldviews going on in the judiciary."

"It's in the form of two different approaches to the Constitution. One is called the original intent approach where the judge tries to discern what the drafters meant by what was the use of those words in English at that time, what were the political writings at that time that spoke about those areas of the law, and then he tries to stay faithful to that in interpreting. On the other side, in stark contrast, is the living document approach where the judges will say this document has to change with time and we're the ones who say in what direction it turns and what direction it changes. This is a fundamental clash of viewpoints, but you can see how the last viewpoint that I just enumerated empowers a judge to be more powerful than a legislator—he becomes a super legislator enabled to determine new direction for our society."

Certainly we have seen too many tragic examples of judges becoming super legislators from the bench. We have also watched the other two branches—largely made up of individuals who also underwent the same un-American indoctrination in American law schools—acquiescing to their decrees. The question remains however—where in the Constitution, or in any of our founding documents for that matter, does it say the judiciary is the final word on what the Constitution means? Where does the Constitution demand the other two branches, or "we the people," to be subservient to a judge's opinion? According to Vieira, it doesn't.

"It doesn't exist, and I think that concept is one that the Founding Fathers would have rejected. If you go back to Sir William Blackstone, he wrote a famous set of books called *Commentaries on the Laws of England.* He was the leading legal commentator on the laws of England during the colonial period, and actually his book was more widely read by American patriots than any other legal book. One of the points that he brings out is that the legislative authority in society is the highest lawmaking authority. Now, if you look at what the legislative authority is in the constitutional system it's we the people. How does the Constitution begin? 'We the people do ordain and establish' the Constitution.

The Constitution predates the establishment of the Supreme Court and before it heard any cases. So did the Constitution not have meaning until the Supreme Court and its opinions came along? Of course not!

The meaning of the Constitution does not depend upon what some judge says it means. The meaning of the Constitution is an objective fact which one derives from looking at the words that were written.

So the idea that a judge making a determination in a particular case as to what the Constitution means somehow thereafter binds everyone else in the world with respect to that interpretation of the Constitution is, I would suggest, nonsense with a capital N."

Vieira is concerned that granting such sweeping powers to the judicial branch erodes the Founders' vision of a "government by the consent of the governed." These changes transform a system where power flows from the bottom up, and instead elevates judges making these decisions to be viewed as uniquely qualified among all living homo sapiens to rule. In this unconstitutional judicial utopia, only they can know what the Constitution means—and only they are immune to the fallen state of human nature that tempts even the best among us to go astray to boot.

"We know for a fact that people are fallible, including judges, so it's certainly possible that judges can make an error in a particular case. We know that the courts make errors. There was a Supreme Court case called *Payne vs. Tennessee*, and it has a footnote note in which the Supreme Court lists earlier opinions of theirs on constitutional points that they have reversed. In other words, earlier opinions that they later admitted were wrong. It's a very long footnote that goes on for a page, so we have seen the recognition by the courts that they make mistakes. If they make mistakes then, how can any particular decision of theirs be the final binding determination of the U.S. Constitution?"

Parker agrees, and says this clash of worldviews within the judiciary leads to a form of judicial oligarchy. He contends this has been going on for longer than we think.

"We have to look historically at what happened to the teaching of law, and it changed at Harvard Law in the late 19th century when the Unitarians gained control and introduced the case law methodology. What they did was move away from studying the Constitution and the legislation, and instead started looking at what judges had to say about it in their written opinions. Once you've moved away from the fixed standard of our founding documents, you begin an evolving system which is slow to change initially, but it gains speed where as now, unfortunately, law schools are teaching their students to be change agents in our society, and that is not the role of the judiciary."

That in and of itself wouldn't be inherently bad, provided the judges rendering the opinions were doing so from a righteous framework. After all, is there a precedent older and more binding than the Ten Commandments or the "Laws of Nature and Nature's God?" However, by allowing the law to be called the law even though it comes from men in authority and not from God who is the highest authority, we have made men out to be our gods.

The problem with that is if only God is good and all men "have gone astray," laws made by men without recognition of God can't be automatically counted on to be good. Peroutka sees this as a key component of understanding our current situation.

"The concept that laws came from God, and that God was the source of our law and our liberty and our rights, is enshrined in our *Declaration of Independence* and all of our founding documents. But once it took hold at Harvard that the law comes from the opinion of judges, it took hold in all the institutions of legal learning, and now is the way that people study law."

Vieira witnessed firsthand what Parker and Peroutka are describing when he attended Harvard Law School.

"I went to Harvard Law School in the 1970s to study Constitutional Law, and I would've thought we'd spend the first two weeks or a month actually reading the Constitution, and going through and studying it as a separate entity. We never did read the Constitution. We started right off reading these decisions from the Supreme Court as if the decisions from the Supreme Court were the things that told us what the Constitution means instead of the Constitution itself.

The legal intellectuals picked up on this idea that came out of the late 1800s, because this was a way to expand their power. So now we have a legal system that's driven not simply by judges, but by these legal intellectuals in the law schools and the various think tanks, and they can insinuate any legal theories they want into our system through the mechanism of judicial interpretation as opposed to what the correct mechanism for changing the law under the Constitution actually is."

Before you roll your eyes at Vieira's assessment, listen to the words of current Supreme Court Justice Sonia Sotomayor:

"All of the legal defense funds out there, they are looking for people with court of appeals experience because the court of appeals is where policy is made." [136]

By the way, what is the supreme appellate court in the United States? You guessed it, the United States Supreme Court. If you stop and think about it, almost all of the "policies" in the past generation that have done the most damage to the Founding Fathers' vision for America have not come not from the Congress, but instead have come from the appellate courts. This despite the constitutional fact that the Congress is the only branch of the federal government granted the enumerated power to make laws. For example:

- School prayer removed—*Engle v. Vitale*
- Legalizing infanticide—*Roe v. Wade*
- Confiscation of private property—*Kelo v. New London*
- Removal of anti-sodomy laws—*Lawrence v. Texas*
- Illegal aliens are entitled to American taxpayer funding—*Plyler v. Doe*
- Homosexuals allowed to marry—*Goodridge v. Department of Public Health* and *Varnum v. Brien*

You will find no record of any bills passed by the U.S. Congress or signed into law by the President of the United States legalizing any of these policies. Sotomayor's assessment of where policy is made in America is tragically true, but is that what the Constitution says should be happening? Vieira says no.

"Article one Section one of the Constitution clearly says all legislative powers herein granted shall be vested in a Congress of the United States. Presidents can't make laws by executive order, and the courts can't make laws through judicial opinions. The Constitution tells us there is no legislative power from a court that attempts to legislate from the bench through an opinion. That opinion is not a law, because the Constitution tells us the courts have no legislative power. How much simpler do you want it?"

Apparently the longer you stay in law school the less simple it becomes. Peroutka believes that nothing which God says is wrong can be "legalized" by men since God alone is the supreme lawgiver. As a result, he refers to this corrupted jurisprudence as "unlaw."

Or, as the aforementioned Blackstone put it:

"This law of nature, being co-equal with mankind and dictated by God himself, is of course superior in obligation to any other. It is binding over all the globe, in all countries, and at all times: no human laws are of any validity, if contrary to this; and such of them as are valid derive all their force, and all their authority, mediately or immediately, from this original."[137]

An unlikely ally in this cause is Rev. Dr. Martin Luther King, Jr., who has ironically become an icon for many who have done the most to perpetuate what Peroutka calls "unlaw."

While behind bars in 1963 for his non-violent civil rights protests, King penned the famous *Letter from a Birmingham Jail* as a response to a group of white clergymen who agreed with King about the evils of racial injustice, but believed the battle for equality should take place in the courts rather than the public domain. King questions whether a system that for centuries enabled racial inequality can suddenly be trusted to act righteously without external pressure:

"There are just laws and there are unjust laws. I would be the first to advocate obeying just laws. One has not only a legal but moral responsibility to obey just laws. Conversely, one has a moral responsibility to disobey unjust laws. I would agree with Saint Augustine that 'An unjust law is no law at all.' Now what is the difference between the two? How does one determine when a law is just or unjust? A just law is a man-made code that squares with the moral law or the law of God. An unjust law is a code that is out of harmony with the moral law. To put it in the terms of Saint Thomas Aquinas, an unjust law is a human law that is not rooted in eternal and natural law...Of course there is nothing new about this kind of civil disobedience. It was seen sublimely in the refusal of Shadrach, Meshach, and Abednego to obey the laws of Nebuchadnezzar because a higher moral law was involved. It was practiced superbly by the early Christians who were willing to face hungry lions and the excruciating pain of chopping blocks, before submitting to certain unjust laws of the Roman Empire."[138]

King, the same man now revered by American liberals who seek to remove all references to the God he acknowledged, is appealing to the highest law as the foundation for his moral crusade for racial equality. King took a stand that you almost never see today's Christian lawyers, activists, politicians, and organizations that ask for your money are willing to take. Instead they often utilize the Left's language with statements like, "the court struck down," and "the court legalized," or "the court's opinion is the law of the land," which accepts the immoral—dare we say pagan—legal positivistic philosophy of the very opponents they're contending with.

In short, they're attempting to play God's game by the devil's rules. Peroutka has a warning for those who look to moral equivocators for godly leadership.

"When we rely on people who call themselves conservatives, that should give it away, because conservative nowadays means you're just conserving yesterday's liberalism. You're not really adhering to a fixed standard. Most conservative talking heads are just trying to slow down liberalism as it moves forward by holding onto its shirtsleeves, but they're really just going off the cliff a little slower than the liberals are.

We need a culture that understands the true meaning behind our *Declaration of Independence* and the worldview behind it. G.K. Chesterton is reported to have written that America might be the only country founded on a creed.

In America we don't as a culture believe that creed anymore, or we don't believe it strong enough to actually have the fortitude to implement it in the political arena."

The U.S. Supreme Court's ruling *Salazar v. Buono* in 2010 is a case in point. The case was heard to determined if allowing a World War I memorial in California's Mojave Desert that included a cross violated the Constitution's establishment clause. By a scant 5-4 majority the court ruled the cross could stay.

Speaking for the majority, Justice Anthony Kennedy said it was wrong to view the cross as strictly a symbol of the Resurrection of Jesus Christ. "Here one Latin cross in the desert evokes far more than religion," Kennedy said. "It evokes thousands of small crosses in foreign fields marking the graves of Americans who fell in battles, battles whose tragedies are compounded if the fallen are forgotten."[139]

Although we doubt it, perhaps Kennedy is unaware that apart from the Christian religion the cross is hardly a symbol of hope and life to place on the graves of the "fallen." Until Christ's resurrection, the cross was a symbol of torture, dread, and death. Does Justice Kennedy really believe those who placed that cross there did so for any reasons other than religious ones?

Sadly, no Christian legal or political organization bothered to make the argument that no court even has the jurisdiction to remove such a monument in the first place. The words "separation of church and state" appear nowhere in the Constitution, right next to the part that doesn't say the courts are the ultimate authority on what the Constitution means, and the part that doesn't say their rulings have the force of law.

The establishment clause of the U.S. Constitution refers specifically to Congress not establishing a state religion. It recognizes the right of every citizen to the freedom *of* religion, not a freedom *from* religion. The Veterans of Foreign Wars who placed that cross there in 1934 aren't the Congress, and they weren't establishing a religion.

In the same way, a school system that wants to acknowledge God at graduation or other school functions shouldn't face threats from the court because it isn't the Congress. Just like a city council that permits public references to Christmas shouldn't face threats from the court because it isn't the U.S. Congress. Just like every other cultural institution the courts have allowed to become secularly sanitized isn't the U.S. Congress.

If only this tomfoolery were an isolated case.

Abortion was never "legalized" in America through the legislative process of a duly elected Congress sending a bill to a duly-elected President for his signature. Instead, the slaughter of babies became an invention of the U.S. Supreme Court. However, instead of adhering to the Constitutional standard both Vieira and Peroutka are advocating, the vast majority of conservative and Christian politicians, activists, and lawyers treat this opinion of the court as if it is the law.

Two states that "legalized" homosexual marriage—Massachusetts and Iowa—each did so virtually the exact same way.

The Iowa Constitution clearly says that "all political power is inherent in the people," while also saying only the legislature shall make law. Yet in 2009 when its State Supreme Court decided the Defense of Marriage Act was unconstitutional, Democrat Governor Chet Culver allowed his executive branch to carry out the Court's wishes and issue marriage licenses to homosexuals.

That practice continues today under Republican Governor Terry

Branstad, despite the fact the law on the books in Iowa—the law that was passed by the actual lawmakers –forbids it. Even as this book was nearing completion the newly updated 2011 Iowa Code, which lists all the laws of the state, still forbids homosexual marriage![140]

That's also what happened during Republican Mitt Romney's term as Governor of Massachusetts. The Constitution of Massachusetts was at least partially written by John Adams himself, and is the oldest constitution in the country. It contains the following wording:[141]

> **Part I, Article X.** *"...the people of this commonwealth are not controllable by any other laws than those to which their constitutional representative body have given their consent."*

> **Part I, Article XX.** *"The power of suspending the laws, or the execution of the laws, ought never to be exercised but by the legislature, or by authority derived from it...."*

> **Part I, Article XXX.** *"In the government of this commonwealth, the legislative department shall never exercise the executive and judicial powers, or either of them: the executive shall never exercise the legislative and judicial powers, or either of them: the judicial shall never exercise the legislative and executive powers, or either of them: to the end it may be a government of laws and not of men."*

> **Part II, Ch. III, Article V.** *"All causes of marriage, divorce, and alimony, and all appeals from the judges of probate shall be heard and determined by the governor and council, until the legislature shall, by law, make other provision."*

Translation: these quotes, taken directly from the Massachusetts' Constitution, explain that it's not a rogue judicial branch led by activist leftist judges that owns the blame for so-called gay marriage happening there. According to the Massachusetts Constitution, it's actually Mitt Romney who deserves the blame. He not only had no authority to carry out the court's opinion in the case, but he actually violated his own sworn oath of office by doing so.

After a while, when evil continues to flourish, you stop blaming only the culprits and start targeting the collaborators. Since you don't ever hear these facts or principles coming from the majority of the most well-known lawyers, politicians, and pundits on "our side," that means we're aiding and abetting evil even while we claim to be working so hard to stop it. This disconnect has far-reaching implications according to Vieira.

"It's extremely dangerous to allow power to be non-accountable and non-responsible. If you go back historically to the founding of the country, I think that the most outspoken individual on this subject was Thomas Jefferson. He warned again and again of the possibility that individual judges could use their offices to gain essentially a kind of legislative power for themselves if the other branches of government did not act in the manner of checks and balances as our system requires them. It's clear that power corrupts and absolute power corrupts absolutely in this case.

If a person in that position is of weak character, he will attempt to usurp authority, but our system depends upon those attempts at usurpation being subject to checks and balances from other branches of government—the legislative branch and the executive branch in the federal system the state versus the federal government at the state level. What we've actually seen here is a decay in the check and balance mechanism, and of course that has encouraged further usurpation by the judges because, my gosh, they get away with it so why not take advantage of it."

There's been a lot of debate in this country in recent years about what kind of judges should be appointed. Do we want strict constructionists or activist judges?

Perhaps the answer is neither.

What we're looking for are *righteous* judges. The kind that know where law comes from, know who the ultimate lawgiver is, and that know who they're eternally accountable to for upholding their sworn oaths of office.

When judges do get out of line, however, there are still two other branches of government, as well as we the people, that have the responsibility to rein them in. Unfortunately, all have been derelict in their duty where those checks and balances are concerned. According to Peroutka, a flawed understanding of proper roles leads to time and energy wasted on activities that inadvertently lend credibility to the flawed understanding.

"I've worked a lot in the pro-life movement and you hear people spend their time and their effort trying to overturn *Roe v. Wade* because they say it's the law of the land. *Roe v. Wade* can't be the law of the land if you read the very first sentence of the Constitution after the preamble. It says all authority to make laws is vested only in the Congress of the United States.

The strategy of electing Republican candidates to appoint conservative judges that will overturn immoral precedents has been an absolute loser. The next time some shill for a RINO candidate tries to lecture you how he's so much better than the Democrat because of the judges he'll nominate, remind him that seven of the nine Supreme Court justices who gave us such infamous rulings as *Roe v. Wade, Lawrence v. Texas,* and *Kelo v. New London* were appointed by Republicans.

Courts don't make law under our Constitution, so we spend all our time trying to undo what should be ignored. I really believe that the ultimate solution, or the practical solution in our age, is for states and local magistrates to stand up and say, 'that doesn't apply here because we know that's not law.'

What happens if a governor says we're not going to carry out that Supreme Court edict because they can't order me to do something that violates the highest law?"

What happens if the governor, or any other official in the executive branch, doesn't do what the court tells them to? Have we ever stopped to ask ourselves if on the day of judgment God will accept "that was the law of the land" or "the supreme court said so" as an excuse for carrying out laws that violate His Word?

For instance, what will God say to a professing Christian governor whose executive branch hands out marriage licenses to homosexuals because a court unconstitutionally ordered him to? Here's another, what will God say to a professing Christian president who signs a budget into law that gives taxpayer money to Planned Parenthood?

We are aware of no Biblical examples where God has excused such behavior. Perhaps we are those extra special American Christians who will be given a "the judicial oligarchy compelled me," or "the devil made me do it" exception?

On the contrary, the Book of Daniel recounts how Daniel refused to carry out the king's ungodly edicts because he feared God and not man, and how God supernaturally rewarded Daniel for his faithfulness. Recall some of the interviews you've read in this book that have addressed why God has not blessed a generation's efforts to restore righteousness in America? Could it be that we don't miraculously see the hand of God as visible as Daniel did in his day because we're not as faithful as Daniel was?

Does God not still hold magistrates and politicians who profess faith in him to that same standard today? If someone like Daniel, living under a dictatorial monarchy before the time of Christ, was called to take such a righteous stand why would God lower His standards for those of us living in an age of grace and in a much freer and less oppressive society today? Peroutka sees instead an eternal God applying eternal standards.

"There are natural moral laws just like there are natural laws of gravity. These are part of the 'Laws of Nature and of Nature's God.' And when you break these laws they really end up breaking you."

It's clear when you look at America today—whether it be economically, morally, or spiritually—we are a nation at the breaking point. We are breaking down as a society because we are breaking laws that aren't supposed to be broken—laws that were embedded into the creation for our own good.

Let's look at an illustration at "the Laws of Nature and Nature's God" in parable form.

There once was a man piloting a plane that was about to crash. Against the advice of the air traffic controllers, those that shepherd the skies if you will, the man had decided he could pilot his plane through a storm and save fuel and time because it was the most direct route to his destination.

He took the easy way. He took a shortcut. He took matters into his own hands.

Sure, there were those that had warned him against flying through the storm. They were, by and large, more experienced flyers than he was so they might have known what they were talking about, but they had no idea that he was in a hurry. He had somewhere he had to be, and he couldn't be late.

Plus, fuel these days isn't cheap and he was on a tight budget. He might've been able to afford the fuel costs of going the safer way, but then once he arrived at his destination he would lack the resources necessary to have the fun he was planning on having once he got there.

"Who are these air traffic controllers anyway," he thought. "Who died and made them boss?"

He had flown in poor weather before, and dodged lightning strikes and turbulence each and every time. He didn't need to learn from the mistakes of others. He knew what he was doing. Besides, those that can't do teach, right?

Unfortunately, now after failing to have his mayday heard because of radio interference from the storm, and with the sad reality confronting him that he had tempted fate recklessly once too often, he still wasn't willing to swallow his pride.

He refused to believe his fait accompli was about to be accomplished. He refused to accept that he couldn't keep his plane airborne. He still believed if it was meant to be then it's up to me.

Then, suddenly, out of the corner of his eye he saw a parachute. It had been gathering mothballs for ages, and he wasn't even sure he remembered how to strap it on and use it. He had always prided himself on never having to abandon ship and his—up until now anyway—perfect flying record.

For a moment all of his pride was stripped away and the conviction that his life was really at stake here entered into his mind. His thoughts began to joust with one another.

One part of him said: "This is silly. Take the parachute. Eject. It's just a plane. It's not worth your life. You're being given a second chance to live here, make up for some things you wish you could do differently. You can choose life. This is a no-brainer. Count this is as a blessing and get rescued."

On the other hand, another part of him said: 'Never give up. You can do it. You've made it this far when others doubted you. When the going gets tough the tough get going. You're not going to surrender now, are you? You're not a weakling. You don't need that parachute to save you. Besides, does the parachute even work anyway? It's been there for so long that it might fail once you jump, and then you've traded one death for another more macabre. At least this way you control your own fate. If you jump, it's all up to the parachute. But if you stay and fight, you've got a fighting chance to live."

Now, guess which side of the man's brain won out?

The man decided the parachute was too risky, and he wasn't going to rely on something else to rescue him. He knew the way to keep the plane airborne, he knew the truth of how to fly all on his own, and he knew this was his best shot to keep his life.

Or so he thought.

He thought wrong.

Hours later, when investigators combed through the wreckage of the man's plane and needed dental records to identify his gruesome remains, the one thing they found intact was the parachute.

One of the investigators said to the other, "Wasn't this man told how he could be saved? Wasn't he trained on how to use the parachute?"

The other investigator pointed out that he must have been trained on how to be saved through the parachute because it's required in order to get a pilot's license. However, there are those who refuse to believe they need rescuing under any circumstances, and just pay lip service to the training as a means to an end.

And then they sadly crash and burn because in their minds it's about being in control and being free. They never consider the fact they're dead because they violated the law of gravity.

Even though they ignore the law of gravity, or act as if they alone have what it takes to defy it, the law of gravity is always there. It never changes. The natural laws existed on this planet before the United States of America, and will be here long after we are gone. Our Founding Fathers weren't all pious saints, but they at least got this basic idea of common grace correct, and these natural laws are the foundation for the system of laws they gave us.

This is why as long as Christian lawyers, politicians, activists, and advocacy organizations continue to labor for cultural revival in America without first and foremost acknowledging, honoring, and obeying "the Laws of Nature and Nature's God," they will continue to labor in vain.

Conclusion

When our Lord and Master, Jesus Christ, said
"Repent" He called for the entire life of believers
to be one of repentance.

−MARTIN LUTHER

⸺⬦⬦⸺

If you've made it this far, you're ready to turn the conversation towards making right that which has gone wrong in the name of righteousness.

So are we.

Compiling the information for this book has been a spiritually exhausting exercise for the two of us, just as it likely was for you to read it. It's never easy to examine yourself or your own side.

That's especially true in politics, when candidates are often judged by being compared to their opponents rather than how good they really are. When you also consider that many contemporary Democrats and liberals promote a moral standard that is completely at odds with what the Bible teaches is right and wrong, the temptation to be self-righteous and judge ourselves not by God's holiness, but instead by how much better we perceive ourselves to be in comparison to our fellow sinner, can be difficult to resist.

However, if we're going to get this country back on the right track, resist it we must, by the grace of God.

As we prayerfully considered what to put in this conclusion we had to resist this temptation ourselves. It would be very easy for us to pronounce judgment on a movement with the benefit of history as the 20/20 hindsight its leaders never had. We also understand that the two of us have not necessarily walked a mile in their shoes, having to make the judgment calls they've had to make at times. We also acknowledge that it is certainly fair to ask: would things be even worse if even the disjointed movement well-chronicled in this book had not been there?

We'll never know the answer to that question, but we do believe it's quite clear that we know for certain that this movement did not accomplish most of what it was intended and founded to do. Even if a singular answer as to why the movement failed is unattainable, no one can reasonably or credibly argue that the failure hasn't happened.

Therefore, as we turn the page and look forward to a new generation of leadership, it is important to remember that those who have not learned from history are doomed to repeat it. This is why rather than providing our input on who those next leaders should be, or what issues they should lead on, we have decided to focus on the foundation rather than the application. We believe that God does not judge us by our works in a utilitarian way, but by our faithfulness to Him in performing them.

Or, as Founding Father John Adams once famously put it, "Duty is ours but outcomes belong to God."

Therefore, we have determined that God has not called us to conclude this book with our own set of plans to replace the failed ones of the past, but rather to get to the heart of the matter—which is the condition of our hearts.

We must put first things first. For there to be reformation in our churches, and revival in our culture, there must first be repentance in our hearts. Throughout the Bible, and the history of how God interacts with human civilization, this is the pattern that seems to lead to cultural renewal: repentance + reformation = revival.

By repentance we, the authors of this book, mean *real* repentance. Real repentance requires humility on behalf of the penitent, and a desire to turn away from that which is wrong to that which is right. All of us, ourselves included, need to live lives of real repentance. A life of real repentance includes real accountability, which also requires the humility to receive it in a way that leads to growth and maturity.

This is especially true if you're charging head-first into the political arena, where you will be more scrutinized and under more pressure to conform to the thoughts and patterns of this world than perhaps at any other point in this culture. Without accountability, and proper understanding of the chain of command that puts God alone at the top, we all will eventually fall short of God's standard. Even worse, without proper accountability, we may decide to play God ourselves by redefining His standard to suit us.

Unfortunately, even as polls show the majority of Americans believe their country is headed down the wrong track, humility remains in short supply in America today. Like the stubborn people in the time of the Old Testament prophet who believed that the Temple remaining in Jerusalem was proof that God was pleased with them regardless of how unfaithful they were to Him, we seem to believe that as long as we plant the flag, take a few Bible verses way out of context, and end our patriotic pleas with "God bless America," He will.

We are playing a very dangerous game.

A God that can speak the universe into existence, and raise the dead to life, is not to be trifled with. His Word and His laws are not to be mocked. He is not putting up with our turning our backs on Him because He is distant, inept, nonexistent, or pleased with our humanistic attempts to curry His blessing. Rather, He is a loving Father being patient with His children, desiring that we would come to repentance.

However, sooner or later that patience will wear out, and the signs are there that His patience is wearing thin. All of the worldly things we put our trust in, such as our economic prosperity, emphasis on education, and military superiority, have failed to restore our hope in the American dream. There are several examples in the Bible of God using that which His people scorned to judge them for their own unfaithfulness and hypocrisy. If you look at who appears to be winning America's so-called culture war, there is at least some evidence that this is exactly what is happening in America today.

We have seen the enemy, and he is us.

We are our own worst enemies, and by "we," the authors of this book really mean *we*—including ourselves. We, the authors of this book, recognize that we are guilty of exactly that which this book seeks to expose. Even as we wrote the preceding pages, we were also exposing our own modern day idolatry. In a very real way, writing this book is a public act of penance for that idolatry.

We have given glory to the G-O-P that was only due to the G-O-D. We have helped to make men who had broken multiple marriage vows out to be the contemporary equivalent of canonized saints, because they were for lower taxes than their more politically liberal opponents who remained faithful to their marriage covenants with their wives. We have bought the lie that America is the last, best hope for mankind, when that is to be found in Christ alone. We have forgotten that only when America recognized that Christ was her last best hope did she become a beacon of hope to the world.

These are just some of the things we need to repent of. Perhaps you do, too, or maybe you need to repent of other things. Regardless, we will not preserve the God-given freedoms and liberties that we have enjoyed for our children and grandchildren until we humble ourselves before Him.

And the people that need to lead the way in repenting are those, like many of us in our churches, who shirked our responsibilities to be watchmen on the wall, and who feared men more than we feared God. We were the ones given the responsibility to disciple the nation, but instead we let the nation disciple us.

Once we have truly repented, we believe there must next be a reformation. In other words, we must go back to worshipping Christ and witnessing for Him in the manner we're commanded to—a manner which puts the emphasis on glorifying God and not ourselves or our associations. Christians must once again be His ambassadors on earth, in accordance with what He commands in His Word, and is worthy of as our Savior, Priest, Prophet, and King. We must seek to glorify and serve Christ and Christ alone. We must return to a place where we make the main thing the main thing.

While neither of us would be considered a master theologian, we do believe God's Word provides an easy-to-understand (but not always so easy to follow on this side of Heaven) framework for what that reformation looks like:

Bring Back the Bible

Imagine a general who went to war expecting to win by voluntarily refusing to use his most fearsome weapon because he was afraid it might offend his enemy if he did.

Sounds asinine right?

Well, that's exactly what we've done for a generation, and as a result the Bible is simply not taken seriously on an intellectual level in the American mainstream anymore. That has been counterproductive to our movement because the very thing we base our entire belief system on is no longer revered. As a result, the Bible holds no place of esteem in our culture, and there's little reason to esteem the stances we do take that are based on the Bible.

And why should it be revered? After all, if its adherents are defensive about its contents and transformational power, why should the unbelieving world revere it?

We believe it is impossible to glorify, worship, and obey God consistently without a reverence for His Word. Any pastor will tell you one of the first questions they'll ask a struggling Christian is, "how often are you reading your Bible?"

The transaction that takes place between the believer and the Word of

God when the two are joined together is nothing short of supernatural. Remove it from the believer's life, and you instantly drain the most immediate power supply a believer has. A believer not in the Bible is like a power plant without electricity. It may still look and sound like a power plant, but it has no real power.

This is why the unbelieving world wants to suppress the truth, and have shunned the Bible and its teachings from the public square. The truth is that without the truth of the Bible, we have no claim on morality or foundation from which to determine what is right and wrong than even the most confused pagan does. Take the Bible away, and we no longer stand for truth, but instead it's just our opinion versus theirs.

Furthermore, casting the Bible aside in the public square has actually made us more divisive, not less so, because without the Word of God present the debate simply becomes an argument between two sets of standards as opposed to what *is* the actual standard—and when there is an actual defined standard there is no argument.

What is more divisive? To have those separated from God's grace argue with their fellow citizen about how to live together as a society, or to get out of the way and let them discuss it with the God who in the life, death, and resurrection of Jesus Christ demonstrated His desire for eternal communion with them?

It has been our experience that most culturally engaged Christians are better at defending Fox News than they are the Bible. Most of them certainly seem more comfortable quoting from their favorite conservative talk radio titan to prove their points than the Bible, as if Glenn Beck can do a better job of changing hearts and minds than can the Holy Spirit.

Even more indicting, when challenged to explain the rationale for their actions and decisions from a Biblical perspective, many Christians engaged in the political/cultural arena aren't able to do so. Instead, they resort to Machiavellian pragmatism to justify their positions or tactics. Sadly, that was demonstrated in some of the most important interviews in this book, including the one we did with Dr. Richard Land of the Southern Baptist Convention, and Tom Minnery with *Focus on the Family*.

That doesn't mean things will just instantly get better if people just stand up and start quoting the Bible.

On the contrary, throughout the Gospels we see examples of Jesus using common vernacular to make his point. Jesus used contemporary culture references from his time like "hypocrites" or "white washed tombs" at times to make his points, and He spoke in parables describing real life circumstances so that those He was speaking to would understand. Yes,

He frequently quoted the Scriptures as well, but He also put them in a contemporary context which the average person could relate to.

Shouldn't we follow His lead?

We should use the Scriptures as the ultimate authority for our arguments, but not as the only authority. For if all truth is God's truth, then we can use everything in philosophy, science, education, etc. to put the eternal Word of God in a contemporary context.

For example, if what God says is wrong is indeed bad, then those who do wrong should suffer consequences for doing so, right? So what does the secular data say about those who engage in homosexual acts, girls who have abortions, children that are born out of wedlock, or whose parents are divorced? Is there any practical evidence that people mired in these situations are better off despite all the clamoring for "tolerance?" No, the exact opposite is true; proving the truth of God's Word in a practical way and demonstrating *why* He forbids us from engaging in such things. It's for the same reason any other parent doesn't allow their children to do what brings them harm—because He loves us and wants to prevent us from doing harm to ourselves and others.

There is no such thing in the Bible as "traditional marriage" or "traditional values." There's just marriage and virtues. Anything else is evil. The word traditional is a double-edged sword anyway, because for many years humankind had "traditions" of polygamy, slavery, and misogyny as well. Why did Christians work to abandon those traditions? Because they were evil according to God's Law, which means they denigrated the inherent value of those created in the image of God.

Thus, it's not about tradition, or any other cute, neutral code words we might devise to disguise what we really mean. It's about what's right and what's wrong. Traditions can be wrong, too, if they don't come from God.

God is a big God. He's got broad shoulders. He's been at this a lot longer than we have. Perhaps we should not assume we can out-think Him, and instead lean on Him and His Word rather than leaning on our own understanding. In all our ways let's acknowledge Him first, and then trust that He will guide the way. I think we can all agree that He couldn't do any worse reaching this culture without our help than we've done the past generation by trying to outwit the Holy Spirit.

Discipleship, Encouragement, and Accountability

Discipleship has become a buzzword in recent years in American Christianity thanks to excellent tools like *The Truth Project*. We finally seem to be waking up to the fact that we've neglected the very core of the Great Commission.

Tools for how to disciple men, women, marriages, children, and even those who want to bring their Christian worldview with them into Corporate America are plentiful, but glaringly absent from this resurgence in discipleship is how to equip those the Bible refers to as "civil magistrates."

If a man goes to his pastor and says he wants to know what the Bible has to say about becoming a better husband or father, most pastors will gladly take that man under his wing. However, if the same man goes to his pastor and says he's thinking about running for elected office, the pastor offers very little in the way of mentoring for fear of being seen as becoming "political."

Irony of ironies, because when we don't apply what the Word of God has to say about how to govern, government and public policy becomes political because it stops being about right and wrong and starts being about right and left.

Nature abhors a vacuum, so once the church vacates her Christ-given jurisdiction to the moral high ground, all we have left to fill the void are political opinions. Look at marriage as just one example. Not too long ago it was recognized culture-wide that marriage was ordained by God, and intended for one man and one woman. Now that the church doesn't want to get "political," the definition of marriage is up for debate. Plus, now we have political parties claiming terms like "moral" or "compassion" when in reality this fallen world doesn't know what those words mean. Apart from Christ and His church, the history of mankind has been anything but moral and compassionate.

By not standing for the Word of God in the public square, out of some misguided notion of not tainting the importance of individual salvation, the church is actually making that salvation harder to come by. That's because whenever a people reject God they always then make the state their god. At that point, the state determines what is right and wrong and not God—meaning it becomes even harder to convict sinners of their need for God's grace since even in their sin they may be right with the state.

It is imperative that the church collectively take discipling those who are called to run for public office seriously, and do so in terms that are defined Biblically. No one political party or human philosophy has a sole claim on God's Word, but they'll all try to claim it if we don't stand up and proclaim God's Word ourselves.

Discipleship must be partnered with encouragement and accountability. Each of us has had the honor of knowing several candidates and elected officials over the years, and through those associations caught a glimpse of the overwhelming pressure they feel to conform to the thoughts and patterns of this world. They need accountability when they get it wrong, and then the encouragement that comes from knowing they are more than conquerors in an age of grace once they admit their error. They also need to be at least as encouraged by those they're serving when they take a bold stand and get it right, as they receive correction from us when they compromise their integrity and get it wrong.

We believe this is also true of leaders of organizations and movements.

In this last generation, some of these leaders became so revered by those of us they were leading that they almost became the political equivalent of vicars of Christ. As a result, it was anathema to dare challenge them. That's not only not good for a movement, but it's also not good for the leaders. We're doing their personal spiritual condition no favors by putting them on such an idolatrous pedestal, and we're feeding the root of all sin— pride. Accountability creates humility, which creates growth that bears fruit. However, pride cometh before the fall, and the headlines have been replete with the fall of many a "Christian leader" in recent decades. How many scandalous revelations were the direct result of a lack of accountability and encouragement—which feeds one's pride in a destructive way?

We should submit to our leaders, but only while they are submitting to God. When they cease submitting to God, they cease being our leaders. And if we continue to follow or fund them at that point, we become just as guilty as they are.

Follow the Chain of Command

We must stop fearing the one that can only destroy the body, and only fear the one that can destroy the body and cast the soul into Hell.[142] To put a finer point on it, we need to be less concerned about worldly retribution and more worried about eternal damnation.

If we want to be "one nation under God," then we have to act like it. We're not one nation under a Supreme Court opinion that says we can't acknowledge God, and we're not one nation allowed to slaughter unborn babies. Nor should Christians in elected office give their primary allegiance to their political party, faction within that political party, or even their constituents. These things are all temporary, but the Word of the Lord stands forever. Hell is a really hot and a really forever place, and we're all going to be dead a lot longer than we were ever alive. How much different would our lives be if we lived moment-by-moment in recognition of that truth?

We believe the reason too many Christians get themselves caught between trying to please two masters is because they frame their dilemma in the form of the question, "what *should* I do?"

Instead, we propose asking the question "what *can* I do."

The former question puts the pressure on you to decide whom to serve and how much/often. It calls believers to live in the shades of grey so often found in the world of politics. To borrow a phrase made popular by the Star Wars movies, that is the path to the dark side of the Force. On the other hand, the latter question is framed as an absolute, which takes the pressure off of the individual because violating one's core convictions isn't an option once you've counted the cost.

For example, you may get very angry at a driver that cuts you off, but when the temptation to respond by running him into a ditch emerges you don't wrestle with whether you should do it because you know the law says you can't without facing dire consequences. Likewise, God's Word has a core set of commandments you aren't allowed to compromise, and when you do you face eternal as well as real-time consequences.

That means the next time someone asks you to look the other way for a candidate or piece of legislation you know is either compromised or corrupt, you can simply say "no" because they're asking you to do something you simply cannot do. Defying these core convictions becomes no more an option for you than is defying gravity.

You may struggle with this concept if you've bought into the myth of the separation of church and state, or if you've been taught a hermeneutically-flawed version of the "two kingdoms" view.

We're not suggesting that the state is like the church, nor do we want it to be. God's Word has granted specific roles and responsibilities to each. However, when in Rome we are not allowed to do as the Romans, and the early Christians were killed because they understood that truth.

Just because the state is called to punish evil, and the church is called to be a redemptive agent, doesn't mean there's one set of rules for the one jurisdiction and another set of rules in the other. The specific jurisdiction limits the authority of the state and the church, but the sovereignty of God is never limited. He makes the rain fall on the just and the unjust just the same. Both the city of man and the city of God are ultimately and always accountable to Him.

Christ says that "all authority in Heaven and on earth"[143] has been granted to Him, which means He is sovereign over all peoples at all times in all places regardless of the circumstances. This means your political/ cultural engagement should be viewed as an act of worship, not a calculated attempt to "get the best deal you can get."

Since God is ultimately in charge, no matter who's running the government, you're not so much lobbying an elected official to do the right thing as much as you're witnessing to him and helping him to understand what the right thing is. The Word of God is quite clear an elected official's job is to be "a minister of God's justice." If they're not governing like one that's not your problem but theirs, and it could be theirs eternally unless they acknowledge the truth.

As Christ said to Pontius Pilate, "You would have no power over me if it were given to you from above. Therefore, the one who handed me over to you is guilty of a greater sin."[144]

Translation: there is no authority except that which God has established, and when His people act as if that earthly authority is greater than His, it makes them even worse sinners than those who are estranged from God.

Motive Matters Most

Liberals like to be judged by their intentions, and conservatives want to be judged by their results, but we believe neither approach is Biblical.

Instead, we believe the Bible teaches that God judges us by our motives.

Intentions are what you meant to do, and results are what you actually did, but your motive is why and/or for whom you did it in the first place. Liberals coerce the state into violating its God-given authority in the interest of tolerance, fairness, and compassion. Although their intentions may be good, they're elevating the state to a status of worship as a source of people's provision in a way it was never Biblically intended to be.

The purpose of helping those in need isn't primarily to meet their material needs, but instead to have their material needs be the means by which they become spiritually fulfilled. Who's more likely to bow the knee to Jesus, the one who is without, or the one who already thinks he has it all?

In God's economy, charity is not simply a secular means of meeting material needs. Instead, charity is a material means of demonstrating the sacred love and mercy of Jesus Christ, who fulfills all our needs beginning with our most immediate one—the need to overcome our own sin and separation from God by His grace.

So while liberals may be out there doing what Christ has called us to do for the less fortunate, if they're not doing it for the purpose of pointing people to Christ, or in a way that brings honor and Glory to Him, there is no reward awaiting them in heaven when their time comes. Ever heard the phrase "the road to Hell is paved with good intentions?" See Matthew 7:21-23 for a further explanation of exactly what that means.

Not to be outdone in their self-righteousness, too many conservatives believe the ends justifies the means, and whatever it takes to make the trains run on time is just fine provided they do.

You can see this philosophy manifest itself in the defensive posture from which they construct many of their arguments. See, modern American conservatism always looks like its playing defense against the liberals because that's exactly what it is doing.

It's little more than free market moralism, which doesn't produce righteousness any more than secular humanism does. Conservatism in America is not predicated on advancing a set of ideals. It's focused on stopping the ones it doesn't like.

Thus, victory is defined as not letting the liberals have everything they want, and as long as conservatives are robbing us or killing us a little less than the "bad guys," it's called a conservative win. When you point out that the Bible says things like we're not to return evil for evil, they become self-righteously indignant that you would waste your time holding them accountable when there are much more wicked liberals who are more deserving of your attention.

Instead of justification by faith, conservatives believe in justification by comparison. As long as they're a little less evil than their political opponents, they're worthy of a heavenly gold star. That's how they justify having Rush Limbaugh spend a decade railing against the presidential peccadilloes of Bill Clinton when the first bishop of conservative talk radio is currently working on his fourth marriage, and he's not a three-time widower.

Conservatism never rolls back what the liberals have done, because it's not in its nature. It has no real alternative to offer. Its compromised itself so often to stop the stuff it's against, that it can no longer define what it's actually for. Hence, conservatism ends up resorting to patriotic platitudes and some generic and meaningless God-talk—waxing poetic about an America that supposedly once was but never actually existed apart from a reverential fear of the God of the Bible it denies.

Even more distressing, when righteousness does arise in the public square it's often conservatism that does its best to thwart it. Conservative voices have become a worried chorus that Biblical principles are "too radical" or "can't win" or "the media and the courts will never go for it." Thus, conservatives often end up proclaiming the modern-day political equivalent of "we have no king but Caesar."

We believe neither of these two paradigms is supported by the Scriptures. Instead, it's the condition of our hearts that is God's first concern.

Over and over again this theme is repeated in the Bible. In the Old Testament, God chastises His people for performing rote religiosity in which they were functionally doing what He commanded them to do, but their motives weren't to worship Him. Instead, the goal was to incur His provision and protection as if He were some sort of intergalactic ATM. In the New Testament we see Christ's own disciples asking Him when He's going to restore Israel's national glory. Unable to see beyond their own cultural biases and preconceived notions regarding what the true mission of the Messiah was, they were missing the point entirely. Sound familiar?

There are many more examples of this in the Bible, and we keep repeating these mistakes in our day. We, the authors of this book, are just as guilty as anyone. We confess that even now we too often see the world as the good guys versus the bad guys as opposed to those who know Christ as Savior and those who need to. We confess that we too often confuse the sheep with the wolves. And we confess that we have spent far more time taking stock in the shortcomings of those we disagree with compared to confessing our own.

We must avoid the trap of making good deeds like saving unborn babies, or helping the poor, the primary means by which we exercise our faith. Rather, we need to make a desire to see God glorified in all that we do our motivation, and allow that to become *why* we want to protect the sanctity of life and help the less fortunate. When the image of God is upheld by his creatures, He is glorified in His creation.

Redeem, Receive, Reject

Before any confrontation begins, one must know the rules of the engagement. And make no mistake, if you plan on taking the Gospel with you into every facet of existence there will be confrontations.

The rules of engagement determine what you can and can't do, and the Bible most certainly provides rules of engagement when it comes to engaging a culture. In general, we believe the Bible breaks culture down into three categories:

- What we can receive.
- What we should reject.
- What needs to be redeemed.

For instance, we can receive sinners no matter how heinous their sin. Prostitutes, homosexuals, adulterers, swindlers, junkies—they should all be received into the church with open arms. We should only reject them once it becomes clear they're not interested in repentance, or when they demand we receive them by conforming the Word of God to their behaviors and desires. Otherwise the goal should be to redeem them.

Yet there are certain things we should reject from the outset, and that's anything that directly contradicts Scripture. We immediately reject things contrary to God's Word and only those things.

The rest we can receive.

We can receive the community's sports teams, most of the community's music –provided it doesn't have explicitly immoral lyrics—and the community's traditions, legends, and customs that don't explicitly contradict God's Word. By receiving them, we develop a relationship with those God has placed around us. While this may involve activities that on the surface don't appear to have any spiritual value, any time you take to connect with those around you that doesn't compromise your Christian integrity is an example of loving your neighbor.

The rest of the culture needs to be redeemed, beginning with its people, and then those people should see the redemption of their neighbors and its institutions as their mission field. It's quite simple: if you want a culture to exhibit righteousness, it requires righteous people. The more unrighteous the people, the more unrighteous the culture. The condition of a culture's institutions is just a manifestation of those who inhabit it, for better or for worse.

Faith with Works, not Works with Faith

In the book of Nehemiah we read that he prays and he plans before he asks the pagan king he serves under to return to his homeland to rebuild the city walls. If only we did the same.

Instead, we have a tendency to tell God what we're going to do and then ask Him to bless it. That's works with faith, not faith with works. We are like contemporary Cains, petulantly giving God the offering we want as opposed to the one He is worthy of.

We scheme and plot with one another, our consultants, fundraisers, strategists, etc. but rarely does anybody bother to suggest we should stop and ask God for guidance. Then, on those rare occasions when we do, if the answer doesn't come when we want it, rather than patiently waiting on Him we just go do our own thing confident that since our intentions are so good there's no way God won't bless it.

Are we deists or Christians? Either we believe that God is intimately and actively at work redeeming His creation (with Christ coming to Earth being the greatest example of that), or we don't. If we do, our actions should demonstrate that. Instead, our actions in cultural and political affairs seem to more often demonstrate the deistic view that God is really just a kid with an ant hill—He's there but disinterested, so we're on our own.

Faith is the currency of God's economy, and when we behave in such a way we become as bankrupt as the federal government. This is the spiritual equivalent of a government decoupling its currency from a fixed commodity of tangible value that defines its worth objectively, and instead just printing it arbitrarily and trusting that the official government seal it carries will ensure no one will ever question it's worth. On the other hand, the more we rely on faith, the more prosperous we become in God's economy, because it's in our faithfulness that He is glorified.

Often we first determine what rules man's system says we have to play by, and then try to do as much for God as we can within those rules. We believe that God is actually looking for is people who first determine what He wants them to do, and then compel man's system to react to that. We believe God is looking for people who will challenge man's fallen system, not play nice with it.

Accommodation not Affirmation

We see many examples in the Bible of God's willingness to accommodate the weaknesses of an individual, or even a society, in order to accomplish His will. What we never see, though, is a single example of God affirming them in a way that compromises His integrity.

For example, many of the patriarchs of the Old Testament were either adulterers or polygamists. While God made accommodations for their sinfulness in order to use them for His righteousness, He never once calls their sin righteous, and they all suffered consequences for those sins. Polygamy may have been a deviant norm in the time of the patriarchs, but if you read the Bible you'll find every one of those saints of old who practiced it still suffered for it despite the work God was willing to do through them.

We used to understand this distinction, and often coined phrases such as "hate the sin but love the sinner" to explain it. Yet nowadays we have lost our way:

- Instead of accommodating our unbelieving neighbors' religious beliefs by giving them the same right of conscience everyone else has, we affirm them by removing ours from the public square to make room for theirs in the name of tolerance.
- Instead of accommodating our neighbor's immoral lifestyle by still treating him with dignity and respect as a human being created in the image of God, we affirm his immorality by welcoming it into our homes, allowing our children to be indoctrinated into accepting it using our own tax dollars, and then we replace his sinful nature with a label of "sexual orientation" saying "he just can't help it."
- Instead of accommodating a political system corrupted by partisanship and co-opting it to advance our agenda, we affirm it by letting it co-opt us to advance theirs.

We must reacquire the ability to accommodate fallen human nature without affirming it, because we're at our best when we're in the world but not of it.

Tone Deaf

One of the most pernicious lies in our culture today is that it's not what Christians are saying but how they're saying it which matters most.

Nothing could be further from the truth.

Those peddling such psychobabble do so because it's an effective red herring designed to produce confusion. All the time we spend on *how* to speak up distracts us from the real challenge of *when* to speak up and *what* to say when we do.

The real truth is that sinful humanity hates God and His Word. So it doesn't matter how many of Miss Manners' rules of etiquette you follow in standing up for it, they're going to hate you for doing so nonetheless. This debate isn't really about where to draw the line as they claim, but it's really about whether to draw the line at all.

Now please don't take that to mean we have no obligation to speak "words of love seasoned with salt," but instead have license to use the power of our tongues to cruelly destroy people because Christ is clear that we don't.

What it does mean is that love is not a tone or a feeling, it's a motive that leads to action. God is love, but love is not God. God defines love, not the other way around, and sometimes He defines it as saving us from our sins, and sometimes He defines it as making us suffer the consequences for them.

Similarly, we unconditionally love our children but that doesn't mean we don't hold them accountable for their wrongdoing. It's because we love them that we hold them accountable. We want them to know the difference between right and wrong so they will live accordingly. The Bible says "the Lord disciplines those He loves"[145] and so do good parents. Do our children like it when we discipline them? Would it make them like it more if we were really nice while grounding them for a week? Probably not, because in the end it's the being grounded part they don't like, not our tone of voice.

Lest you fall prey to the urban myth of the hippy Jesus, whom the culture reduces to little more than coffee shop shaman in guru garb tiptoeing through the tulips of Galilee, dispensing pithy sayings that boost our self esteem, know that some of the snarkiest, harshest, and most confrontational language found in the Scriptures comes from Christ himself. The point of this language and tone isn't to be salacious; it's to awaken a spiritually complacent people from their slumber before it's too late.

If your motive for being provocative is the same then so be it, especially since the motive most have for rejecting truth isn't your tone, but that they don't like the implications of accepting what you're saying as true no matter how you say it.

Don't Surrender the High Ground

In the past generation we believe that Christians have surrendered the moral high ground on almost every battlefront, and any good tactician will tell you whoever possesses the high ground is going to win the battle.

Here are just three examples of many:

- We surrender to so-called "exceptions" on the sanctity of life up front. That means we're really pro-choice, too, but just for fewer choices than the abortionists want. When we agree with their premise that in certain circumstances life isn't sacred, we are different in degree but not in kind.

• We no longer seek to define homosexuality as immoral, but instead fight to preserve the definition of marriage as one man and one woman. However, in a culture that increasingly fails to see homosexual behavior as immoral that is a lost cause, because if you're denying someone access to a societal benefit you're guilty of discrimination unless you're denying them that access on the basis that what they're doing is immoral. Only in that case have they forfeited their access by their very actions. We don't deny individuals or groups access to privileges based on a state of being (i.e. race or gender) but rather on the basis of immoral behavior, and that's the only basis by which to deny marriage to same sex relationships.

• We use phrases like "the courts struck down," or the "court made legal," when there isn't a single founding document in the history of this nation where such language is utilized or endorsed. Our Founding Fathers were clear that courts don't make law, and that any man-made edict or statute that contradicts the Law of God is no law at all. Anything to the contrary is purely un-American pagan propaganda perpetuated by the Left, plain and simple. Instead of calling it what it is, we actually go along with it, and send money each year to Christian legal groups who do the same.

We must admit to ourselves that we've lost the premise of every one of our arguments, but that it wasn't because we were out-maneuvered. Instead, out of fear, we decided to surrender first before it was too late.

There is not a single example we know of in all of the Bible of God accepting the premise of those opposed to righteousness. So why are we doing it? We know some of you reading this will say, "But we don't want a theocracy, do we?"

Actually that's exactly what we want, and whether you like it or not, that's exactly what we already have.

Every government in the history of humankind has been a theocracy, and every decision we make is a theological one. The only debate here isn't whether we'll have a theocracy, but who or what the "theo" will be.

We've seen ample evidence in the past few decades that just because Christians have been gracious enough to surrender the core of their beliefs doesn't mean the Left or Islamo-fascists are willing to do the same.

Make it about Issues and not Personalities

The American political system thrives on cults of personalities and identity-based politics, because that stymies critical thinking and instead produces emotion-based devotion. The Bible has a word for this, by the way.

Idolatry.

How many black ministers who preach fire and brimstone from their pulpits voted for Barack Obama despite the long list of his unbiblical beliefs simply because they shared the same skin color? How many evangelicals voted for Mike Huckabee just because he once was a Baptist minister but never vetted him on the issues? How many women support a Hillary Clinton or a Sarah Palin just because they share the same gender? In 2008 we kept hearing how Christians wouldn't support Mitt Romney because he was a Mormon, when the question that should've been asked is how could any serious Mormon support someone whose record as governor and a U.S. Senate candidate repudiates almost all of Mormonism's moral teachings?

When we make it about us, and not about God, this is what happens—idolatry happens. We will all worship something because we're built for worship, and if we don't worship the one, true living God we'll create for ourselves worldly saviors. More often than not they'll look like us and/or talk like us because absent the unity in diversity found only in the Body of Christ, humankind always breaks down into tribalism. That unhealthy tribalism creates factions that are more interested in maintaining their status, access, or relationships than anything else.

Jeepers, sounds like we just described the current American political landscape, doesn't it? That's because we did.

Christians cannot be successful under this paradigm, because at the core of our very message is personal transformation. The blind are made to see. The poor become rich. The sinner becomes a saint.

Tribalism and cults of personality, on the other hand, don't allow for those sorts of transformations, but rather seek to pigeon-hole people into convenient little enclaves of groupthink they can't ever break free from. Those who try are labeled traitors. Then the media appoints for each group its own leaders that they then permit to speak for everyone.

Case in point: the system doesn't see us as Christians standing for transcendent truth, but instead as social conservatives within the Republican Party.

That relegates the Word of God to just another political agenda no different than any other special interest group's pet cause. That also means the media never bothers to cover the story of whether or not what we stand for is true, but instead just focuses on the horse race aspect of the story. That almost always results in stories on the so-called conflict between Christians and moderates within the Republican Party. Then, when the media covers that story, you already know which "leaders" will be giving comments on both sides of this fruitless, futile, and phony debate, because they're the same ones we see every time the story is told.

These are the very definition of "foolish controversies" that the Bible warns us to avoid because they are "unprofitable and worthless."

Allowing the Word of God to be branded by the culture in this way is not only bad for our own integrity, but it's even worse for a decaying culture desperately in need of the healing power of the Word of God.

There's no room for a Saul to become a Paul under this personality-driven system, or for a Peter to transition from a coward to a courageous leader. You're either a Democrat, Republican, conservative, liberal, or assigned to some issue-advocacy special interest group that makes it convenient to label you.

In contrast, Christians are called to be holy. We are to be set apart from such schemes. Our identity is in Christ alone. We follow God, not a man or a movement. That doesn't mean we can't be Democrats or Republicans. Far from it, there are few organizations that need more true Christians in their ranks than those two. However, it does mean that if you choose to go that route, you don't buy into the groupthink, and you maintain your identity in Christ rather than in your association with the group—you better be prepared to be called lots of nasty names from those that do.

The best way to circumvent this flawed premise is to remove as much of the emotion-based attachments, connection to personalities, and tribalism as possible so you can focus on the issues. If you base your support for a candidate, cause, or leader on a cult of personality or tribalism, you'll constantly find yourself contorting your integrity to justify your emotions. We believe what God prefers is that we hold our candidates, causes, and leaders up to His objective standard, which is easier to do when you just look clinically and critically at where they're at on the issues.

Don't worry as much about what they say, but spend more time examining what they actually do. Spend at least as much time looking at their methodology as you do their ideology. In other words, examine how a candidate acts on what they say they believe just as much as you do what they're saying.

Put Principles ahead of the Process

Have you ever asked a Christian why they're supporting a candidate only to have them tell you, "because I believe they can win."

Have you ever been a part of a Christian organization that wrestled with who to invite to speak that could draw a big crowd at a fundraiser in order to cover a budget shortfall more than they wrestled with the reasons why they're experiencing that budget shortfall in the first place?

Ever been to a conference that spent more time plotting how to get more people to church than how to disciple those people if they actually showed up, let alone the ones that are already there?

These aren't isolated examples, because in our Western mindset we are more enamored with the methodology than the missiology. Our freedom and discretionary income has fed our prideful belief that we can be like God—masters of our fates, architects of outcomes, and determiners of our destiny.

The Bible has a word for such thinking: foolishness.

As the great prophets Bill and Ted once keenly observed, "All we are is dust in the wind, dude." We're behaving like Martha in a Mary world. The ruler of all creation lives in our hearts, but instead of stopping to contemplate what that means for a creation groaning with sin, we're too busy tidying up the place and performing menial rather than eternal tasks.

Just think of the time, talent, and treasure that has been squandered by Christian candidates, causes, and leaders on working the process in comparison to what was spent on standing for our principles? No audit is enjoyable, but we're guessing that one might be especially painful.

After a generation of political activism, it's obvious more time was spent on the process than the principles, because pretty much everyone follows the same partisan paradigm but not much headway was made in terms of policy.

We need to flip the script and worry less about who gets the money and the credit and instead focus more on what they're doing with it and whether or not they deserve it. Ronald Reagan reportedly had a sign on his desk in the oval office during his presidency which read: "It's amazing what you can get done when don't care who gets the credit for it."

Moreover, we need to spend more time discerning who *should* win than who *could* win, and when we Biblically discern who should win we should do whatever we can to support that person. If you think about it, more often than not, the reason that person "can't win" is because we create self-fulfilling prophecies by looking for "the winner," who is often the biggest loser when it comes to our principles.

Focus on the most righteousness you can do, not the lesser of two evils

Several times in this book we asked Christian leaders to tell us how much evil a Christian can support and still call themselves the lesser of two evils? If you read this book all the way through, you likely didn't get a satisfactory answer to that question, and we're guessing that's because there isn't one.

Nowhere does the Bible condone such Machiavellian pragmatism. In fact, it often condemns it. More specifically, the Christian is commanded not to focus on evil but instead "take captive every thought to make it obedient to Christ."[146]

There is power in the Word. The Bible says through the Word God spoke the heavens and the earth into existence. Christ is the Word made flesh. Our words have the power to hurt or to heal. When Christians even verbally capitulate to any semblance of evil, it is counter-productive to our witness.

We are supposed to be a light to the world, not just a less dingy darkness than what the devil would drown us in. Spending our time calculating the lesser of two evils is what the devil would have us do. God would rather we focus on how much good we can do.

If there were only two women in town available to marry your son, and one of them was a prostitute and the other was a devil-worshipper, would you have your son marry and produce your grandchildren with "the lesser of two evils?"

Besides, how would you even define that? Perhaps the devil-worshipper is a good cook and promises to remain sexually faithful to your son. On the other hand, the prostitute doesn't worship the devil per se, she just behaves in private with other men like she does. So which one is the lesser of two evils? And just imagine if they were both registered Republicans! Then you'd have a really hard time making that determination!

Most of us wouldn't let our son marry either one of these women, but would instead wait for something better to come along, or move our son to a town where there was something better. We wouldn't dare so dangerously water down our standards when it came to our children and grandchildren. If only we were willing to have this same attitude about the leaders who make decisions every day that will impact our children and grandchildren. God might actually grant us a real leader one of these days.

By defining the contest as the lesser of two evils, the candidates get away with campaigning on how bad their opponents are, not on how much good they're willing to do. By defining the contest as the lesser of two evils, we perpetuate the very kind of moral compromise we're claiming to oppose in other cultural venues. By defining the contest as the lesser of two evils, we miss an opportunity to witness to the culture at-large by explaining exactly what righteousness is.

This is why we propose to banish from our lexicon the phrase, "the lesser of two evils," and instead incentivize the system to compete for our support on the basis of who will do the most righteousness.

Suppose we did that in the 2008 presidential election when we had one candidate (John McCain) who was inconsistent at best on the pro-life issue and another (Barack Obama) who was downright hostile to it. When we frame the debate as the lesser of two evils, we never encourage McCain to rise above his moral inconsistency because that moral inconsistency looks mighty moral in comparison to outright immorality. But next to God's standard of righteousness, McCain is weighed, measured, and found severely wanting.

What if we had framed the debate around who will do the most righteousness instead? That would force McCain to explain why he accepts the premise that life is sacred but isn't willing to apply that principle consistently across-the-board. Instead of letting him get away with just being less evil than someone that repudiates everything we believe in, we might have compelled him to raise his game.

This model takes the pressure off of we the people to determine how much we can compromise God's integrity while maintaining our own. Instead, it puts the pressure where it belongs—on the candidate, cause, or leader whose duty it is to prove that they're worthy of our trust. It also makes the election less about the personalities of the two candidates and the various factions supporting them, and more about where they're at the on the issues.

In the military, do we allow soldiers to attain rank simply on the basis of being better than those they're competing with, or are there objective criteria for reaching those positions? Does a pro athlete with average stats make the Hall of Fame because his mediocrity was better in his era than someone else's putridity? When your child comes to you and says he'd like to start smoking crack cocaine to fit in with his friends, do you encourage him to get drunk instead because that's not quite as bad?

Of course when we look at it like this, we can't help but chuckle at how stupid these analogies all sound. Why then are we so willing to engage in this sort of silliness when it comes to electing our leaders?

God is sovereign, and in His sovereignty He has granted us the opportunity to have some say in determining what our government looks like. That doesn't mean we're on our own and free to do what is right in our own eyes. When a father loans his son the keys to the car on a Friday night that doesn't mean ownership of the car changes hands. It's still dad's car, he's just granting his son the freedom to use it as he sees fit within the boundaries set forth. Should the son violate those boundaries, his driving privileges will be revoked.

This is why it's no coincidence that as our nation drifts further and further away from its providential heritage, we are losing our liberties at the exact same time. We originally established this republic to protect those God-given freedoms, but now that we place our hope and trust in the state, which redistributes our wealth and enables our moral depravity, the state giveth and the state taketh away.

To borrow a line from *Seinfeld*, "We're killing independent George." We're taking that which belongs to God and rendering it unto Caesar, and when these worlds collide catastrophe ensues.

History records there are two things almost every once great civilization on earth had in common. The first is an abandonment of moral certainty and absolute truth right down to its most basic foundations. The second is that in their arrogance they never saw their downfall coming.

John Adams once asked his friend Thomas Jefferson in a letter if "any nation can recover its virtue once it's been lost." For America to recover hers she must first repent of her willful disobedience, and then reform her practices in a way that demonstrates that repentance was sincere. Then, perhaps, by the grace of God He will be merciful enough to send us another Great Awakening to revive us.

We believe this process must begin with Christians, since we are the ones called to model repentance, humility, forgiveness, and obedience—by His grace—to those who are living outside of it.

Blessed is the nation whose God is the LORD, the people he chose for his inheritance. From heaven the LORD looks down and sees all mankind; from his dwelling place he watches all who live on earth—he who forms the hearts of all, who considers everything they do.

No king is saved by the size of his army; no warrior escapes by his great strength. A horse is a vain hope for deliverance; despite all its great strength it cannot save. But the eyes of the LORD are on those who fear him, on those whose hope is in his unfailing love, to deliver them from death and keep them alive in famine.

We wait in hope for the LORD; he is our help and our shield. In him our hearts rejoice, for we trust in his holy name. May your unfailing love be with us, LORD, even as we put our hope in you.[147]

Amen.

Appendix A—History & The Judiciary

On July 12, 2008, the late Paul Weyrich published one of his final columns for *Townhall.com*. He died on December 18, 2008.

Ghost-written by our mutual friend John Haskins, Weyrich wrote this piece as simultaneously a retrospective and a warning to the Christian Conservative movement he helped found in the 1970s.

In this piece, Weyrich asserts the central premise of this book—that the movement formed to stop the Left from dismantling our constitutional republic undergirded by Christian moral values, is actually doing more harm to its own cause than the Left could ever dare to imagine. Considering the magnitude of the source of this accusation, we felt it was a fitting addendum to this book.

History and the Judiciary[148]
By Paul Weyrich

I am neither an attorney nor an expert in Constitutional Law. Others have been good enough to say I am a good strategist. If so, then I would like to share my perspective of the current state of the judiciary. I have listened as a debate is occurring over the proper powers of the courts and the tendency of some Americans to cede to the advocates of unrestrained judicial power victories to which they are not entitled.

I am occasionally referred to as a "founder of the modern conservative movement." Such an honor places upon me and others to whom such a description applies a special duty to warn our fellow citizens. Americans today are witnesses to the realization of the great fear of our Founding Fathers: the passing away of government "of the people, by the people, for the people," as President Abraham Lincoln stated, in the United States of America. With respect to the courts, we need a revival of the rule of law based upon the constitutional principles laid down by those who founded this nation.

Our forefathers gave their lives to liberate us from the rule of a British Parliament unelected by the American colonists:

Governments are instituted among Men, deriving their just powers from the consent of the governed.... But when a long train of abuses and usurpations, pursuing invariably the same Object evinces a design to reduce them under absolute Despotism, it is their right, it is their duty, to throw off such Government.... (Emphasis added.)

The grand formalities of American election rituals hide a glaring fact: Americans can no longer claim that we are our own rulers in every circumstance in which we are empowered to be. Regardless of our votes, the defining judgments in our collective and personal destinies often are made by persons whom the American people have not elected to rule.

We gave judges their robes and gavels so that they might resolve specific disputes between specific plaintiffs and defendants. We never gave them authority to issue commands to our elected lawmakers, forcing us down roads which we have not chosen to travel. Judges have no constitutional authority to make laws or to amend our national and state constitutions. They have no authority to redefine words and concepts in our laws to mean what they and their ideological partisans wish for them to mean.

To Americans of previous generations this was obvious and fundamental. But for many in America today, this is meaningless, a mere technicality: judges are supreme because, well, because they just are.

When several judges opined that there ought to be no more prayer in American schools, lawyers, politicians and journalists told us that after three centuries of prayer in our schools, judges had suddenly "outlawed" it. Court opinions interpreting law and social custom magically became the law itself.

After three centuries of Americans exercising their right to control their communities as citizens and to keep pornography out of public view, several judges opined that the Founding Fathers had given pornographers a right to pollute us and our children, a right that does not exist in the United States Constitution. They put us on a course that has almost obliterated the ideal of fidelity of body, mind, imagination and the heart, upon which marriage, family and child-rearing are built.

Nevertheless, lawyers, journalists and politicians announced that this opinion was to be the new law though it had no basis in the Constitution or in any law authorized by the American people via their chosen lawmakers.

Likewise, judges—acting on behalf of a tiny, anti-constitutional, self-styled cultural "elite" dedicated to turning America into an ideological utopia—opined that the American people may neither protect children from violent murder in their mother's womb, nor outlaw sodomy, nor restrict their civic blessing upon marriage to nature's definition of it, nor ensure that parentless children are placed with parents as nature defines them: one father and one mother.

Nor should I forget to mention judicial disregard for centuries of customary, legal and constitutional protection of private property in order to provide legal sanction for powerful, corrupt politicians lusting after other men's land or buildings. "Take what you please," they said in essence. And this was now the law. One hand washes the other.

Many of us received in shock and sadness the *Goodridge v. the Department of Public Health of Massachusetts* opinion on homosexual marriage. Why do self-styled "conservatives," lawyers, politician and pundits among them, spread the assertion that judges have powers that the American people have never given them?

The truth is that the ruthlessly enforced illusion of judicial supremacy did not merely empower judges and disenfranchise the American people. It made journalists, lawyers and clever politicians more influential culturally. Most, after all, are of the same ideological bent as many judges. And those who were not, the "conservatives," played within the new rules: judges' opinions are the law in the United States of America.

If Americans paid attention, understood what is at stake and agreed upon the solution, their long-term strategy would require:

- A string of primary victories by candidates who fully grasp the fact that judges have no authority to change our laws and who aggressively will oppose all claims to the contrary.
- An unbroken series of triumphs by such constitutionalist candidates in general elections, year after year.
- An unbroken series of nominations of judges who will interpret the law and will reject the noxious and absurd myth that previous court opinions are "the law of the land"; (Presidents Ronald W. Reagan and George H. W. Bush gave us activists such as Sandra Day O'Connor, Anthony Kennedy and David Souter!).
- An unbroken series of Senate confirmations of originalist judges.
- Unwavering constitutionalism by originalist judges in their years on the bench, withstanding daily assault by infuriated cultural "elites" who grew accustomed to using legally void and impotent court opinions as bulldozers to deceive and enslave Americans via a-moral, anti-constitutional and increasingly tyrannical judicial delusions.

Not a single signer of the Constitution (or of the *Declaration of Independence*) would have taken seriously the purportedly "conservative" view today that to restrain judges we need to replace them through attrition over decades. That view, in my opinion, guarantees a victory of the far left because it implies that the judicial branch is the final authority on the law.

In his book and British Broadcasting Corporation series *Civilization*, historian Sir Kenneth Clarke noted that after the dissolution of the Roman Empire, scattered pockets of normalcy continued for a surprisingly long time. How will we know, living in such "pockets of normalcy," when our republic has collapsed? Has it already? Are we prisoners who still think themselves free?

For the sake of this republic I urge my friends, fellow leaders and Americans emphatically to repudiate the devastating myth that judges have the power to make and redefine our laws. We should do so rapidly and forcefully before our republic is replaced by the irresistible tyranny of men and women who believe that nihilist elites should make the rules and pass them to judges for formal announcement when the time is ripe for the latest step into the post-rule of law, post-moral abyss. Otherwise our "conservatism" will continue to be merely the rearguard for subtle left-wing revolution.

The tragedy of how we have reached this point: in our desire for social acceptance and respectability among the anti-constitutional, anti-rule of law, anti-Christian, anti-family nihilist left, "conservative" elites have abandoned the core principles of our Constitution. We have flouted the warnings of the likes of Thomas Jefferson, who wrote:

"To consider the judges as the ultimate arbiters of all constitutional questions [is] a very dangerous doctrine indeed, and one which would place us under the despotism of an oligarchy. ...The Constitution has erected no such single tribunal, knowing that to whatever hands confided, with the corruptions of time and party, its members would become despots."

Alexander Hamilton was perhaps the strongest advocate of "judicial review"—the right of judges to opine on our Constitution. But an opinion on the meaning of the Constitution is merely an advisory opinion to the legislative and executive branches of government. Not even Hamilton imagined that the right to opine is a power to rule. Courts, he pointed out, intentionally have been given no means of enforcing their opinions, noting that the executive and legislative branches are not compelled to obey false or dubious opinions. Therefore, he wrote:

...The judiciary, from the nature of its functions, will always be the least dangerous to the political rights of the Constitution. ... [T]he judiciary... has no influence over either the sword or purse; no direction either of the strength or of the wealth of the society; and can take no active resolution whatever. It may truly be said to have neither force nor will....

Abraham Lincoln acknowledged that court opinions were binding upon the specific parties involved and "entitled to very high respect and consideration...by all other departments of the government." But like the Founding Fathers, he utterly rejected the myth that judges' opinions are the law of the land:

...If the policy of the government, upon vital questions, affecting the whole people, is to be irrevocably fixed by decisions of the Supreme Court, the instant they are made, in ordinary litigation between parties, in personal actions, the people will have ceased, to be their own rulers, having, to that extent, practically resigned their government, into the hands of that eminent tribunal.

In the last century cultural elites created an illusion of judicial power that would be unrecognizable to earlier Americans, lawyers and laymen. After the American Revolution, the framers of the Constitution rejected any judicial authority over the other branches of government.

I fear the conservative elites are putting the final nail in our coffin. I know these men. They mean well. They are not pursuing their view out of malice. They believe what they are doing is right. Nor do I associate myself with some of their critics who often are accusatory, judgmental and angry. I look at results, and it seems to me that proponents of the status quo are allowing the legal profession and the courts to impose moral and civil codes which cannot pass federal and state legislatures. They foolishly are handing absolute power to anti-Judeo-Christian, anti-family ideologues.

This is where the trajectory of the post-constitutional pragmatism undergirding the "conservative revolution" has taken us. The story is not yet complete, but if we continue on this trajectory we may reach the point of tyranny and persecution. History reveals this to be true.

Many of those with whom I have worked for years unwittingly are aiding the far left in the destruction of America. It is time for our presidents, governors, legislatures and prominent citizens to call the bluff of impotent judges as Jefferson did and to ask them, as President Andrew

Jackson did, how they will enforce their impotent opinions. The myth of judicial supremacy cannot justify governors violating state and federal constitutions, their oaths of office and the sovereignty of the American people. Look at the way so-called gay marriage has been imposed by judicial fiat, running ruthlessly over elected legislatures and the will of the people.

The Massachusetts Constitution contains the quintessential statement of the American form of government: "The power of suspending the laws, or the execution of the laws, ought never to be exercised but by the legislature...." (Part the First, Article XX.) "[T]he people...are not controllable by any other laws than those to which their constitutional representative body have given their consent." (Part the First, Article X.) "The judicial shall never exercise the legislative and executive powers, or either of them: to the end it may be a government of laws and not of men." (Part the First, Article XXX.) "All the laws which have heretofore been adopted, used and approved...shall still remain and be in full force, until altered or repealed by the legislature...." (Part the Second, Article VI.)

Americans must debunk the Orwellian lie that has obliterated self-government in the United States and acknowledge Lincoln's words at Gettysburg in 1863:

> *Now we are engaged in a great civil war, testing whether that nation, or any nation so conceived and so dedicated, can long endure.... It is for us the living...to be here dedicated to the great task remaining before us—that from these honored dead we take increased devotion to that cause for which they gave the last full measure of devotion—that we here highly resolve that these dead shall not have died in vain—that this nation, under God, shall have a new birth of freedom—and that government of the people, by the people, for the people, shall not perish from the earth.*

Appendix B—Faith to Action: A Cautionary Tale

As the finishing touches were added to this book, a battle was raging a few miles from co-author Steve Deace's home under the golden dome of the Iowa capitol. As the authors reviewed the interviews compiled in this work one last time, the Iowa legislature offered an illustration that goes right to the heart of the message of *We Won't Get Fooled Again*.

Fresh off winning a new 60-seat House majority, Republicans went from the political wilderness to control of both the governor's office and the House of Representatives following the 2010 election. This political shift occurred just as a vicious late-term abortionist announced his intention to move his infanticide operation from Nebraska to Iowa. A new day had dawned, and even before the new legislature was sworn in, an opportunity presented itself for the newly elected Republican leaders to put campaign rhetoric into action and use their majority to push truly pro-life legislation. Unfortunately, instead of taking advantage of an opportunity to do something that was both righteous and politically advantageous, Republican leadership chose a path that ended up creating a schism in the pro-life movement in the first-in-the-nation caucus state that is likely to take years to mend.

It's not that the leadership didn't know how to properly pander to pro-life activists, instead this self-inflicted wound was the direct result of their inability to understand that "we the people" had elected a new type of legislator in 2010. The political applecart was upset by three freshmen state legislators who stepped forward and asked a very simple, yet salient question—if we all say we're pro-life, and the first plank in the Iowa Republican Platform says that life is worthy of legal protection from the point of conception, how come a Republican majority doesn't begin the legislative process from that perspective?

Those three freshmen state legislators—Tom Shaw, Kim Pearson, and Glen Massie—not only refused to vote for what they viewed as a compromise over the sanctity of life, but they eventually used a controversial process to force their own leadership to hold a vote on a bill defining life at conception (personhood). Every member of the Republican leadership in the Iowa House voted against the life at conception bill. In the end, only 23 of their Republican colleagues, and one Democrat Representative, voted with the three pro-life freshmen.[149]

The story of what happened to these three freshmen state legislators, who took a principled stand for righteousness in public office, is a cautionary tale for the next generation of potential leaders that will follow in their footsteps. These three freshmen learned a valuable lesson, and now know firsthand that it's not as simple as "Republicans are good" and "Democrats are bad" when it comes to standing up for what's right.

They learned that the real fight isn't so much right versus left as it is right versus wrong.

First, a little about these three who were courageous enough to stand up to a tidal wave of pressure to compromise on that which God says we cannot.

State Rep. Tom Shaw spent 20 years in the Navy, where he was stationed in 20 different ports around the world. Seeing how everyone else lived, in contrast to his own experience, gave him a greater appreciation for the principles found in the writings and documents that forged America.

> "Travelling the world in the Navy, I learned that once you lose liberty you lose your rights, and you almost never regain them. Like muscles, we need to exercise our rights and fight for them, otherwise we lose them."

State Rep. Kim Pearson has a law degree, but has spent most of her adult years as a stay-at-home wife and home-schooling mother. She said she decided to run for office when she realized her long-term state legislator didn't represent her views. She says she ignored the advice of Republican Party pooh-bahs who told her to moderate her views to win an urban seat that had been held by Democrats for decades.

> "I decided that I needed to put myself out there, and I ran completely to the right in the primary and I stayed there in the general. I stayed to the right on all the fiscal and social issues, as well as issues of constitutional integrity, and by God's grace pulled out a victory in a so-called Democratic seat. When I was knocking on doors during the campaign, I think the people found it refreshing to hear me say I'm a Christian first, then a constitutionalist, and then a conservative Republican."

State Rep. Glen Massie also comes from humble origins. A self-described "blue collar worker," Massie's hands and fingers feature the calluses and blisters to back that up. Like Pearson, he also homeschools his children, and says it's the education he's given his children that motivated him to run for office.

"Probably the reason I ran is because of the years of teaching my children about our Constitution, particularly our Bill of Rights. After a while, I felt like I was teaching them lies, because I was watching those inalienable rights being violated left and right. I recognized that if I wanted to do anything about it, I was going to have to run for office."

Despite the fact the pundits and political party elites said the 2010 election was only about jobs and the economy, these three freshmen state legislators from different parts of the state each proudly campaigned on a pro-life platform. All three were from long-time Democrat districts with different demographics. Shaw represents a largely rural district. Pearson represents the east side of Des Moines, Iowa's capitol city. Massie represents several working-class, Democrat-leaning small towns just south of Des Moines.

Each of them explained how they defined themselves to voters as pro-life, beginning with Massie.

"One thing I said was the right to life for people like Terri Schiavo, who had the state order that her food and water be taken away. I very much talked about that when people talked about jobs and the economy. I pointed out, yes, jobs and the economy are important, but if we use our freedom and liberty and the things that set America apart from other republics, we'll go down just like they did. I don't want to be a republic like Russia or China. They are a Republic rule of law, too. I didn't want to live in a republic like that. I want to be a republic like what our founders gave us—one that's based on natural law."

Pearson said she made it a point to make the sanctity of life an issue on the campaign trail in her Democrat-leaning district.

"I worked on the party platform. That's how I got started in politics. I was so tired of Republicans going in there and saying one thing to get my vote, and then turning around and doing nothing. So I didn't hide that life was an important issue for me, as well as marriage between one man and one woman. There were only a couple of staunch Democrats that I ran into with a problem with that. Now, I'm finding more Republicans that have an issue with that.

I told the voters I wanted to protect life from the moment of natural conception to the moment of natural death. And that I would go forth and put up a life at conception bill, and that I was going to work hard to pass it."

Shaw said he made the sanctity of life and the Second Amendment constants in his campaign.

"It was in all my literature and I never hid from the issue. I flat out told the voters I would not vote for compromised life bills, and the only thing I would vote for is personhood because that is the only way that we're going to end abortion. I can tell you that on every life survey I received, I lined though all the questions and I wrote off into the margin that I will vote only for personhood bills so that innocent life in the womb will receive protection under the fourteenth amendment. As a result, I got calls from pro-life groups saying they didn't know how to score me because I didn't fit into their little box.

Everyone says that *Roe v. Wade* is the law of the land which it's not, because judges don't make law. Besides, Justice Blackmun in his decision gave us the key. He says if you recognize that life in the womb as a person, all the protections of the fourteenth amendment would apply. He gave us the key to unlock the door. But, what we have done since 1973 is we set the key aside and we're sitting there trying to pick the lock. It's time to stop, back up, pick the key up and unlock the door, and let's end this slaughter now."

Massie had been urging pro-lifers to cease regulating abortion for years, and instead focus their fight around the principle that all life is sacred. He even wrote a white paper on the subject after researching what the Bible has to say about the sanctity of life.

"The people that supported me, from my Republican central committee, knew for 16 years I've been taking this stance that life begins at conception, and that's where we should be fighting. After 38 years of incrementalism, where has it gotten us? But it really comes back to what our founders believe and that's the natural law. They even went as far as saying that any law that contradicted God's law was no law at all, and that's why the incrementalism doesn't work for me. What right do I have to say that these innocent lives deserve to be protected and these don't. That's to take on the mantle of God. I don't have that right. I don't have that ability.

Jesus Christ is my Lord and Savior, but Gandhi recognized that in these types of battles first they'll ignore you, and we've been ignored for a number of years. Then they'll laugh at you, then they'll fight with you, which is what's happening now—and then you win. So, I feel we're in the fighting mode now. I don't measure victory as one day we'll overturn *Roe v. Wade*. Although that would be victorious, but every time we elevate the subject and the taking of innocent life, people's minds are changed."

One of the interesting aspects of this trio's story is that they didn't even know each other before they ran for office and got elected. Thus, this wasn't a coordinated effort on their part. Rather, each of them arrived at this principled conclusion individually. For example, since finishing his 20-year stint in the Navy, Shaw has worked in local law enforcement. And he says his experience as a cop seared his conscience on the issue.

"I'm going to go public here with a story that I've told a couple times privately. I say it hesitantly because I can't describe the circumstances where I found myself in this situation. In the course of a police investigation I had to go to a Planned Parenthood and retrieve evidence for a case. Well, when that little plastic bag was put in my hand, that's when the light bulb went off for me. I can't even describe it. I went to my squad car. I had a little cooler packed with ice and I put it in there. I'm driving two or three hours and I kept looking at that little cooler thinking there's a murdered baby in my car with me. That image was seared into my mind and it haunts me today. That's (voice trails off)…it's just got to stop. I don't know how else to say it."

Fast forward now to January 2011 and the start of a new legislative session in Iowa.

Each of these three freshmen state legislators had resolved to act on their moral conviction that life begins at conception. Reality hit them hard when instead of receiving the Republican leadership's blessing to act on the courage of their conviction, which is also coincidentally enshrined in their party platform, those leaders tried to get them to vote for a bill that would supposedly ban one late-term abortionist from coming to Iowa. The argument was that the Democrat-controlled state senate was supposedly willing to allow a vote on the compromise bill—something they never did.

Massie points out the fallacy of banning abortions under certain situations like length of gestation, fetal pain, or if a heartbeat is detectable. He notes that the state must almost always rely on the reporting of the abortionist to acknowledge if such thresholds are being met. That means some pro-lifers are willing to take the word of those who are shamelessly slaughtering children for money that the law is being obeyed. Massie says relying on the integrity of those who commit baby-murder doesn't exactly give him a warm fuzzy.

> "From the very beginning I let the author of the bill know that with the language of the bill, there's no way we'll fight to protect this bill since it doesn't necessarily protect anyone. We were surrendering to the Democrats up front. Why fight for the compromise when you haven't even fought for the principle? Fight for the principle first before you fight for the compromise. So, we were quite adamant and quite clear. We didn't come up here to fight for this. We came to fight for innocent life."

Shaw said the bill, while well-intentioned, missed the real point of the pro-life movement in the first place.

> "The whole problem is it doesn't ask the right question. The question is not 'does the fetus feel pain?' The question should be 'is that a person or not?' If it is a person, forget about 20 weeks or a heartbeat, or when it's breathing, or when you can hear it cry. If it is a person from the moment of conception until natural death, that life must be protected. It is our duty to uphold the Constitution. The purpose of government in this country, which makes us unique, is that our government is supposed to be protecting individual rights. That's why it was formed, and to allow this abortion industry to continue means government is failing. It is not protecting the inalienable right to life.

Shaw said an attempt by leadership to address the concerns of the three uncompromising pro-life lawmakers backfired when the author of the bill added language stating that life begins at conception. In other words, the

Republican leadership in the Iowa House was willing to codify that life begins at conception into the law, but then do nothing to protect it.

"We put out a public statement saying that that bill was worse than *Roe v. Wade* because in *Roe v. Wade* the justices said it's not a person so you can kill it. Here we're saying it is a person, but go ahead and kill it anyway."

Massie believed the compromised "life" bill backed by his Republican leadership in the Iowa House was more immoral than the so-called "three-fifths compromise" of the slavery era.

"We used to consider slaves to be three-fifths of a person. So I did some figuring here and discovered that meant we thought slaves were a person 60% of the time. This bill that sought to ban abortions after 20 weeks in Iowa is interesting. Since normal gestation from conception is about 38 weeks on average, this late term abortion ban after 20 weeks was saying a person is a person 48% of the time. So a slave used to be 60% of a person and now life in the womb is 48%. Slaves had more rights."

Where were the pro-life groups in Iowa as this battle for the sanctity of life was taking place within the Republican caucus? Shaw says not only was support for their efforts few and far between, but two pro-family groups actually opposed them.

"Some words were spoken between the lobbyist of the Iowa Christian Alliance (now a part of Ralph Reed's Faith and Freedom Coalition) and myself. They and the Iowa Catholic Conference were opposed to personhood. Although they said they personally believed in it, they were worried the judges would just throw it out. They don't want to fight the fight because they just believe in the judiciary and not the legislature. So, they're fighting what is the judge going to rule and that's how we should write our legislation. That's what I took away from it."

Imagine if the 19th century abolitionists would've ceased their efforts to free the slaves after *Dred Scott* because you "couldn't get it past the judges." Makes you wonder why we have a legislative branch at all if we're just going to continue allowing unelected judges to make all the decisions.

Still, those pro-lifers who make such arguments really do have a desire to save those babies from being slaughtered. Oftentimes to justify their compromises they use analogies like coming upon a burning building and trying to save as many lives as they can. Shaw says he heard all of the clichéd pragmatic arguments while he was standing for personhood in the Iowa Legislature.

"How about for once we prevent the building from starting on fire in the first place, or make arson illegal? The other one I got was Schindler in Germany saving some of the Jews, so like him Schindler I'm going to do what I can. The flaw in that argument is that Schindler was a private business man. He was not making policy. He didn't go to Hitler and say it's ok, keep killing all the rest of the Jews, if you let me keep my workers."

Massie said the other fallacy in the burning building or Nazi Germany argument is that in this country we vote for our leaders, so there's no need to consent to these moral compromises. Do we tell an arsonist to go ahead and burn the whole orphanage down provided he lets us save a few babies first, or do we try to stop the arsonist?

Nor are pro-lifers who regulate abortion anything at all like Schindler, according to Massie, because Schindler was living under the oppressive dictatorship of Nazi Germany. To the contrary, we are a free country with a government by the consent of the governed. We're not oppressed by our leaders, for we play an active role in selecting them.

"Our job as legislators is to make law that would match with God's law. It is not my job to be on the street as a firefighter trying to save the lives that I can as a legislator. If I was on the street, sure save as many as I can. But here in the legislature it's my job to make law that protects all innocent life. End of assignment. That's my job here."

Shaw also said the personhood debate seemed to awaken pastors and churches in Iowa to the need to take a principled, righteous stand.

"Pastors started coming to the capitol and praying with us. They knew some tough votes on the life issue were coming up, and pastors were coming and praying with us and for us to have God's guidance."

Massie added that not only were some pastors inspired, but some long-serving principled legislators who had gone dormant over the years were reawakened by the fight. They had begun to believe there was little hope in actually doing something principled or standing boldly while awash in a sea of compromise.

"Alexander Solzhenitsyn said when you realize you're in bondage to a tyrant, and you have to resist at some point and go and fight, and there's a machine gun nest on their side, they're going to pick off the first wave and some of the second wave, but it inspires others to stand up and charge also because they realize that continuing this present situation is unacceptable and I will not stay here. You take up, and you charge, and do the right thing, even if it costs you everything. We saw this very thing play out at the legislature over this issue.

I believe with a little more nurturing that we could build an army. We need an army because with this whole issue of fighting for life, we are storming the gates of Hell. It is a spiritual battle. The devil is not going to surrender it easily. It's going to be a difficult battle, but you only win it by fighting it from a righteous point of view."

The three also say there were plenty of discouraging events during the time they were taking this stand. Shaw said that ironically, one in particular came from a "Christian" organization. The *Iowa Christian Alliance*, which is affiliated with Ralph Reed, and whose president is Iowa's Republican National Committeeman Steve Scheffler, actually sent out an email urging its members to contact them. However, the e-mail didn't urge their fellow Christians to encourage the stand for all life, but instead pressured lawmakers to compromise their moral conscience.

"I just relied on a lot of prayer and a lot of talking to the Lord. My wife gave me so much support, as did (Massie and Pearson). We have become a little family. A lot of times we'd go in the back and sit on one of the benches and think this is crazy, what are we going to do here. I think we did a good job of upholding each other. I referenced the pastors coming to the capitol. They knew we were hurting and needed guidance and support. I got a lot of emails on the compromised bill when it first came out, asking me to vote for it. As I started emailing back, explaining the flaws in the bill, people were like 'wow, thanks for letting us know.' Those people would send encouragement. I ended up receiving a lot of support."

Pearson said the most discouraging time for her was when she was attacked by some of her fellow Republicans for forcing the vote on the life at conception bill, despite having followed all the protocols leadership had asked her to obey up to that point.

"I think my low point is when we were going to do the bill the next day and the screaming began. It was the fact that we had gone down the route that was prescribed by our leaders. We did it exactly how they asked us to do it, and then they left us—they hung us out to dry. That was the lowest spot for me. We did exactly what they told us to do and they left us."

Massie said the vote itself, as well as the circumstances leading up to it, were both the high and low point for him.

"It's an interesting thing because the low and the high point were both at the same time for me. The low point was leading up to the vote because there was so much resistance and yelling, but then there was peace because we were willing to do the right thing. There was so much support. I say it with tears in my eyes. You can't believe how much I covet your prayers because that place is a den of vipers and snakes. This was the most emotionally, spiritually, physically draining task that I've ever taken on in my lifetime. To be there, and I don't have the physical strength, so it has to be somebody out there with their prayers carrying us through the day."

Both Pearson and Shaw nodded their heads as Massie described how difficult it is to swim against the tide. They each had advice for a future generation of leaders looking to put their faith into principled action. Shaw said support, honesty, and accountability are the keys to him maintaining his witness as well as sanity.

"First off, without that family support you can't do this. Secondly, say what you stand for and be honest with the people because that saves us from a lot of criticism when I go back to my district. If they're upset with the way I vote, I say did I not say I will only vote for personhood. I have lived up to my end of the bargain. I even put it in writing. When I was door knocking people were always saying that candidates would say one thing and then get there and do another.

I'd say I'm handing you a score card. Right here is everything I stand for. You can keep track of everything I'm doing for accountability. We are all human. We are all prone to error, and we've each had our moments where one or two of us have had to pull the other one along because you do get isolated sometimes. You have to allow yourself to be accountable to others and make them keep you accountable."

Pearson said recognition of the real chain of command helped her have the courage to stand.

"I think one of the most important things is you have to know who the leader is. Because if you go down there and don't know who the ultimate leader is, your Lord and Savior Jesus Christ, you're going to fall into follow the leader and your party leader becomes your leader. They also have to be prepared that there's an incredible spirit of fear in politics. It's a fear of rejection. They want to get reelected. It's all a fear of man instead of the fear of God."

So where's the hope? Where's the optimism? Pearson said it comes from "Christ alone."

"I believe in God's sovereign grace. If he's calling you to run, you will not have peace if you don't do it. He will give you the strength and the wisdom to do it. That's the victory. Every day stepping forward and honoring Him. If we stand firm in it we encourage some and make some more willing to listen."

Shaw also found some inspiration from a Clint Eastwood film.

"I got this line from a Clint Eastwood movie: 'we must endeavor to persevere.' I've always loved that line. We have to keep at it."

In the end, Massie says trusting in God regardless of the outcome is the best advice he would give to those that follow in his footsteps.

"I worked hard as if it depended on me, and trusted the results to God. If I won, praise God. If I lost, praise God. In the end what we all want to hear is 'well done, good and faithful servant.'"

Footnotes

1   *American Right To Life Analysis of the George W. Bush Abortion Legacy*, http://americanrtl.org/news/prolife-profile-george-w-bush

2   Associated Press, *Cheney at Odds With Bush on Gay Marriage*, http://www.msnbc.msn.com/id/5817720/ns/politics/ (August 25, 2004)

3   Good Morning America, *Bush Backs Civil Unions*, http://www.youtube.com/watch?V=ql5qsiw3luq (October 26, 2004)

4   NPR, *Roberts' Pro Bono Work Raises Eyebrows*, http://www.npr.org/templates/story/story.php?Storyid=4785876 (August 4, 2005)

5   Kevin Eckstrom, *Conservative Christians Criticize Bush on Gay AIDS Appointee*, http://www.beliefnet.com/News/Gender-and-Sexuality/Conservative-Christians-Criticize-Bush-On-Gay-AIDS-Appointee.aspx (April 11, 2001)

6   ABC, *Bush on Religion and God*, http://abcnews.go.com/Politics/story?Id=193746&page=1(October 26, 2004)

7   "Bush: Bible 'probably not' literally true", *The Washington Times*, December 9, 2008

8   "Philippians 3:8-9," Holy Bible -NIV, (Grand Rapids, Michigan: Zondervan Bible Publishers, 1982) p. 1261

9   "James 2:26," Holy Bible—NIV, (Grand Rapids, Michigan: Zondervan Bible Publishers, 1982) p. 1303

10 "Luke 12:48b," Holy Bible—NIV, (Grand Rapids, Michigan: Zondervan Bible Publishers, 1982) p. 1119

11 "Matthew 7:1-2," Holy Bible—NIV, (Grand Rapids, Michigan: Zondervan Bible Publishers, 1982) p. 1041

12 "I Peter 4:17," Holy Bible—NIV, (Grand Rapids, Michigan: Zondervan Bible Publishers, 1982) p. 1309

13 *Barna Survey Examines Changes in Worldview Among Christians over the Past 13 Years*, http://www.barna.org/barna-update/article/12-faithspirituality/252-barna-survey-examines-changes-in-worldview-among-christians-over-the-past-13-years(March 6, 2009)

14 Gary Langer, ABC, *Poll: Most Americans Say They're Christian Varies Greatly From the World at Large*, http://abcnews.go.com/sections/us/dailynews/beliefnet_poll_010718.html (July 18, 2002)

15 Paul E. Rondeau, "Planned Parenthood Leaves Unprofitable Communities Despite Record Revenues and Subsidies," http://www.all.org/article/index/id/odczmq/, (March 29, 2011)

16 "Facts on Induced Abortion in the United States," http://www.guttmacher.org/pubs/fb_induced_abortion.html, (January, 2011)

17 Steven Ertelt, "Planned Parenthood President Says Telemed Abortion Scheme Going Nationwide,"http://www.lifenews.com/2010/05/21/state-5111/

18 Joshua Green, "They Won't Know What Hit Them," http://nomblog.com/wp-content/uploads/2011/03/They-Won%E2%80%99t-Know-What-Hit-Them-Magazine-The-Atlantic.pdf(March 2007)

19 KeyWiki, http://www.keywiki.org/index.php/Tim_Gill

20 Joe Kovacs, "America's Pro-Homosexual Giants: 2010," http://www.wnd.com/?Pageid=114304, (October 28, 2009)

21 Warner Todd Huston, "10% of Americans Are Gay—Urban Myth Explored," http://www.renewamerica.com/columns/huston/060314 (March 14, 2006)

22   Liz Goodwin, "Poll: Majority of Americans Support Gay Marriage," http://news.yahoo.com/s/yblog_upshot/20100812/pl_yblog_upshot/poll-majority-of-americans-support-gay-marriage, (August 12, 2010)

23 John Berthoud, "NEA: 30 Years of Lobbying Democrats," http://www.humanevents.com/article.php?Id=11785 (January 23, 2006)

24 "NEA & RW Bastards," http://www.youtube.com/watch?V=Ahb8rBMuDDs (August 26, 2009)

25 Catherine Snow, "Federal Judge Strikes Down Prop 8; One Man, One Woman Marriage 'Irrational,'" http://www.citizenlink.com/2010/08/04/federal-judge-strikes-down-prop-8-one-man-one-women-marriage-irrational/ (August 4, 2010)

26 Bill Mears, "Supreme Court Backs Municipal Land Grabs," http://articles.cnn.com/2005-06-24/justice/scotus.property_1_eminent-domain-tax-revenue-susette-kelo?_s=PM:LAW (June 24, 2005)

27 US Supreme Court, "Plyer v Doe, 457 U.S. 202" http://caselaw.lp.findlaw.com/cgi-bin/getcase.pl?Court=us&vol=457&invol=202 (June 15, 1982)

28 Jack Cashill, "Why California Homeschooling Is In Peril," http://www.wnd.com/index.php?Fa=PAGE.view&pageid=58712 (March 13, 2008)

29 Adam Liptak, "Ginsburg Shares Views on Influence of Foreign Law on Her Court, and Vice Versa,"http://www.nytimes.com/2009/04/12/us/12ginsburg.html, (April 11, 2009)

30 Duncan Hollis, "Justice Ginsburg on Using Foreign and International Law in Constitutional Adjudication," http://opiniojuris.org/2010/08/02/justice-ginsburg-on-using-foreign-and-international-law-in-constitutional-adjudication/ (August 2, 2010)

31 Budget of the United States Government, "Historical Tables," http://www.gpoaccess.gov/usbudget/fy09/pdf/hist.pdf (Fiscal Year 2009) P. 30

32 Budget of the United States Government, "Historical Tables," http://www.gpoaccess.gov/usbudget/fy10/pdf/hist.pdf (Fiscal Year 2010) P. 31

33 Steve Deace, "Branstad Barnstorms Again," The Washington Times, http://www.washingtontimes.com/news/2010/apr/27/branstad-barnstorms-again/ (April 27, 2010)

34 Conn Carroll, "Bush Deficit vs. Obama Deficit in Pictures," The Heritage Foundation,http://blog.heritage.org/2009/03/24/bush-deficit-vs-obama-deficit-in-pictures/ (March 24, 2009)

35 US Office of Budget and Management, http://www.whitehouse.gov/sites/
default/files/omb/budget/fy2012/assets/hist01z1.xls

36 Eric Zimmermann, "IMF: U.S. Debt Nearing 100 Percent of GDP," http://the-
hill.com/blogs/on-the-money/budget/98047-imf-us-debt-approaching-100-
of-gdp (May 15, 2010)

37 AP, "Study: 1 in 7 U.S. Babies Born to Moms 35+," http://www.cbsnews.com/
stories/2010/05/06/health/main6465326.shtml (May 6, 2010)

38 George A Akerlof, "An Analysis of Out-Of-Wedlock Births in the United
States," http://www.brookings.edu/papers/1996/08childrenfamilies_akerlof.
aspx (August, 1996)

39 "Divorce Rates In America," http://marriage101.org/divorce-rates-in-america/

40 "Divorce and Death: Their Social & Social-Psychological Impacts," http://
www.trinity.edu/MKEARL/fam-div.html

41 Sam Roberts, New York Times, "To Be Married Means To Be Outnumbered,"
http://www.nytimes.com/2006/10/15/us/15census.html (October 15, 2006)

42 Center for Media and Public Affairs, "TV Goes PG But Movies Are Still R
Rated" Volume XVI No. 2, (March/April 2002)

43 Kaiser Family Foundation, "Sex on TV 3: TV Sex Getting Safer," http://
www.kff.org/entmedia/loader.cfm?Url=/commonspot/security/getfile.
cfm&pageid=14211 (February 4, 2003)

44 Family Safe Media, "Pornography Statistics," http://www.familysafemedia.
com/pornography_statistics.html

45 "Study: Violent Video Game Play Makes More Aggressive Kids,"http://www.
usnews.com/science/articles/2010/03/03/study-proves-conclusively-that-vio-
lent-video-game-play-makes-more-aggressive-kids (March 3, 2010)

46 CNN, "McCain: Same-Sex Marriage Ban Is Un-Republican," http://articles.
cnn.com/2004-07-14/politics/mccain.marriage_1_amendment-defense-of-
marriage-act-marriage-ban?_s=PM:ALLPOLITICS (July 14, 2004)

47 Alex Knapp, "John McCain Re-Emphasizes Support for Stem Cell Research,"
http://www.outsidethebeltway.com/john_mccain_re-emphasizes_support_
for_stem_cell_research/ (September 16, 2008)

48 Congressional Record—Senate, http://www.loc.gov/law/find/nominations/
ginsburg/vote.pdf (August 3, 1993)

49 Holly Bailey, Newsweek, "No Prize To The Noble Loser," ," http://www.news-
week.com/2008/10/10/no-prize-to-the-noble-loser.html, (October 11, 2008)

50 Marc Ambinder, "Bush Campaign Chief and Former RNC Chair Ken Mehlman: I'm Gay," http://www.theatlantic.com/politics/archive/2010/08/bush-
campaign-chief-and-former-rnc-chair-ken-mehlman-im-gay/62065, (August
25, 2010)

51 Melanie Mason, "Cornyn, Sessions to Receive Award from Gay and Lesbian
GOP Group," http://trailblazersblog.dallasnews.com/archives/2010/09/
cornyn-sessions-to-receive-awa.html, (September 21, 2010)

52 John-Henry Westen, "Why Rush Limbaugh is Wrong to Support Homosexual Civil Unions," http://www.lifesitenews.com/news/archive/ldn/2010/
jul/10073011 (July 30, 2010)

53   John-Henry Westen, "First Rush, then Coulter, and Now Glenn Beck...
     What's Happening?," http://www.lifesitenews.com/news/archive/ldn/2010/
     aug/10081315 (August 13, 2010)
54   The Church of Jesus Christ of Latter-Day Saints, "Our Values—Strengthening
     Families," http://mormon.org/family/
55   MormonWiki, http://www.mormonwiki.com/Family
56   Sam Stein, "Cheney Offers Support for Gay Marriage," http://www.huffing-
     tonpost.com/2009/06/01/cheney-offers-his-support_n_209869.html, (June 1,
     2009)
57   David Weigel, "Grover Norquist Joins GOProud," Washington Post,http://
     voices.washingtonpost.com/right-now/2010/06/grover_norquist_joins_
     goproud.html, (June 15, 2010)
58   Jennifer Riley, "Laura Bush: Gay Marriage, Abortion Should be Legal," Chris-
     tian Post, http://www.christianpost.com/news/laura-bush-gay-marriage-abor-
     tion-should-be-legal-45144/, (May 13, 2010)
59   Bob Unruh, "Conservatives Alarmed by 'Gay' Sponsorship of CPAC," World
     Net Daily, http://www.wnd.com/index.php?Fa=PAGE.view&pageid=119848
     (December 22, 2009)
60   Brian Fitzpatrick, "Biggest Conservative Names Bidding Goodbye to CPAC,"
     World Net Daily, http://www.wnd.com/?Pageid=244741 (December 27, 2010)
61   Lydia Saad, "More Americans 'Pro-Life' than 'Pro-Choice' for First Time," Gal-
     lup, (May 15, 2009)
62   "Isaiah 55:11," Holy Bible—NKJV, (Nashville, Tennessee: Thomas Nelson,
     INC., 1982) p. 300
63   "Acts 20:29-31," Holy Bible—NKJV, (Nashville, Tennessee: Thomas Nelson,
     INC., 1982) p. 452
64   "I John 4:1," Holy Bible—NKJV, (Nashville, Tennessee: Thomas Nelson, INC.,
     1982) p. 494
65   "Hosea 4:6," Holy Bible—NIV, (Grand Rapids, Michigan: Zondervan Bible
     Publishers, 1982) p. 966
66   *Mitt Romney CPAC 2007 Transcript*, http://mittromneycentral.com/speeches/
     cpac-2007/ (March 2, 2007)
67   "Romney Created 'Gay' Marriage, Family Groups Say" *World Net Daily*, http://
     www.wnd.com/news/article.asp?ARTICLE_ID=53787 (January 16, 2007)
68   *Romney—$50 Abortions in Massachusetts*, Christian News Wire, http://christi-
     annewswire.com/news/962685067.html (December 12, 2007)
69   Rick Klein, "Romney's Pro-Life Conversion: Myth or Reality?," ABC News,
     http://abcnews.go.com/Politics/story?Id=3279653&page=1 (June 14, 2007)
70   Brian Camenker, *The Mitt Romney Deception*, http://www.massresistance.org/
     docs/marriage/romney/record/ (November 20, 2006)
71   "Will Introduces Giuliani At CPAC," http://www.youtube.com/watch?V=
     rzfieha7euk (March 2, 2007)
72   "Giuliani on Public Funding of Abortion," http://www.youtube.com/
     watch?V=aldfwxiyux0 (November 3, 1989)

73 John Hawkins, "Conservative Case Against Rudy Giuliani," http://www.humanevents.com/article.php?id=16762 (August 30, 2006)
74 Garance Franke-Ruta, "Enemy Lines," The American Prospect, http://prospect.org/cs/articles?articleid=7186 (March 1, 2004)
75 Mitt Romney, 1994 US Senate Debate, "Romney on Abortion—1994," http://www.youtube.com/watch?v=ueqgobiggqy
76 Mitt Romney, 2002 Gubernatorial Debate, "Romney on Abortion—2002," http://www.youtube.com/watch?v=P_w9pquznG4
77 *Romney—$50 Abortions in Massachusetts*, Christian News Wire, http://christiannewswire.com/news/962685067.html (December 12, 2007)
78 Daniel Larison, "No To Mitt," The American Conservative, http://www.amconmag.com/larison/2008/04/04/no-to-mitt/ (April 4, 2008)
79 Massachusetts Health Benefits and Copay details https://www.mahealthconnector.org/portal/binary/com.epicentric.contentmanagement.servlet.ContentDeliveryServlet/About%2520Us/Connector%2520Programs/Additional%2520Resources/cc_benefits1220_pt234.pdf
80 "Joint Letter to Governor Mitt Romney from Pro-Family Leaders,"http://www.massresistance.org/docs/marriage/romney/dec_letter/letter.pdf, (December 20, 2006)
81 Steve LeBlanc, "Romney's Record On Gay Rights, Social Issues In Cross-Hairs," http://www.boston.com/news/local/massachusetts/articles/2007/01/12/romneys_record_on_gay_rights_social_issues_in_cross_hairs/, (January 12, 2007)
82 Brian Camenker, "The Mitt Romney Deception," http://www.massresistance.org/docs/marriage/romney/record/, (November 20, 2006)
83 Rudy Giuliani, "Giuliani on Public Funding of Abortion," Comments made at a Women's Coalition for Giuliani event, (November 3, 1989)
84 Rudy Giuliani, "Will the Real Rudy Show Up At CPAC?" http://www.youtube.com/watch?v=rvbtpirelem (February 27, 2007)
85 Orlando Sentinel, "First Lady, Giuliani Join Gay Pride Celebration," (June26, 2000)
86 "Rudy Giuliani in Drag—Dude Looks Like A Lady," http://www.youtube.com/watch?v=E_90nrroxk8&NR=1&feature=fvwp, (August 2, 2007)
87 Brian Camenker, "The Mitt Romney Deception,"http://massresistance.org/docs/marriage/romney/record/, (November 20, 2006)
88 "Luke 11:39," Holy Bible—KJV, (Nashville, Tennessee: Thomas Nelson, INC., 1977) p. 570
89 "Luke 11:43-44," Holy Bible—KJV, (Nashville, Tennessee: Thomas Nelson, INC., 1977) p. 570
90 "Luke 11:45," Holy Bible—KJV, (Nashville, Tennessee: Thomas Nelson, INC., 1977) p. 570
91 "Luke 11:46," Holy Bible—KJV, (Nashville, Tennessee: Thomas Nelson, INC., 1977) p. 570
92 "Luke 11:52," Holy Bible—KJV, (Nashville, Tennessee: Thomas Nelson, INC., 1977) p. 571

93   World Net Daily, "Ann Coulter on WND: 'They're a bunch of fake Christians,'" http://www.wnd.com/?pageid=194229 (August 21, 2010)

94   John-Henry Westen, "Why Rush Limbaugh is Wrong to Support Homosexual Civil Unions," http://catholicexchange.com/2010/08/02/132930/ (August 2nd, 2010)

95   "Why Glenn Beck Doesn't Cover Social Issues," http://www.youtube.com/watch?v=d5u4cg00oay, (August 14, 2010)

96   "McCain Favors Embryonic Stem Cell Research," http://www.youtube.com/watch?v=gjbuouhhujq, The Bob Dutko Show, (April 13, 2007)

97   Rham Emanuel, "Rham Emanuel on the Opportunities of Crisis," speaking to the Wall street Journal CEO Council, http://www.youtube.com/watch?v=_mzcbXi1Tkk&feature=related, (November 19, 2008)

98   C-SPAN, "Richard Land, Southern Baptist Convention Ethics & Religious Liberty Commission," http://www.c-span.org/Events/Richard-Land-Southern-Baptist-Convention-Ethics-amp-Religious-Liberty-Commission/8411/, (October 7, 2007)

99   WKRN, "Breaking: Romney Caught on Video Refuting Human Life Amendment on 3/6/07," http://archive.redstate.com/blogs/perico/2007/nov/16/breaking_romney_caught_on_video_refuting_human_life_amendment_on_3_6_07, (March 6, 2007)

100 Massachusetts Health Connector, https://www.mahealthconnector.org/portal/binary/com.epicentric.contentmanagement.servlet.ContentDeliveryServlet/About%2520Us/Connector%2520Programs/Additional%2520Resources/cc_benefits1220_pt234.pdf

101 "Obama, McCain both vote 'Yes' on Senate bailout bill," http://archive.redstate.com/blogs/perico/2007/nov/16/breaking_romney_caught_on_video_refuting_human_life_amendment_on_3_6_07, (March 6, 2007)

102 CNN, "McCain: Same-sex marriage ban is un-Republican," http://articles.cnn.com/2004-07-14/politics/mccain.marriage_1_amendment-defense-of-marriage-act-marriage-ban?_s=PM:ALLPOLITICS, (July 14, 2004)

103 Catholic News Agency, "John McCain Still Supports Embryonic Stem Cell Research," http://www.catholic.org/politics/story.php?id=26574, (January 25, 2008)

104 "Romans 13:1," Holy Bible—NIV, (Grand Rapids, Michigan: Zondervan Bible Publishers, 1982) p. 1217

105 CFR Membership Roster, http://www.cfr.org/about/membership/roster.html?Letter=L, (as of May 19, 2011)

106 Council on Foreign Relations, "Global Governance," http://www.cfr.org/issue/global-governance/ri23

107 "John 15:5," Holy Bible—NIV, (Grand Rapids, Michigan: Zondervan Bible Publishers, 1982) p. 1158

108 American Right To Life Action, "Dr. Dobson Broke His Pledge Made Before God," http://www.youtube.com/watch?gl=US&feature=related&hl=iw&v=RbkRJ-A2ZPI

109 Dr. James Dobson, interview on the Frank Pastore Radio Show, http://www.

youtube.com/watch?v=4v6czoexiu4, (May 18, 2007) & Dr. James Dobson, interview on The Dennis Prager Show, "Dennis Talks To Dr. James Dobson About Who He Will And Won't Vote For, http://www.dennisprager.com/transcripts.aspx?id=1137, (February 5, 2008)

110   "James 2:10," Holy Bible—NIV, (Grand Rapids, Michigan: Zondervan Bible Publishers, 1982) p. 1302

111   "Luke 20:25," Holy Bible—NKJV, (Nashville, Tennessee: Thomas Nelson, INC., 1982) p. 428

112   John Quincy Adams, http://www.quotesea.com/quote/dutyisoursresultsare

113   Justice Sonia Sotomayor, "Sonia Sotomayor: Court Of Appeals Is Where Policy Is Made," http://www.youtube.com/watch?v=gdsk8ehtcmg (2005)

114   "Psalm 14:1," Holy Bible—NKJV, (Nashville, Tennessee: Thomas Nelson, INC., 1982) p. 223

115   "Leviticus 18:5," Holy Bible—NIV, (Grand Rapids, Michigan: Zondervan Bible Publishers, 1982) p. 124

116   "Leviticus 19:37," Holy Bible—NIV, (Grand Rapids, Michigan: Zondervan Bible Publishers, 1982) p. 126

117   "Leviticus 25:18," Holy Bible—NIV, (Grand Rapids, Michigan: Zondervan Bible Publishers, 1982) p. 133

118   "Deuteronomy 4:8," Holy Bible—NIV, (Grand Rapids, Michigan: Zondervan Bible Publishers, 1982) p. 191

119   "Deuteronomy 8:11," Holy Bible—NIV, (Grand Rapids, Michigan: Zondervan Bible Publishers, 1982) p. 196

120   "Deuteronomy 27:26," Holy Bible—NIV, (Grand Rapids, Michigan: Zondervan Bible Publishers, 1982) p. 214

121   "Deuteronomy 29:29," Holy Bible—NIV, (Grand Rapids, Michigan: Zondervan Bible Publishers, 1982) p. 218

122   "Nehemiah 9:13," Holy Bible—NIV, (Grand Rapids, Michigan: Zondervan Bible Publishers, 1982) p. 524

123   "Psalm 1:1," Holy Bible—NIV, (Grand Rapids, Michigan: Zondervan Bible Publishers, 1982) p. 579

124   "Psalm 19:7," Holy Bible—NIV, (Grand Rapids, Michigan: Zondervan Bible Publishers, 1982) p. 589

125   "Psalm 119:91," Holy Bible—NIV, (Grand Rapids, Michigan: Zondervan Bible Publishers, 1982) p. 663

126   "Psalm 119:142," Holy Bible—NIV, (Grand Rapids, Michigan: Zondervan Bible Publishers, 1982) p. 664

127   "Psalm 119:160," Holy Bible—NIV, (Grand Rapids, Michigan: Zondervan Bible Publishers, 1982) p. 665

128   "Isaiah 10:1," Holy Bible—NIV, (Grand Rapids, Michigan: Zondervan Bible Publishers, 1982) p. 743

129   "Isaiah 42:21," Holy Bible—NIV, (Grand Rapids, Michigan: Zondervan Bible Publishers, 1982) p. 779

130   "Jeremiah 6:19," Holy Bible—NIV, (Grand Rapids, Michigan: Zondervan Bible Publishers, 1982) p. 818

131 "Hosea 4:6," Holy Bible—NIV, (Grand Rapids, Michigan: Zondervan Bible Publishers, 1982) p. 966

132 "Matthew 5:17," Holy Bible—NIV, (Grand Rapids, Michigan: Zondervan Bible Publishers, 1982) p. 1039

133 "Romans 2:13," Holy Bible—NIV, (Grand Rapids, Michigan: Zondervan Bible Publishers, 1982) p. 1206

134 "James 1:25," Holy Bible—NIV, (Grand Rapids, Michigan: Zondervan Bible Publishers, 1982) p. 1301

135 John Adams, http://www.quotedb.com/quotes/3659

136 Sonia Sotomayor, "Sonia Sotomayor Says Courts Make Policy," http://www.youtube.com/watch?v=ZiAnWLUMmYg&feature=player_embedded

137 William Blackstone, Commentaries on the Laws of England, Introduction, Section 2, http://ebooks.adelaide.edu.au/b/blackstone/william/comment/introduction2.html

138 Rev. Dr. Martin Luther King Jr., "Letter From Birmingham Jail," http://mlkkpp01.stanford.edu/index.php/resources/article/annotated_letter_from_birmingham/, (April 16, 1963)

139 Justice Kennedy, Supreme Court of the United States No. 08-472, http://www.supremecourt.gov/opinions/09pdf/08-472.pdf, P 22, (April 28, 2010)

140 Iowa Code 595.2, Gender-Age, http://www.legis.iowa.gov/IowaLaw/statutoryLaw.aspx

141 Constitution of the Commonwealth of Masachusetts, http://www.malegislature.gov/Laws/Constitution#cp21s00.htm

142 "Matthew 10:28," Holy Bible—NIV, (Grand Rapids, Michigan: Zondervan Bible Publishers, 1982) p. 1046

143 "Matthew 28:18," Holy Bible—NIV, (Grand Rapids, Michigan: Zondervan Bible Publishers, 1982) p. 1072

144 "John 19:11," Holy Bible—NIV, (Grand Rapids, Michigan: Zondervan Bible Publishers, 1982) p. 1163

145 "Hebrews 12:6," Holy Bible—NIV, (Grand Rapids, Michigan: Zondervan Bible Publishers, 1982) p. 1298

146 "II Corinthians 10:5," Holy Bible—NIV, (Grand Rapids, Michigan: Zondervan Bible Publishers, 1982) p. 1243

147 "Psalm 33:12-22," Holy Bible—NIV, (Grand Rapids, Michigan: Zondervan Bible Publishers, 1982) p. 598

148 John Haskins and Paul Weyrich, "History and the Judiciary," Townhall.com, http://townhall.com/columnists/paulweyrich/2008/07/12/history_and_the_judiciary, (July 12, 2008)*Ghost written by John Haskins

149 Steve Deace, "Kill Them All," http://stevedeace.com/news/iowa-politics/killthem-all/, (May 10, 2011)